Ukrainian Otherlands

FOLKLORE STUDIES
IN A MULTICULTURAL
WORLD

The Folklore Studies in a Multicultural World series is a collaborative venture of the University of Illinois Press, the University Press of Mississippi, the University of Wisconsin Press, and the American Folklore Society, made possible by a generous grant from the Andrew W. Mellon Foundation. The series emphasizes the interdisciplinary and international nature of current folklore scholarship, documenting connections between communities and their cultural production. Series volumes highlight aspects of folklore studies such as world folk cultures, folk art and music, foodways, dance, African American and ethnic studies, gender and queer studies, and popular culture.

Ukrainian Otherlands

Diaspora, Homeland, and Folk Imagination in the Twentieth Century

Natalia Khanenko-Friesen

The University of Wisconsin Press

Publication of this volume has been made possible, in part, through support from the **Andrew W. Mellon Foundation**.

The University of Wisconsin Press
1930 Monroe Street, 3rd Floor
Madison, Wisconsin 53711-2059
uwpress.wisc.edu

3 Henrietta Street, Covent Garden
London WC2E 8LU, United Kingdom
eurospanbookstore.com

Library of Congress Cataloging-in-Publication Data

Khanenko-Friesen, Natalia, author.
Ukrainian otherlands: diaspora, homeland, and folk imagination in the twentieth century /
Natalia Khanenko-Friesen.
pages   cm — (Folklore studies in a multicultural world)
ISBN 978-0-299-30344-0 (pbk.: alk. paper)
ISBN 978-0-299-30343-3 (e-book)
1. Ukrainian diaspora.   2. Ukrainians—Ethnic identity.
3. Ukrainians—Canada—Ethnic identity.   4. Ukrainians—Canada—Folklore.
I. Title.   II. Series: Folklore studies in a multicultural world.
DK508.44.K49   2015
909'.0491791082—dc23
2014040214

To
Tim
and
Adrian

Contents

Illustrations

Preface

Many people have been my inspiration and the reason why this book was written. With some, I spent years conversing about the meanings of diaspora and home and the sources of their longing for each other. With others, I contemplated the challenges of stitching together the torn mesh of transatlantic family relations. Some people I only met briefly, but those fleeting encounters proved to be memorable and crucial for my understanding of diaspora-homeland encounters. Fleeting or prolonged, these engagements helped me to craft the arguments presented in this book, and I find myself in debt to each individual for steering me, most often unknowingly, toward better arguments. I also express my gratitude to all the individuals mentioned in the book, either under their real names or pseudonyms, who shared with me their experiences of departure and separation from and longing for their "other" kin in faraway places.

Several Ukrainian Canadian academics from the University of Alberta were also my inspiration in this work. Bohdan Medwidsky, Andriy Nahachewsky, and Frances Swyripa of the University of Alberta introduced me to the field of Ukrainian Canadian studies in ways more than just academic. Bohdan, I hope this book could offer further answers to that poignant question of what it feels like to live in more than one world. Andriy and Frances, thank you for sharing with me your knowledge of and love for the prairies, a feeling I now share with you.

My words of gratitude also go to those who assisted me in my fieldwork in practical terms, welcomed me into their communities, let me stay in their homes, and made sure I had access to the right people and the right resources while conducting my research. The Bakus'ko family in Hrytsevolia, Ukraine, put up with me, a stranger in their home, during my two prolonged stays in their house and made me feel like a part of their family. Brenda Prins, Mary Shelast, Marlyn Mandiuk, and Iryna and Bogdan Pyvovarchuk of Mundare,

Alberta, Canada, over the course of four years kept taking me into their homes so I could do my work in town without having to commute back to the city or worry about driving back in dangerous conditions in winter. In Edmonton, over the years, Mary and Fred Paranchych became my Canadian family, accommodating me on my return trips to the city for various interviews and archival work. Mary and Fred, thank you for letting me into your life. Olena Husar, head of the Department of the Ukrainian Language at Ternopil National Pedagogical University, generously re-created the feel of home for me when I worked in her city several summers in a row coordinating the study abroad program for Canadian students and pursuing my research at the same time. Thanks to Olena, I met many people in Ukraine who directly contributed to my book. Marta Madych welcomed me to her home on my many trips to L'viv to conduct further interviews for this project. Iryna Hlibovych of Nebyliw, who hosted me in her home having only just met me at the bus stop when I arrived for the first time, was indispensable to my exploration of Nebyliw's connections to Canada. On several occasions Bohdan and Lida Struk of Burshtyn, Ukraine, hosted me and took me around their region, including the village of Bili Oslavy so I could conduct further interviews. In the United States, my Harvard colleague Vera Andrushkiv nearly adopted me into her family over the course of several summers that we taught together in the Harvard Ukrainian Research Institute. I spent many days in Vera's summer home in the Catskill Mountains in upstate New York, where I had the privilege to experience firsthand the intimate workings of some established Ukrainian American families and their networks. The stories of homecoming you shared with me, Vera, made me appreciate the complexity of these trips in a new light and prompted me to explore this topic further. In Lisbon, Portugal, Teresa Carvalho was keen to introduce me to several Ukrainian migrants working in her father's estate while also letting me stay in her home in the city. Pavlo Sadokha, Lidia Hall, Nadia Baranovs'ka, and Yuriy Unhurian of Lisbon were most helpful guides and guardians in my explorations of Ukrainian culture of Portugal. In Rome, His Excellency Hlib Lonchyna, Bishop of the Ukrainian Greek Catholic Church and Apostolic Visitor for Ukrainian Catholics in Italy (2003–2008), ensured I received the best reception in the Ukrainian Greek Catholic community of Rome. The editorial team of *Do Svitla*, Lida Dukas and Father Vasyl' Potochniak, helped me with my earliest explorations of Italian Ukrainian culture, and later Marianna Soronevych, the editor of Italy's *Ukrainska Gazeta*, took me under her wing, exposing me to the community life of Ukrainians in Rome. It would have been impossible to see and explore as much of Ukrainian culture as I did in Italy without their kind support and interest in my work.

While writing this book has been a recent undertaking, the research discussed here spans some two decades. Over the course of those years, I received
a number of grants that supported projects that led to this monograph, including
a University of Alberta Doctoral Scholarship (1994–96), a Social Sciences and
Humanities Research Council Doctoral Fellowship (1997–98), and a Helen Dar-
covich Doctoral Fellowship from the Canadian Institute of Ukrainian Studies
(1998–99). The preparation of this book and further research toward its production were supported by Canada's Social Sciences and Humanities Research
Council, through its standard research grant (2006–9). St. Thomas More College at the University of Saskatchewan supported my research on this book
through a variety of research grants (2003–11). Saskatchewan's Centennial
Student Employment Program supported "Oral History of Sociocultural
Change on the Prairies: The Ukrainian Canadian Experience" (2002), the
interviews from which I analyze in this book. The Prairie Centre for the Study
of Ukrainian Heritage at St. Thomas More College provided ongoing financial
support to the Oral History Program and Personal Archives Sources that I
founded in 2007. Both programs now house several research projects profiled
in the book. My appreciation goes to Orysia Ehrmantraut, Maria Melenchuk,
Nadya Foty, and Yuriy Kirushok, who in their capacity of graduate research
assistants were involved in the production and maintenance of research data
examined in this monograph. I shall thank Yuriy also for helping me with the
final preparation of the manuscript for publication. I thank the anonymous
reviewers, who provided critical feedback that helped me to improve the narrative and scholarship of this monograph. Natalka Husar, I cannot thank you
enough, for offering my most cherished art pieces from your art portfolio as
illustrations for this book and for the stories they brought to life during our
several visits. The University of Wisconsin Press editorial team of Sheila Leary,
Gwen Walker, and Adam Mehring has been capably steering this project toward
its completion. My copyeditor MJ Devaney applied her amazing skills to my
narrative to make it more coherent and to the point. Thank you all at UW
Press for your high professionalism and utmost attention to my book. Working
with you has been a pleasure. At the end, let me state that while so many people
have contributed to my work presented here, any of the book's shortcomings or
weaknesses are my sole responsibility. Finally, I thank Tim and Adrian, for
being the core and the backbone of my universe, for always keeping my spirits
high, making me laugh, and showing how to keep things in perspective.

Ukrainian Otherlands

Figure 0.1. Natalka Husar, *Grotto*, 1987, oil/linen, 203 × 64 cm. Photo by Chris Chown. Courtesy of Natalka Husar.

Introduction

Homeland-Diaspora Imaginations and the Roots of Their Mutual Attraction

*I*n the early morning on a July day, Tim and I disembarked from our train at the Melitopol station in South Ukraine. The year was 2005, and this was the first time Tim was visiting Ukraine, the land once populated by his ancestors. I was excited to arrange this trip to the country's south. It promised us a healthy dose of adventure and discovery. As an ethnographer who had been born and raised in Ukraine and who possessed local knowledge and language skills, I spent years traveling throughout Ukraine's countryside, and was looking forward to exploring yet another field site. Tim, with his family history going back to the south frontiers of the Russian Empire of the nineteenth century, marveled at the prospect of finally setting foot on the land his ancestors left for America in 1874. We unloaded our heavy backpacks full of climbing gear, the climbing trip to the Crimea being over, on a wood bench facing the rail tracks and pulled out our maps. Mine were contemporary maps of Ukraine; Tim's were the photocopies of the maps of times bygone, carefully folded out and laminated.

Combining our knowledge of the geography of the current Ukraine and the layout of its frontier communities in the nineteenth century, we soon decided on an itinerary through the Molochansk district of Melitopol Oblast, known locally as a "German" territory and in Canada as one of the largest Mennonite settlements in South Ukraine. The next thing was to find a vehicle. A dozen weathered Zhigulis were lined up in front of the main entry to the train station. Soon, we picked out a driver from among the handful standing around. Nikolai was a fifty-year-old plumber who was trying to make extra cash for his family on the weekends by driving tourists to their vacation destinations on the shores of the Black sea some fifty kilometers south of Melitopol. Nikolai struck us as both an entrepreneurial and knowledgeable person, and I reckoned he would become our local guide through the communities we planned to visit that day.

3

As we headed out of town, surrounded by the vast fields and orchards—
sunflowers in full bloom, cherries, peaches, apples pulling the tree branches
toward the ground—I could not stop thinking about how exactly we would
navigate through this vast rural terrain so similar in its looks to the Canadian
prairies where I now live and work and to where many German settlers from
south Ukraine have immigrated. Neither Tim nor I have ever been to this land.
In the eighteenth and nineteenth centuries it was home to the German settlements that were once spread far apart from each other and then all renamed
and collectivized during the USSR years, many of which no longer exist. Nikolai's knowledge of the surroundings would come in handy indeed, I thought.

Several formerly German communities on our list were small roadside
villages, adjacent households facing the same road from both its sides. There was
nothing German about them anymore. Still, like many other modern pilgrims
from Canada in search of their roots in ancestral lands, Tim got out of the car,
took pictures and commented on how his grandmother would be thrilled to see
that her front yard flowerbeds were identical to the flowerbeds he was photo-
graphing at the moment in front of local village homes. The largest community
on our agenda was the town of Molochansk, with many streets but few street
signs. This was a typical situation in contemporary Ukraine at the time—street
signs, made of steel, were often, shall I say, "recycled" by anonymous entrepreneurial recyclists, and as a result, the town streets and country roads became
less easy to navigate, especially by those from afar.

In Molochansk, the plan was to see important landmarks built by the
German settlers in the eighteenth and the nineteenth centuries. Equipped with
a list of these landmarks, we followed the town's streets, whose contours were
obscured by mature and densely planted trees. It was a relief to find ourselves
away from the hot July sun, but also a challenge, as the tree branches prevented
us from seeing far ahead. Self-appointed guides, Nikolai and I took it upon
ourselves to identify former German businesses and buildings and find our way
to them. The task involved not only translating between German, English, and
Ukrainian but getting out of the car and asking pedestrians for directions. Not
one passerby was able to identify the old German buildings, and soon I felt that
the whole enterprise of Tim's homecoming so carefully orchestrated by us was
in danger of stalling out.

At this very moment, when I found myself unable to find what my friend
flew all the way from Canada to see, the group dynamics in our team abruptly
changed. Suddenly, Tim took the initiative. His instructions were precise, and
detailed. "Go straight for a block." "Turn left." "Go straight for two blocks."
"Make a right turn. Here." And there we were, in front of the main entry to the

old milk factory building, one of many on our list. I found myself in a state of profound puzzlement and wonder—how on earth did Tim know his way around Molochansk!?

According to Tim, the answer to this question was simple. While we were driving around the Molochansk streets and chatting with the locals, he saw a tall structure in a brief opening in the tree branches, which he quickly identified as a chimney stack of the old German milk factory that he remembered seeing on photographs in various Mennonite Canadian history books on the Molochansk settlement area. Right then he promptly realized his whereabouts in Molochansk, since he knew the location of other German buildings in town in relationship to each other. It was only a matter of putting things together in his head—his understanding of the physical environment of the past and his perception of the physical environment of the present—and then he was able to quickly bring us, his guides in this country, to one of his sought-after destinations.

Yet the reasons for Tim's familiarity with Molochansk are far more complicated. How did it happen that a person born and raised in pre-internet and pre-Google Map times who has never been to a place on the opposite side of the globe, could know its geography so intimately and far better than many local people? What informed his detailed knowledge of this Ukrainian town?

On another hot July afternoon in 2009, this time in Canada, my friend Ann took me to the home of George and Janet Zenkiw, who live in one of the picturesque valleys of North Okanagan of interior British Columbia.[1] George, a well-known and successful grower of vegetables, is a Ukrainian Canadian proud of his ethnic roots and prairie upbringing. Ann and George had known each other for a while professionally, and this connection helped them to form a bond that went beyond their professional relationship. You have to interview George, Ann would tell me on many occasions, his stories are fascinating, he is a reflective storyteller and can crack more than one good joke. In my research center, Prairie Centre for the Study of Ukrainian Heritage at St. Thomas More College at the University of Saskatchewan, we have introduced a number of oral history research initiatives. An interview with George, I thought, would fit into one of these projects, "The Oral History of Sociocultural Change on the Prairies: Ukrainian Canadian Experience." His story would, I believed, make a good addition to our collection of interviews, for George is one of a large number of Ukrainian Canadians who over the years "emigrated" from their rural homes on the Canadian prairies to the interior mountains of British Columbia. So I flew to Vernon to meet the Zenkiws.

In his fifties at the time of the interview, George carefully wove his narrative about his childhood on the prairies, his extended Ukrainian family that comprised his social universe for a long time, his move to the mountains and life there, and his understanding of what it means to be a Ukrainian. To describe his ancestors, he consulted the local history book from Wildwood, Alberta, which contains a chapter about his grandparents on both sides. Throughout our conversation, to which Ann and Janet were also active contributors, George reiterated many times that for him, being a Ukrainian meant being a part of the large network of an extended family who all shared the same culture, language, and religion, and what I would call clan consciousness. I could not help thinking that his sense of Ukrainian identity did not really arise from an attachment to place, a land, a territory, a homeland, but rather from an emotional attachment to his own people, his immediate extended family who live in the same historical moment as he does. Where would the "old country" fit into his story, I wondered, but decided against asking him this question directly.

Meanwhile, with George's encouragement, Janet took over our conversation, and the interview promptly shifted away from George's life. A good narrator with an excellent sense of story development, Janet gladly ventured into the life story of her own. And suddenly, the room around us transformed. With Janet's soft voice in the foreground, my mind was swinging back and forth in time and space, from the seventeen hundreds to the nineteenth century, from tsarist Russia to rural Saskatchewan at the turn of the twentieth century, from Louis XIV and medieval France to Canada's north in times of fur trade and Hudson Bay Company's expansion. What initially was to be a life story of Janet Zenkiw, a local pharmacist, a wife of a farmer, and a Russian Canadian living in the remote area of rural British Columbia, soon evolved into a fascinating adventure narrative, a family saga spanning the continents, cultures, ethnicities, and centuries. To follow her story was not an easy undertaking, given its swiftly changing scenes and densely populated plots. I was also puzzled by the scope of her life story and the expansion of its time and space horizons. While still immersed in the world of Janet's ancestors, I realized that unlike George, who chose to maintain his ethnic identity as monolithic, his wife, having been swept along by the powerful tide of ever growing genealogical movement, has completely undone her lifelong identity as a Russian Canadian. Having spent hundreds of hours on the internet as a member of many genealogical online research communities, she has discovered that her family tree contains many other roots than the Russian ones—German, French, and Métis being most pronounced. Together with her siblings, to the dismay of her Russian mother, she is now trying to obtain Métis status.

Unlike George, whose sense of Ukrainianness had been reinforced through his relationship with the extended family of here and now, horizontally, Janet's sense of self-identity was grounded in her relationship to her kin in her family tree. Janet's personal identity had also been constructed vis-à-vis her extended kin, but vertically. And despite the fact that their self-identities were dominated by the connection to people rather than to places, both George and Janet brought up the topic of their ancestral lands. George announced that he planned to go to Ukraine one day, even though he understands his Ukrainian ethnicity as belonging to his Canadian family clan. And Janet, to bring herself closer to the fascinating characters she has encountered on her metaphorical journey into the past, with more than one ethnic homeland under her belt, now wants to travel to Russia, France, Germany, and Quebec.

The search for ancestors—actively pursued by Tim in Ukraine, lived out by Janet in front of her computer in a quiet rural valley of interior British Columbia, and being tentatively considered by Janet's husband, George—is one of the foundational features of modern identities. It has also been recognized by scholars of diaspora studies as a common trait of modern diasporic cultures and communities. Searching for one's roots, David Lowenthal asserts, has become a commonplace and is a natural response to a persistent sense of displacement instigated by the global mass migration of the twentieth century.[2] Diaspora cultures, points out James Clifford, "mediate, in a lived tension, the experiences of separation and entanglement, of living here and remembering/desiring another place."[3] Different people from different ethnic backgrounds, Canada's Mennonites, Russians, or Ukrainians, would follow their own unique paths in their quest for cultural rootedness and genealogical continuity, but ultimately, their pursuit speaks to a unique cultural phenomenon of modern times.

This kind of preoccupation with ancestors and ancestral homeland leads us to other important questions about the meaning and makeup of modern identities. In this book, as someone familiar with Ukrainian culture in its various diasporic manifestations, I explore this preoccupation as it has developed in the context of the Ukrainian diaspora, focusing primarily on Ukrainian Canadian culture. Yet the book goes beyond the analysis of how ancestral homeland is imagined, understood, and dealt with in the diaspora. This would already be a familiar, though a relatively novel, undertaking in the field of diaspora studies and cultural anthropology. What I propose involves also an analysis of how diaspora has been imagined in the homeland.

What makes my approach different is that I consider this longing to be only a part of a larger social phenomenon of displacement and separation as experienced by ordinary people on both ends of what can be called a cultural *binomial* of homeland-diaspora. Here I borrow the term "diaspora-homeland binomial" from Oksana Pakhl'iovs'ka.[4] In linguistics, "binomial" refers to a sequence of two or more words, all from the same grammatical category, bound in a semantic relationship and joined by one or another syntactic device, such as "and" or "or." As such, "binomial" can serve as an apt metaphor for the immutable interconnectedness that defines the relationship between diaspora and its ancestral homeland. To understand the meaning of one half of a binomial requires one to look at the other half. The set of attitudes that people in diaspora develop toward their ancestral homelands has an important counterpart in the attitudes that people in their ancestral homelands form over the years toward the diaspora. Together they constitute a unique modern phenomenon of folk nostalgia for the cultural "same" in various Ukrainian lands. Thus, given their inseparability, in order to understand the meanings and outcomes of longing for the ancestral homeland in ethnic communities born out of immigrant populations, one needs to identify and examine the longings for the departed folk as they developed in ancestral homelands.

The longings for these "other Ukrainians" in both the diaspora and its ancestral homeland may come across as mirroring each other. After all, people in both settings appear to share the same roots, culture, and ancestry. Yet my long term ethnographic involvement with the two sides of the binomial has demonstrated to me that these longings are rather mismatched, having grown apart over the course of a century against the background of two civilizations, the West, on the one hand, and the former socialist bloc, on the other. Informed by their particular historical and sociocultural circumstances, Ukrainian "brothers" and "sisters" on each side of the binomial have developed their own unique expressive forms and cultural practices. Incongruence between the two kinds of imagining often leads to real-life misunderstandings between the people from both worlds in their encounters with each other. Those who were imagined as "the same people" have long become "the others," ultimately becoming the Ukrainian "diasporic others," whom I will refer to as the "other Ukrainians."

In effort to understand the reasons for this incongruence this book explores the diasporic dimension of ethnicity in the Ukrainian diasporic and Ukrainian homeland cultures, focusing on ordinary people's encounters with and popular imaginings of each other. In the context of Ukrainian Canadian ethnicity, these noninstitutionalized sites of interaction between the two worlds have not been granted sustained academic attention, despite the fact that the fundamental aspects of, and differences between, the cultures of homeland and diaspora are generated, practiced, and contested within them. In post-Soviet Ukraine, diaspora studies is a relatively new intellectual undertaking focusing primarily on rediscovery of the already well-established individual Ukrainian diasporas and their organizational histories. It displays little interest so far in mapping non-institutional expressions of diasporic longing for the Ukrainian "otherland." At the same time, there is much public debate about current labor migration, as new Ukrainian communities are emerging today in various corners of the globe, and separation and displacement, so familiar to rural Western Ukrainians at the turn of the twentieth century, has once again entered the lives of millions of ordinary Ukrainians at the turn of the twenty-first century, injecting into their lives new diasporic experiences.

Let me elaborate what I mean by "diasporic dimension of ethnicity," "diasporic consciousness," and "diasporic imagination." Longing for homeland is seen here not only as a universal feature of modern identity but as a particular dimension of both ethnic culture and the consciousness of individual people. Both are responsible for a long-lived diasporic imagination expressed in a variety of ways in the cultures of the homeland and the diaspora. A number of scholars in the field of diaspora studies utilize the notions of diasporic consciousness and diasporic imagination, some leaving them mostly unexplained, others elaborating on their meanings in their own analyses of diaspora-homeland relations.[5] In some cases, the term diasporic imagination refers to how cultural minorities see and understand the world rather than the homeland.[6] In more recent explorations of diasporic consciousness and imagination scholars typically focus on the diaspora and its attitudes toward the homeland. In my project, I address the imaginings of Ukrainians on both ends of the diaspora-homeland binomial, I argue for the presence of diasporic consciousness and diasporic imagination in both cultural settings, in both the homeland and the diaspora. I understand diasporic consciousness as a set of cultural values that are present and may be dominant in a community, implicitly governing people's lives in such a way as to make them feel bound to the so-called other Ukrainians occupying the so-called diasporic otherlands. Such consciousness inevitably leads to a particular kind of what Arjun Appadurai has called "social imagination," the novel ability of a modern person, informed by all kinds of modern technologies of communication, to imagine and fantasize about the world beyond his or her life-world that emerged in the second half of the twentieth century.[7] In my project here, I see diasporic imagination as a process and its outcome as a set of cultural practices and representations concerning people's understanding of their ethnic otherlands and their diasporic others.

It is also important to mention that when I speak of diasporic consciousness and diasporic imaginations, I do not suggest that all individuals who share a Ukrainian heritage are going to be endowed with such consciousness or exercise such an imagination. Neither do I suggest that the term "diaspora" is the only term that can be used vis-à-vis various Ukrainian communities in the world. As many researchers of Ukrainian Canadian culture (especially concerns scholars of Ukrainian Canadian folklore) have pointed out, Ukrainian culture in Canada cannot be seen as solely exported from the Ukrainian lands. Asserting that over the course of time it has become firmly rooted in Canadian soil, these scholars emphasize the localized, or ethnic, nature of this culture and shun the use of the word "diaspora" to describe Ukrainian Canadians. In addition, Ukrainian Canadians who have been interviewed for various folklore studies projects, especially in Western Canada, tend not to speak of themselves as members of diaspora but as members of local ethnic communities. Ukrainian Canadian culture and especially vernacular culture, they say, long time ago evolved into something of its own and is not anymore solely Ukraine oriented.

I fully share this understanding of a Canadian Ukrainian culture as a unique, made-in-Canada ethnicity. In my own research in Western Canada many of my respondents, like George Zenkiw, highlighted the Canadian core of their Ukrainian identities. Whether or not we apply the adjective "diasporic" to a well-established ethnic culture is a matter of perspective, though. While a Ukrainian Canadian person or a local organization may be predominantly concerned with Canadian issues, their local lives are often informed by matters and preoccupations external to their immediate environment, as with Tim and Janet. In addition to living in their immediate social worlds, their lives have also been unfolding in a domain that extends beyond the here and now, a domain framed by the itineraries and dispersion of their real families and imagined genealogies. This domain often provides people with life-changing and meaning-ful experiences, as demonstrated by the story of Janet's metaphorical journey through the past. These kinds of experiences and preoccupations with family history position Ukrainian Canadians in relation to not only their ancestral lands but, by default, today's Ukraine.

This book also addresses private feelings about the diaspora that emerged in the twentieth century in Ukraine. Here, I also concentrate on noninstitutional, vernacular contexts where these sentiments develop and present themselves. I mostly focus on the attitudes toward and imaginings of diaspora in Western Ukrainian rural settings, in communities that experienced significant loss in local population due to various waves of emigration that began as early as last quarter of the nineteenth century and continued throughout the twentieth. During the Soviet period, when contact with the Western world was extremely limited and allowed only under the surveillance by the Soviet authorities, real connections between the villagers and their overseas kin were almost cut com-pletely, initiating a period of disinvolvement, supplemented by imaginings of and longing for the lost kin. As new generations grew further apart from each other these imaginings and longing resulted in the formation of the unique body of knowledge and practices that underscored the perseverance of a diasporic dimension in the otherwise local lives of Western Ukrainian villagers. It is important to mention here that in Ukraine my ethnographic work took place in rural communities populated predominantly by ethnic Ukrainians. Thus, in the context of my discussion of the imaginings of diaspora among ethnic Ukrainians in rural Western Ukraine, the word "ethnicity," meaning an ethnic group, is quite applicable, allowing me to use the term "ethnicity" in my account of diasporic consciousness among both Ukrainian Canadians and Ukrainians in Ukraine.

To examine the vernacular foundations of diasporic imaginings of "other Ukrainians," I undertake two parallel yet related avenues of investigation. The first concerns the exploration of cultural manifestations of diasporic dimension of ethnicity. Between 2007 and 2010, as a holder of Canada's Social Sciences and Humanities Research Council grant, I was able to return to this long-term research initiative and concentrate on the grassroots origins of diaspora constructions of the homeland and homeland constructions of the diaspora in Ukrainian culture in the twentieth century. Throughout the grant period I continued collecting and analyzing Ukrainian diaspora-homeland folklore of the twentieth century, such as folk songs, oral narratives, and folk beliefs.

The second avenue concerns the study of diasporic practices. Such study encompasses the analysis of vernacular diasporic practices engaged in by ordinary Ukrainians in various transnational settings and draws on my own fieldwork in Canada, Ukraine, and Italy. Many of these diasporic practices— transatlantic family correspondence, the establishment of kinship networks, modern practices of homecoming, diaspora visiting, family history research, and immigrant poetry writing—have not been explored yet by Ukrainian or Canadian scholars. Ultimately, rather than simply identifying such practices this book aims to explain "vernacular" mechanisms and principles responsible for the persistence of a diasporic dimension of ethnic cultures in a complex society.

To attest to the longevity of the vernacular reflexivity of modern diasporas in the context of ongoing globalization, in the concluding part of the book, I turn to "new" Ukrainian diasporas that formed in the last decade of the twentieth century in southwestern Europe. The current mass labor migration to southern Europe (especially Portugal, Spain, and Italy but other countries as well) has its roots in the same rural Western Ukrainian communities that witnessed the emigration of their folk to the Americas a century earlier. And just like over a century ago when Ukrainians were channeled by the Canadian government to settle and develop the western Canadian frontier, Ukrainian migrants today have been filling marginal yet crucial sectors of national economies, such as, the construction and agriculture industries in Portugal and the domestic sector in Italy and Spain.[8] The immigrants were followed by their churches. The Greek Catholic Church was the first Ukrainian church to arrive on the prairies at the turn of the twentieth century, and it was the first to set up Ukrainian parishes in Portugal and Italy at the turn of the twenty-first century.[9] Similar to their predecessors who went to the Americas, contemporary migrants turn en masse to poetry writing (Italy and Portugal are excellent examples). Will these diasporas have enough vernacular creativity to build their future mythologies of homeland the way Ukrainian Canadians have? Or, given the exponential development of new technologies of information, communication, and travel, will these diasporas be spared the traditional social practices of imagining the homeland? While sociological exploration of this new global dispersion of Ukrainians began in the early 2000s, no research is being conducted into the nature of symbolic relations between these potentially very powerful diasporic communities and their homeland.[10] By adding a comparative perspective to the study of the sociocultural organization of imaginary of the diaspora in times of modernity (Ukrainian Canadian case) and late modernity (Ukrainian Portuguese case), this book, benefiting from my field research in all these settings, seeks to offer answers to these questions as well.

The proposed focus of this study—the vernacular foundations of how those in the diaspora imagine the ancestral homeland and how those in the homeland imagine the diaspora—is also informed by the recent shift in understanding of contemporary cultures that has taken place in the humanities and social science over the last two decades. As I have suggested, I see these processes of imagination, unfolding in completely different countries, geographies, societies, continents, and, if I may, civilizations, as manifestation of the same cultural phenomenon of social displacement, separation, and longing experienced by a particular cultural group, in our case by Ukrainians. The focus here is not on a territorially bound culture but rather on a culture that has long detached itself from a plot of land and reorganized itself as a global phenomenon.

With the ever-accelerating compression of the modern world's space/time parameters, the increasing migration of populations, and more accessible communication, it has become plausible to argue that "the notion of the fixity of cultures is an illusion; and that the fashioning of homogenous societies is unrealizable, if not undesirable."[11] Today's peoples increasingly operate outside defined national boundaries and interests, having been immersed already for some time in a variety of globally circulating cultural flows consisting of mass commodities, "patchwork of folk or ethnic styles and motifs stripped of their context, some general ideological discourses concerned with 'human rights and values'" and a variety of standardized languages of communication.[12] Real or virtual, these commodities, styles, discourses, and languages move easily across national borders, having little connection to any national project or national cultural domain. Ukrainians have long participated in these new global cultural flows of ideas and commodities. In fact, their diasporic practices preceded the emergence of this new world order, linked by many to the swift transformation of communication technologies in post-1980s. In the field sites of my research, it appears these practices are directly linked to the initial separation experiences that followed on the early waves of emigration in the last quarter of the nineteenth century. As such, they are deeply rooted in traditional culture and in the social institutions of homeland that were the organizing principles of villagers' lives at a time, with kinship and *zemliatstvo* being primary examples.[13] These vernacular practices were predominantly shaped *prior* to the fundamental global shifts in global economy of the last quarter in the twentieth century, arose in particular social geographies, and had their own agents.

In this study, I question how instrumental these traditional social institutions of kinship and *zemliatstvo* are and how influential the traditional practices of imagination are in the construction of contemporary diasporic mythologies of homeland and diaspora. I argue here that, cognitively, in the Ukrainian and Ukrainian Canadian contexts, the imaginings of overseas Ukrainians have been influenced by different concepts of kinship and community that developed in both the diaspora and the homeland and have been informed by distinctive notions of time and space that Ukrainians have applied differentially to their own lifeworld and the world of "other Ukrainians" and that these imaginings are supported by novel modern rituals of homecoming and diaspora visiting and sustained by unique bodies of local mythologies in diaspora about homeland and vice versa.

To understand today's intensified and not always smooth interaction between the Ukrainians in the world one needs to look into these vernacular constructions of diaspora in homeland and of homeland in diaspora as they developed throughout the twentieth century. I find it important to consider specifically vernacular foundations of diasporic imagination for the following reasons. Enhanced by modern technologies of communication, diasporic imagination is rooted in those domains of human beliefs and practices that cultural anthropologists routinely characterize as culture-specific systems of knowledge that inform sets of practices. Jerome Bruner, renowned American psychologist, speaks of such culture-specific systems as folk social science or folk psychology that informs and governs people's experiences in, knowledge about, and transactions with the social world. All cultures have their own folk psychology, "a set of more or less connected, more or less normative descriptions about how human beings 'tick,' what our own and other minds are like, what one can expect situated action to be like, what are possible modes of life, how one commits oneself to them, and so on."[14] Bruner uses the word "folk" in its broadest philosophical sense. "Folk" in his interpretation does not stand for a localized group of people, such as villagers for example. Rather, it indicates the presence of shared cultural values and predispositions among many people defined as a cultural group.

To be as persistent as they are in a culture, these shared cultural values and predispositions have to be deeply rooted in time and space. The issue of the rootedness of some elements of culture in a so-called deep history has been actively pursued across social sciences since the Annales school raised the topic in the mid-twentieth century. Fernand Braudel, one of the founders of this school of thought, writes convincingly of different historic temporalities underlying and informing different patterns of people's social actions and cultural practices.[15] There is no need to revisit fully this theory here, but a brief outline, even if simplified, will help us to further our discussion on diasporic imagination. According to the Annales, at least three time horizons define the entangled flows of events, ideas, ideologies and values every human society lives by: the short time horizon, the longest and slowest time horizon, or *longue durée,* and the medium range time-horizon occupying the position in between.

The short time horizon is constituted by and experienced through the sequence of various events, both routine and occasional, which take place in our lives. Applying Braudel's findings in a different context, William Mott refers to the short time horizon as an "event time," and I would like to borrow his term for our discussion.[16] The medium-range time horizon is also actively shaping our lives. Certain cultural values, such as that reflected in the Soviet motto "the collective comes before the person," become dominant in a society over a relatively short period of time and are associated with the ruling ideologies of that time. With the change of ideological foundations of the society, the values change as well, normally when the new generation comes of age under a new ideology. Contemporary Ukrainians, whose country "exited" socialism more than two decades ago, do not believe in the primacy of the collective in their lives as much as they did twenty years ago. After Mott, I refer to this temporality as "social time." The longest time horizon is responsible for most persistent values in the society. The most persistent features of culture, its most fundamental values, take shape over the longest period of time, millennia and beyond.

Such values as embodied in dictums like "do not kill" and "respect your neighbor" last throughout the history of many societies, revealing the workings of the slowest and longest temporality, or *longue durée*.

Mott reminds us that unlike event time and social time, the time horizon of *longue durée* runs far into the past and is expected to run far into the future.[17] Thus, we may assume that the worlds of several previous generations and several future generations will be still defined by the same fundamental cultural values as our own contemporary world. This is relevant to my explorations in this book, as the folk system of beliefs and practices, being one of the most powerful constitutive instruments of culture, is a product of *longue durée* and so will continue manifesting itself, through modification and change, in our present and, by default, in some near future. This quality of folk psychology, its capacity for extending itself deeply into the past and further into the future, is of importance to my own argument. Diasporic imagination as lived and practiced among Ukrainians on both ends of the diaspora-homeland binomial has been taking shaping over some 150 years. Its "components," referenced in vernacular texts, are especially marked by the workings of two historic temporalities, of *longue durée* and the medium-range time horizon, or social time, to employ Mott's terminology. Those aspects of diasporic reflectivity rooted in the deep history of *longue durée* will most likely continue to affect future encounters between the Ukrainians in the diaspora and the homeland, while other aspects will be short lived. I return to this matter in my discussion about how over the course of the twentieth century the two Ukrainian worlds developed their own frameworks for understanding and imagining their respective otherlands.

On the other hand, it is difficult to directly apply this understanding of the workings of various historic temporalities to human societies of modern times. A modern person's actions are informed not only by her own culture with its elements shaped under the impact of various historic temporalities but also by a broad range of continuingly emerging discourses and ideas that are not culture specific. Originating elsewhere, these discourses are nowadays easily accessed and get appropriated by various local worlds. Trying to identify those external flows of ideas as well as those inherent in a culture and explain their complex interrelatedness is hugely important. My project here is different, though. Recognizing the complex nature of contemporary imaginings of and desires and beliefs about "other Ukrainians" and realizing the complexity of their sources, I strive to locate those aspects of diasporic modes of imagining and knowing that predate the most recent cultural knowledge that modern and external discourses have imparted to Ukrainians. In doing so, I seek to map a culture-specific understanding of two metaphoric ethnic otherlands as they have been materializing among Ukrainians in the homeland and in the diaspora. I refer to this understanding, which is rooted in both the *longue durée* and a social time, as modern vernacular principle of the diasporic imagination.

Bruner's perspective on folk psychology is relevant for the purposes of my discussion for yet another reason. An important observation that Bruner makes with respect to folk social science is that by its nature this system of knowledge is *not* organized analytically, categorically, or conceptually, but rather narratively and I would add, perceptually and intuitively. As Bruner emphasizes, the critical point about folk psychology that it is narrative in nature rather than logical or categorical.[18] In the context of my fieldwork, ordinary Ukrainians, both in Ukraine and in Canada, communicate their interest in and their imaginings of their respective ethnic otherland most commonly in narrative forms. They do so explicitly when they share their family stories across the dining table, or record a song on a tape recorder to send to a loved one overseas, or compose a poem about the home they left, as Ukrainian labor migrants did in Italy and Portugal in the 1990s, or when they are being interviewed by the researchers. They do this implicitly as well when their experiences and understanding of "other Ukrainians" and their otherlands enter cultural texts such as memoirs, family history, community history books, or even cookbooks, all of which seek to meet current public expectations of how these texts should be put together. Either explicitly or implicitly, these experiences and imaginings are conveyed with the help of the narrative, orally and in writing, and display the same qualities as folk psychology in being less categorical and conceptual and more perceptual and intuitive. The narrative forms of these experiences and ideas, therefore, serve as important points of entry into the logic of the diasporic imagination, and that is why I am interested in documenting and examining such narrative representations on both ends of the diapora-homeland binomial.

It might be argued that in order to understand the roots of vernacular imaginings of the "other Ukrainian world," one also has to consider vernacular representations not only of other worlds but of the same world. However, this would be a rather challenging task, for if departures, separation, death, war, and other disruptive events are regularly "profiled" in folklore texts, songs, stories, folktales, and alike, representations of connectedness, being together, and happiness feature in traditional folk narratives and modern vernacular discourses far less often. This is not surprising, since narratives concerning loss and longing emerge when the status quo is disturbed and the normal course of life is jeopardized by extraordinary events and happenings in the community.[19] It is when the familiar and familial worlds are crumbling that the family and homeland come to the foreground.

The anxieties of initial separation are well documented in the early emigrant folklore, and in chapter 1, "Separation: Songs of Departure," I explore folk songs about emigration from the Ukrainian rural communities from the turn of the twentieth century, showing how unique the experience of separation brought about by the mass migration of the villagers across the ocean was for them. Reviewing homeland folksongs about departure and separation and those born in the new world, I seek to register in these vernacular representations of separation and social displacement a certain transition from the old, village-bound, longing for reconnection and reunion to the qualitatively new longing for one's own folk, now absent from marriage, family, kin, and the community. Representations of separation and longing for the absent *svoii* (our own), as documented in original emigrant/immigrant folklore, are unmediated expressions of folk psychology and serve us as an excellent entry into the domain of ordinary people's anxieties over the emerging new global order. The point here is to analyze the vernacular conceptualizations of the "split" of one kin into two branches, as this split becomes a defining feature of the new global Ukrainian culture. The absence of persons from the habitual social worlds of family and community and begins to define much of Ukrainian culture on both sides of the Atlantic at the turn of the twentieth century. Emigrant folklore was the reaction to this abrupt change in the foundations of culture: on the one hand, it was a means for comprehending this change; on the other, it was the first record, unmediated by other cultural discourses, of its aftermath.

With time, separation in Ukraine acquired the meaning and the feeling of absence. Chapter 2, "Mediating Absence in Ukraine," immerses us into the rural world of twentieth-century Western Ukraine. In this chapter, I focus on the question of how families and communities in Ukraine understood the new kinds of separation that the mass migration from homeland introduced to their lives and how over the course of several generations they have been managing the absence of their kin folk from their local lifeworlds. In the rural community of Hrytsevolia, where over the course of several summers (1998–2003) I conducted my ethnographic research, the reader meets villagers who negotiate their relationship with long-departed kin, along with *zemliaky*, or covillagers, in a variety of ways. As one might expect, in the second part of the twentieth century, common conceptions of the diaspora in Soviet Ukraine were very much shaped by the Soviet official discourse on the diaspora. The Soviet official discourse on the Ukrainian diaspora presented Ukrainians in the diaspora as a hard-working class of laborers and farmers trying to make it in the oppressive world of capitalism, thus offering an ideologically tinted version of overseas others to families who remained in the homeland. At the same time, the Soviet authorities systematically deprived the local people of any opportunity to stay in touch with their overseas relatives and friends and censored personal correspondence. As a result, it was only in their private lives that local villagers could give expression to their longing for overseas kin and imagine Ukrainians in the diaspora. They developed their own perspective of their extended kin overseas, a perspective deeply rooted in traditional culture and a traditional understanding of kinship and kinship responsibilities. Importantly, this chapter argues that in historical circumstances such as that of Soviet rule in Ukraine overseas kin symbolically come to occupy a unique position in the local lifeworld, a position I call a "present absence," characterized by both unmediated absence from the real life of the villagers and sustained presence in the traditionally conceived world of kinship and *zemliatstvo*.

Chapter 3, "Constructing Longing in Canada," examines how the Ukrainians in Canada dealt with the sense of separation by utilizing the idea of homeland in various public discourses. In Ukraine the experience of separation from kin was initially given voice in folklore and for political reasons, throughout the twentieth century, it was dealt with almost exclusively in the domain of private lives. In Canada, however, with time going by and new kin being born, the experience of separation from the overseas kin moved quickly into the public domain. The chapter thus explores the continuity of vernacular dimensions and foundations of diasporic imaginings as they entered into various public practices and discourses of the diaspora in the twentieth century.[20]

Here, I first focus on well established Ukrainian Canadian public rituals and community celebrations, which serve to provide background for the subsequent discussion on how the ethnic homeland is imagined in a particular local Canadian setting. Turning to a local history book produced in 1980 by the community of Mundare in western Canada, I examine how local Ukrainian Canadians define their locality by weaving their personal understanding of Ukraine into their representations and narratives of locality and how their local lifeworld ultimately gets defined against the imagined and mythologized virtues of their ethnic homeland. In doing so, I continue documenting the impact of the split and separation from and absence of kin on Ukrainian Canadians' understanding of their own ethnic identity. This identity, as well as their understanding of their locality, is effectively framed by the continued reliance on the dichotomies of here/there and us/them that underline the narrative development of local history narratives. This further supports my claim that split, separation, and absence have indeed become distinctive features not only of Ukrainian Canadian culture but of Ukrainian Canadian folk psychology as well.

The primary means by which the Ukrainians on both sides of the Atlantic Ocean remained in touch with each other was the personal letter. Chapter 4,

"Enveloping Distance," delves into the understudied cultural practice of letter writing between Ukrainians in the diaspora and those who stayed in Ukraine. Distance became a new aspect of the relationship between the two groups, and it came to be experienced in a variety of way, first in terms of geography, then in terms of personal identity, and eventually in genealogical terms. When considered in its totality, the personal correspondence between the Ukrainians in the homeland and those in the diaspora reveals that over the time the experience of absence of individual actors (personally known to the writers) began giving way to the experience of a distance between the corporate groups, the two branches of the kin. This chapter proceeds to discuss personal letters written by ordinary Ukrainian families in various times (from the beginning of the emigration through the 1990s). Of interest to us here is not only the content, form, and folkloric flare of such personal correspondence but how it became a zone of reconnection with kin and how the practice of reconnection grew into a ritual undertaking that attempted to resolve but in the end sustained the experience of distance. In addition to analyzing the specifically "Ukrainian" characteristics of these letters from the diaspora to the homeland and from the homeland to the diaspora, I also explore the role of transcontinental correspondence in the emergence and sustenance of long-distance imaginings of the two groups of Ukrainians.

Chapters 1 through 4 explore the impact of splitting, absence, separation, and distance on the folk psychology of the Ukrainians on both ends of the diaspora-homeland binomial. In one way or another the discussion in these chapters touches on the matters of family and kinship. Chapter 5, "Imagining Kinship in Canada," picks up where chapter 2 leaves off, turning to diasporic side of the binomial and investigating how transatlantic kinship is was constructed and practiced by many Ukrainian Canadians throughout the twentieth century and how it continues to be represented. Here I also examine the changes that took place in these constructions over the course of a century as a result of various local and global developments that affected the Ukrainian ethnic culture in Canada. If the earliest immigrants considered themselves members of their own extended families that for the most part remained in Ukraine, with time, the distance between the kin here and there resulted in the development of a new sense that the relatives back home were not the same kind of relatives as their relatives in Canada. To account for this movement from being the same to becoming other, I start with an analysis of the notion of generation and its impact on conceptions of transatlantic kinship. Then I proceed to examine the set of family histories written up by various Ukrainian Canadian families in preparation for various anniversaries and look closer at those families' centenary celebrations. These texts offer the researcher a unique entry point into the way such matters as kinship, family, and belonging informed the vernacular subjectivity of the Ukrainian Canadians in the last quarter of the twentieth century.

In response to the chain of important global transformations that began taking place in the 1960s and that continue to unfold today, and with the subsequent exponential growth of communication technologies at the end of the twentieth century, Ukrainian Canadians were able to renegotiate their sense of kinship and belonging via new cultural means, such as popular genealogy. Contemporary genealogical research, now internet enhanced, has helped many reconsider the distance between themselves and overseas kin. This has led to a reconceptualization of transatlantic kinship. Instead of considering the kin on both sides of the binomial as two distinct genealogical entities, one lived and known and the other one imagined and distant, genealogists reimagine them as one large and connected kin group. I illustrate this transition by showing how genealogical research has been pursued by Ukrainian Canadians, beginning with the earliest grassroots initiative that emerged in the late 1970s and continuing with most recent and more institutionalized genealogical practices.

These recent reconceptualizations of transatlantic kinship were preceded by a long period during which a true sense of transatlantic belonging and kinship was not easy to imagine or pursue. During the second part of the twentieth century and especially between the 1960s and the 1980s the relationship between diaspora and homeland was characterized by the extensive efforts of Ukrainians in the diaspora and those in Soviet Ukraine and to symbolically mediate absence and distance in vernacular discourses in the light of highly limited communication between them. In those times new kinds of diasporic practices directed at dealing with the distance between homeland and diaspora emerged. In addition to permitting a highly circumvented practice of state-censored letter writing, the Soviet authorities also eventually allowed Ukrainian Canadians finally to return to Ukraine for a visit, albeit, not surprisingly, a highly controlled visit. Chapter 6, "Homecoming," follows the grassroots itineraries of these preindependent Ukrainian diasporic homecomings, all organized as official tours to Ukraine, and explores the ritual and symbolic nature of these journeys. While the tours made it appear that diaspora Ukrainians were coming to the Soviet Ukraine and the Soviet Union to explore its majestic social and cultural achievements, in reality many of these "tourists" were driven by the desire to visit their ancestral homelands and to reconnect with their kin. For many Ukrainian Canadians who went on these tours and who continue to use organized tourism outlets for their travel needs to Ukraine today, meeting their relatives and visiting the ancestral villages were the highlights of their overseas travel. Exploring Ukrainian Canadians' recollections of their "once-in-a-life-time" journeys to the ancestral villages in Ukraine and analyzing their encounters with and attitudes toward the ancestral land, I develop an argument here that these encounters have evolved into a modern ritual of diasporic homecoming and have become an important rite of passage for Ukrainian Canadians. The question I address here concerns the ability of ritual to bring the two groups together. As I have observed through my own participation in such rituals, homecomings do not automatically serve as closure to separation, split, and absence and do not bring the two branches of the kin into the real contact; on the contrary, they tend to accentuate the symbolic distance between the two. The chapter is based on various reminiscences about homecoming I recorded in North America as well as on my direct fieldwork in various communities of Western Ukraine.

As I researched how Ukrainians on both ends of the diaspora-homeland binomial imagine "other Ukrainians," I was aware that I would risk imposing some sort of artificial closure on this cultural structure that continues to unfold in time and space if I were to only focus on the twentieth century. The 1990s brought about dramatic changes in the lives of Ukrainians across the world. As Ukraine exited the Soviet era and became an independent state and new large scale emigration from it began, the diaspora-homeland binomial came to the foreground once again in Ukrainian culture. To avoid this kind of imposition of a closure, I knew it would only be appropriate to look into the future, into the twenty-first century, in order to estimate the vitality of diasporic vernacular principles in ever-modernizing contexts.

The new wave of emigration from Ukraine in the 1990s that first affected its western regions and the subsequent establishment of new Ukrainian diaspora communities outside of Ukraine prompted me to wonder whether new experiences of separation and longing for kin on the other side of the diaspora-homeland binomial display any continuity with experiences of separation and cultural practices of diasporic imagination that evolved a century earlier. One might assume that new technologies like the mobile phone and the internet would alleviate and minimize the pain of separation from and longing for departed kin. In reality, things are more complicated, though. Throughout the 1990s, most Ukrainian migrants running away from the economic deprivation in their hometowns and villages could not afford, at least initially, to use these and other technologies, and, moreover, these technologies had not yet penetrated society. In addition the overwhelming majority of these migrants went abroad illegally and so were afraid to openly maintain contact with their families back home for fear of being discovered by the authorities and being deported.

As an outcome, the longing and separation engendered by migration was dramatically revived in Ukrainian culture. This profoundly painful experience was attested by extensive media coverage of the labor migration from Ukraine in the late 1990s. And like early twentieth-century Ukrainians dealing with matters of family split, absence and separation, Ukrainian labor migrants of the 1990s also turned en masse to poetry writing in order to overcome their challenges.

Chapter 7, "Into the Twenty-First Century," addresses this modern practice of contemporary immigrant poetry writing. Focusing first on the emerging phenomenon of immigrant poetry writing among Ukrainians in new diasporas in southwestern Europe (specifically in Italy and Portugal), I claim that vernacular poetry writing by contemporary Ukrainian emigrants is a modern manifestation of the vitality of folk psychology among Ukrainians as well as a contemporary affirmation of the old folk tradition. The case study here is poetry written by Ukrainian migrants in Italy and Portugal in the early stages of their diasporic lives. Folk poetry as an expressive vernacular practice can be seen as the least mediated expression of folk psychology. As such, it serves us as the most appropriate point of reentry into the world of vernacular beliefs and practices, in our case those pertaining to Ukrainians' imaginings (and folklorization) of their respective ethnic otherlands. Chapter 7, while opening up a new dialogue on the nature of folk expression in times of late modernity, in a certain way brings us back to the very beginning of the book's argument about the vernacular foundations of diaspora-homeland imaginings.

The book concludes with an epilogue, in which I return to the book's thesis that much of today's diaspora-homeland interaction is informed by centuries-old vernacular practices that emerged before the recent explosion in transnational communications. Contextualizing once more the case of Ukrainian diaspora-homeland imaginings in time and history, I question the vitality of established practices of such imaginings and their underlying vernacular principles as history unfolds into the new millennium.

1

///////////////////////////////////////

Separation

Songs of Departure

The afternoon of January 31, 2001, was cold and brisk, a familiar feel for a small town on the Canadian prairies in the middle of winter. The glittering snow, which had gripped the prairies for months, was blinding, and there was no escape from its glow even inside Maria Genek's house.[1] Perhaps it is because of this backdrop of sunlit yet eerie quietness of the barren winter horizon hiding behind a few houses in front of the living room window that Maria's voice sounded so crystal clear. In her home, we got together on several occasions. At the time, I was conducting field research for my doctoral project on noninstitutional Ukrainian transnationalism and was interested in learning how various people stayed engaged with their ethnic homelands. Maria, in her early sixties, who was born and raised in a small village near the town of Luzhany in Western Ukraine and who had some thirty years prior to our interview married into the Ukrainian Canadian community of Mundare in East Central Alberta, offered me her story of how one may simultaneously live in both worlds, that of homeland and diaspora. Her story unfolds from the 1970s through the 1990s, when for the most part, letter writing and one's own imagination were for many people the only means of staying in touch with the homeland side of their private worlds.

She was happy to share her life story with me. An excellent narrator of a Western Ukrainian rural experience with a unique Bukovinian touch to it, Maria was fluent not only in her own past but that of her kin, remembering the twists and turns of life itineraries of her parents, relatives, friends, and covillagers. Her storytelling techniques were remarkable, the Bukovinian dialect spicing them up even more. Her voice, rolling out in a strong rhythm of its own, betrayed not only good narrating skills but a singing talent. "Oh, Natalko," she would exclaim to me as she described her life in Ukraine, "it has been years since I sang all these songs, years! Every Sunday I used to sing, every Sunday! I was regularly invited for the weddings to cook, and I sang, sang away."[2] Maria

Figure 1.1. William Kurelek, *The Ukrainian Pioneer, No. 2*, 1971–76, acrylic, graphite, colored pencil, watercolor? on Masonite, 152.3 × 121.6 cm. National Gallery of Canada, Acc. #30836.2. Copyright of the Estate of William Kurelek, courtesy of the Wynick/Tuck Gallery, Toronto.

went on and on, describing to me the numerous village weddings, the plentiful pots of *hostyna* (festive meal) she would be cooking for these weddings as the most respected village cook, the dancing that she would join in or initiate once the party began, and the songs she would be singing when the time came for the inevitable chorus during a wedding. "And yeah, we sang those *kanads'ki* songs then, too," she said, not letting me guess whether those were the songs about or from Canada.

"Wait," she said, interrupting my request to clarify the reference to the Canadian songs, "I can sure sing it to you, but wait." She disappeared into the bedroom only to come out a minute later with her own tape recorder. I mentally smiled at yet another episode of what I learned to call "the fusion ethnography of technological age" that I often found myself doing on the Canadian prairies. This fusion ethnography, relying on modern practices of vernacular reflexivity and enhanced by various communicative devices, such as voice recorders, video players, and the internet, ultimately subverts the traditional relationship between the out-of-town ethnographer and the local informant, confusing the roles of researcher and the researched. My prairie informants oftentimes provided me with the recorded results of their own explorations into the subject matter of my academic inquiries, offering me their own research findings or videos or audio recordings of the events I was interested in, thus inevitably becoming the full coauthors of my scholarly pursuits. Would this be the case again, I wondered?

What I was about to experience was not just another case of fusion ethnography, though, but an equally puzzling act of participant observation of a virtual kind. The tape she started playing turned out to be the audio Easter letter that her family and friends back in Luzhany sent to Maria on the occasion of Easter 2000. The voices on the tape now filled the room:

> May we? If we may—we are now entering your home. We came to you for a visit from faraway and beautiful Bukovina. Christ has risen! Maria, Vasyl', and *svat* Pavel. We wish you happiness, health and many fruitful years ahead of you, so you will live and reach the same day the next year. We gathered here, at Sida Marchuchka's, the "ensemble," Vera Kasianivna, Shtefka Hurnia, Olia Mushuk. . . . We are sending you as a gift the joyful Easter song "Christ is Risen." Listen but don't cry.[3]

As the chorus began, I quickly forgot that it was already late and that I had to get back to the city for some other evening engagements. Instead, Maria and I both immersed ourselves in a singing event removed from us in real time and space, yet so immediate in its virtual presence. The modern technologies of communication that made the audio letter possible compressed these distances in time and space, transforming Maria's living room into a fundamentally new ethnographic site, enveloped by the sounds of an "elsewhere" party, of people's laughs, singing, coughs, household noises from across the ocean. Maria started crying.

It was an unsolicited letter and Maria had not requested that any particular songs be sung into the tape recorder. Perhaps, to mark (or to bridge?) the distance between Luzhany and Maria, the singers continued on with the following song:

> Oï shcho ia sobi maiu,
> Shcho ia tak daleko
> Vid ridnoho kraiu,
> Shcho ia tak daleko
> Vid ridnoho kraiu.
>
> Vid ridnoho kraiu,
> Vid ridnoï ridni,
> Shcho ia tak daleko
> Na chuzhiï storoni,
> Shcho ia tak daleko
> Na chuzhiï storoni.
>
> Na chuzhiï storoni
> Tiazhko prozhyla ty,
> Navit' nema koly
> Lystok napysaty,
> Navit' nema koly
> Lystok napysaty.
>
> Lystok napysala,
> Sl'ozamy sia vmyla.
> Oï, shcho zh tam dumaie,
> Oï, shcho zh tam hadaie
> Vsia moia rodyna?
> Oï, shcho zh tam dumaie,
> Oï, shcho zh tam hadaie
> Vsia moia rodyna?
>
> Ne plach ridnia ne plach,
> Ne plach ne zhurysia.
> Zdorova budu ia,
> Shchaslyva budu ia,
> Dodomu vernusia.

Zdorova budu ia,
Shchaslyva budu ia,
Dodomu vernusia.

Ia pryĭdu dodomu,
Budu povidaty
Iak tam na chuzhyni,
Iak tam na chuzhyni
Tiazhko prozhyla ty.
Iak tam na chuzhyni,
Iak tam na chuzhyni,
Tiazhko prozhyla ty.

What a fate I have
That I am so far away
From my native country,
That I am so far away
From my native country.

From my native country,
From my native kin,
That I am so far away
In foreign lands.
That I am so far away
In foreign lands.

In foreign lands
You have lived very hard
And had no time
To write us a letter,
And had no time
To write us a letter.

I have written you a letter
And it got washed in tears.
Oh, what is all my family
Out there now reckoning,
Out there now thinking?
Oh, what is all my family
Out there now reckoning,
Out there now thinking?

Do not cry, my family,
Don't cry and don't be sad.
I will persevere,

I will be happy
And will return home.
I will persevere,
I will be happy
And will return home.

I will arrive home
And will tell you
What life is like in faraway lands,
What life is like in faraway lands,
And how hard you have lived
In faraway lands,
And how hard you have lived
In faraway lands.

Giving voice to the nagging pain of separation that emigration introduced into so many peoples' lives, this song presents the folklorist with an interesting array of characteristics, in many ways distinct from the characteristics of the so-called Ukrainian emigrant songs from the turn of the twentieth century. Its melody is not original, and the lyrics at times lack internal rhythm and do not scan.[4] The atypical epithet-noun pair such as "ridna ridnia" ("native kin" as in second stanza, *vid ridnoï ridni*[5]) and the inconsistency in the usage of verb tenses in the narrative suggest that the song presented by the singers is composed later than the emigrant songs born in the time of mass emigration of Western Ukrainians at the turn of the twentieth century.

Yet in many ways, Luzhany's "Canada" song is an excellent example of a cultural practice that has kept overseas kin present in the lives of Western Ukrainian villagers long after the mass migration at the turn of the twentieth century came to an end.[6] Marked by the use of the past tense—about the life already spent in foreign lands—this song speaks of the ongoing effort of rural Ukrainians to deal with, and resolve, narratively and emotionally, the sense of a split—between themselves (at home) and their kin (overseas). Though the two narrative voices in the song reveal no significant details about the two protagonists engaged in the dialogue, the dialogue itself effectively attests to the fact that the number of years they have been separated and the ever-widening "kinship" gap between them has not made the separation less painful.

With its lyrics devoid of details and specific references either to geography or to a family member (mother, husband, a sibling, etc.), the song stands in sharp contrast to the texts composed during the era of mass migration (the end of the 1800s through the early 1900s). Early immigration songs commonly registered the immediacy of separation and the experience of immigration in a highly detailed fashion. This discrepancy underscores the somewhat different role the Luzhany song has been playing in the communities of its circulation, where the distances in space and time between the kin "here" and "there" have grown to be perceived as insurmountable and irreversible.

Still, no matter what expressive and artistic qualities songs like the one from Luzhany present us with, it is not those qualities that define its importance to the study of diaspora-homeland longings. Rather its importance lies in the fact that it shows that such texts have remained a part of the folk domain. Sofiia Hrytsa, a renowned Ukrainian folklorist whose expertise lies in the analysis of emigrant folk song cycles, has repeatedly stated throughout her academic career (which has been unfolding in both Soviet and post-Soviet Ukraine) that emigrant songs were a rarity in otherwise rich folk song repertoire of the Ukrainians.[7] Yet my ethnographic involvement with various communities of Western Ukraine of the last twenty or so years tells a different story. It is true that the repertoire of the so-called emigrant songs is not vast. Still, in Western Ukraine certain songs concerning those overseas (such as "Oĭ Kanado Kanadon'ko, Iaka Ty Zradlyva" and "Heĭ Hop Kanada") were well known to many Western Ukrainians during the Soviet years, even if not all of them could recite the lyrics.

Despite the fact that open discussion of the diaspora was suppressed in Soviet Ukrainian public discourse, the folk memory of and the longing for "other Ukrainians" never ceased in western Ukrainian lands. In the twentieth century, which brought many technological advancements in the sphere of human communication, this folk memory eventually came to be communicated via different channels rather than remaining the exclusive domain of folk singing. I explore these channels in chapter 6, but for now, let us return to the earliest encodings of longing for "other Ukrainians," the longing that later would indeed grow to become the folk memory and the folk imagination of the Ukrainian diasporic other.

During the period of mass migration though, it was the folk song that came to serve as the primary vehicle for conveying the emotional burden of immigration to others. At the turn of the twentieth century, when villagers in western Ukrainian lands actively pursued emigration and working overseas was a lived experience for many, vernacular reflections on emigration and its outcomes began to proliferate. Like many other parts of Europe, Ukrainian rural societies during the second part of the nineteenth century and in the early twentieth century were still under the strong hold of oral culture. The most immediate and familiar means available to people to relate their experiences and to process the range of emotions displacement and separation engendered were the song, the storytelling (*perekaz*), and other vernacular narrative genres (the ballad, the saying, the anecdote, gossip, etc.). People shared news and stories about emigration by using familiar verbal formulas, which in their turn, were defined by narrative practices of their culture and of their time. Singing while socializing or working even today remains for many Ukrainians a powerful means of bonding, and it is not surprising that in times of mass migration Ukrainians composed many songs about their immigration experiences and shared those songs with others in a number of ways that were available to them.

Ukrainians at the turn of the twentieth century also used technologies of communication of the day to share their experiences, the personal letter and public media being the most pronounced ones. Many songs about the immigration experience that have entered the folksong repertoire of Ukrainian villagers arrived from overseas in letters and were read outloud in a circle of family, neighbors, and friends.[8] Oftentimes letters contained poetic recitations of real events of emigration and new experiences abroad, as is the case with one of the first known emigration sagas concerning Brazil, documented by scholars as "The year of 1895" and also known as "Song about Brazil." This song was sent from Brazil back to Western Ukraine to a local *lirnyk*, or lira player, by his cousin in a letter, with a request that it be sung in public to deter local people from emigrating to Brazil. Soon after, the Brazil song was recorded by a folklorist and eventually published in 1898 in a popular academic journal in Lviv.[9] Various other Ukrainian periodicals in Ukraine and others that sprung up in the Americas at the turn of the twentieth century began actively publishing letters concerning immigration and emigration, thus spreading the word—and the songs—about immigration beyond local village audiences.[10]

Seen as an attestation to a never-failing strength of vernacular creativity, these emigrant songs attracted the attention of researchers, who went on to classify them, explore their formal structures, and discuss their role in the changing society.[11] Early scholarly reflections on emigrant folksongs started to appear at the end of the nineteenth century. Volodymyr Hnatiuk, Mykhaïlo Pavlyk, and later Filaret Kolessa, among many others, were active collectors of the new emigrant folklore as well as thoughtful analysts of it who saw in emigrant songs evidence of the perseverance of the vernacular creativity of the Ukrainian folk, now facing a profound sociocultural change.[12] Soviet Ukrainian scholars later continued on with this work, further classifying this folklore, usually on the basis of its themes and motifs. Bound by the ideology of their time, Soviet folklorists had to rely in their analysis of emigrant folklore on the so called Marxist-Leninist approach to the study of folklore with its emphasis on the study of history as the history of social classes of "oppressors" and "oppressed" and their power struggles. The writings of these researchers therefore attest not so much to the perseverance of the folk creativity of Ukrainians but to the perseverance of the creativity of the social class of peasantry oppressed by the capitalist system.[13] Ukrainian folklore scholars outside of the Soviet folklore studies, and especially Canadian scholars of the twentieth century, produced pioneering studies of Ukrainian immigrant folklore, in some ways elaborating on the classificatory analysis of these songs, many of which were recorded from the Ukrainians in North America and Canada specifically. The songs about immigration and settlement in Canada were actively collected, especially in the second part of the twentieth century, and there are numerous fine collections of this folklore available today.[14]

All in all, the noble and highly valuable task of collecting and classifying this kind of folklore has been already accomplished by my colleagues and predecessors on both sides of the Atlantic. I don't see the necessity here to fully review their findings. Bearing in mind the central point of our discussion—the formation of the so-called diasporic imagination in Ukrainian culture, my goal here is different. In revisiting the earliest emigrant folklore, specifically departure songs and songs about traveling overseas, I hope to show how these songs convey the important shift that began to take place in the folk psychology of Ukrainians in the last quarter of the nineteenth century as Western Ukrainian villagers got hit by powerful and mighty emigration waves. Irreversible changes in how Ukrainians began to see themselves in relation to the changing nature of family and community took place, changes that eventually became responsible for current prominence of a sense of a split—between those *here* and *there*, *us* and *them*—in the lives of many individuals and many communities.

It is important to mention here what prompted me to concentrate on the songs of departure among the range of other immigration songs. In my research practice over the years I encountered many Ukrainian Canadian narratives of coming to Canada. Throughout the second part of the twentieth century, after having been in Canada for more than half a century, Ukrainian Canadians whose ancestors arrived with the first immigration wave (1891–1914) began actively producing personal and community narratives describing in detail the establishment of their families and communities in Canada. Personal memoirs, family histories, and biography write-ups for various commemorative publications such as family reunion publications and yearbooks of various organizations have been retelling, over and over again, a particular metastory of the beginning, in which the authors shared bits and pieces of information of who had left the homeland village, when the family arrived in Canada, where they settled, how hard they had it before they finally established themselves in a new country and so on. These origin narratives, to tap into Anthony Smith's discussion of the emerging mythological qualities of many communal stories of immigrant beginnings, when considered in their totality, are highly repetitive in their organization and content presentation, despite all the diversity of facts they present.[15] The focus in them is usually on the early Canadian years of one's ancestors, that is, on arrival and settlement rather than on departure and the journey from the homeland.[16]

The absence in these narratives of detailed accounts of ancestors' journeys to Canada made me think about the cultural importance (or unimportance) of the motif of departure for Ukrainian Canadian identity at the end of the twentieth century. Before considering the reasons why departure narratives do not figure heavily in contemporary Ukrainian Canadians' imaginings of their ancestors' immigrant experiences, I want to revisit the period when departure narratives came to great prominence among Ukrainians on both sides of the Atlantic. After all, these were the times when departures to the new world affected many a family, bringing into focus the sense of a divide that future Ukrainian clans in both the homeland and the diaspora would experience.

Since in those times oral culture and vernacular means of expressing emotions and feelings about emigration were highly prominent, it is important to explore how these popular folk means conveyed, recorded, and perhaps even constructed the sense of separation and splitting experienced by the kin groups whose members where emigrating. To pursue this goal, I first discuss the place of separation in traditional Ukrainian oral lore in general. Second, I consider textual representations of partings, departures and farewells as they are presented in the earliest emigrant songs from the turn of the twentieth century. Finally, I turn to a discussion of what these representations meant to singers and listeners during the period when these songs were in active circulation and what their legacy has been to Ukrainian culture in general and to Ukrainian families specifically.

In his pioneering study on the experiences of separation in Chinese culture, Charles Stafford, an anthropologist who focuses on Chinese culture, rightly points out that partings, be they physical or symbolic, momentous or long term, mundane or dramatic, longed for or deeply regretted, constitute an important horizon of human lives in every human culture. The experience of separation, he writes, is not marginal in human relationships but, on the contrary, a defining feature of them. As such, separation experiences are of deep interest to the discipline of psychology.[17] Anthropology, however, has not explored this fundamental aspect of human life nearly enough. Repeated physical separations in various forms, Stafford argues, including ultimately death, stand in a complex relationship with various forms of emotional and social separation and distance.[18] While the repetitive nature of separation is universal, the forms of dealing with emotional and social separation are culture- and time-specific. Stafford discusses both the universally present experience of separation and various theoretical approaches to it, attempting to advance in his book new ways to conceptualize what he calls a "separation constraint."[19] Because separation is a universal principle of social existence, it is possible, claims Stafford, to describe it as "constraint," or a structure that both channels and generates culturally appropriate responses to it.

Stafford's approach to separation is refreshing in anthropology. Like Stafford, I would like to suggest, that rather than seeing separation only as something to be overcome (how folklore and folk psychology tend to see it), it should be also understood as a productive and constructive aspect of a culture.

The Ukrainian oral tradition and many of its texts attest to the historic longevity of separation experiences in Ukrainian culture. In his discussion of Ukrainian folksongs circulating in Canada, Bohdan Medwidsky points out that social uprooting, marriage and death—among other forms of separation—are commonly lamented in them.[20] Other folklorists have also attested to the long presence of separation in traditional Ukrainian culture.[21] Sofiia Hrytsa comments that the motif of "departure to the other land" ("vidïzd v chuzhu storonon'ku") long ago established itself in various genres of the Ukrainian folk song repertoire. This motif is especially common in folk songs concerning seasonal labor migration (in *strokarsk'i, chumats'ki, naïmyts'ki, burlats'ki,* and *zarobitchans'ki* songs), a common practice in Ukraine long before the mass migrations of the nineteenth century, and recruitment to the army (as in *rekruts'ki* songs).[22] In light of growing industrialization during the eighteenth and nineteenth centuries and increased seasonal labor migration, it is not surprising that separation became an equally pronounced motif of the Ukrainian folksongs. In the following song dating back more than three hundred years, a young maiden is taking off to serve as a hired help in a different community:

Ta v nediliu rano-poranen'ko, da iak sontse ne vskhodylo
Da z'ïzhdzhalasia vsia moia rodyna, vona mene da vyprodovzhala.
—Vyprovozhaiesh, moia rodynon'ko, da chy ne zhal' tobi bude
Iak ia poïdu na tu Ukraïnu, da mezhdu chuzhyie liudy.
Da zhadaï mene, moia stara nene, sidaiuchy da obidaty:
"Des' moia dytyna na chuzhiï storoni, da nikomu odvidaty . . ."
Oï, zhadaï mene, stara nene, iak siadesh uvecheri ïsty:
"Des' moia dytyna na chuzhiï storoni, da nemaie od neï visti.

Early on Sunday, before the rise of the sun
All my family gathered, they were bidding farewell to me.
Say your goodbyes, my dear family, will you not feel sorry for me

When I am gone to those far lands, [to be] among strangers?
Think of me, my dear old mother, when you sit down to a dinner:
"My child is far away in the foreign lands, there is no one to visit her there."
Think of me, my dear old mother, when you sit down to a supper:
"My child is far away in the foreign lands, and there are no news from her."[23]

Yet the motif of separation, carried over from one text to another, cannot be linked exclusively to the various kinds of physical separation discussed by Medwidsky, because separation is also routinely experienced by those undergoing various rites of passage. Scholars of ritual, beginning with Arnold Van Gennep in the early twentieth century and continuing with Terence Turner, Victor Turner, Maurice Bloch, Valeriia Eremina, and Al'bert Baĭburin, have elaborated, among others, on the prominence of separation in ritual.[24] In many traditional and posttraditional cultures, individuals are subject to special rituals that mark their entry into a new phase of their lives. Thus, in a traditional context, girls undergoing the ritual transformation into maidenhood, usually under the close supervision of knowledgeable agents of ritual, would often be physically and ritually separated from the dominion of young girls. In a posttraditional context, an early twenty-first-century initiation ritual in a student dormitory at the University of Saskatchewan requires first-year residents wear distinct (and ridiculous) clothing and act very submissively, as if they have been stripped of their status as fully independent individuals. Separation from the normalcy of everyday life is marked by the actions of all ritual participants during a given ritual.[25] The folk songs that accompanied rites of passage in traditional cultural contexts—the wedding songs, the funeral laments, the initiation lore—all deal with separation, inevitably resulting in the presence in this lore of the motif of separation. Hrytsa observes that a motif of separation (especially of a daughter from her mother) is found in many wedding songs, as women undergo a profound ritual separation in the course of the wedding ceremony, emerging from it as bearers of a different social status altogether.[26]

In his analysis of Ukrainian Canadian songs, which he calls "the songs of homesickness," Medwidsky offers a detailed list of the narrative means by which the sense of separation experienced en masse by the early immigrants to Canada is conveyed. These songs, Medwidsky notes, are characterized by three distinct elements: loneliness, longing for one's family, and symbols that represent the desire to communicate with the absent loved ones. The mood of loneliness is conveyed with the help of many single words or phrases, such as "chuzhyna" ("foreign land"), "chuzhyĭ kraĭ" ("foreign land"), "chuzhi liudy" ("strangers"), "daleka storona" ("faraway lands"), "lykha dolia" ("evil fate"),

"neshchastia" ("misfortune"), "chorni dni" ("black days"), "bida" ("calamity"),
"propasty" ("to disappear"), "marne" ("in vain"), "plakaty" ("to cry"), "sl'ozy"
("tears"), "syrotyna" ("orphan"), "sam" ("alone"), "rozluka" ("parting"),
"sumno" ("sadly"), "neveselo" ("sadly"), "zhal'" ("sorrow"), "sumni svieta"
("sad holidays"), among others. The longing for family is communicated
through the frequent use of terms denoting relatives. Symbols of communication with those left behind include the birds (many different kinds), the letter,
the flower and others.[27]

Although departure, separation, longing for family, loneliness, and farewells were all well represented in the Ukrainian oral tradition across many
generations of folk songs, the very scope of the late nineteenth to early twentieth
century emigration, its pace and the distances involved, offered a new context
for the separation constraint to play itself out in, and this is what was unique,
new and novel about the emigration songs of the turn of the twentieth century.
Separation due to emigration resulted in prolonged absences or even the
complete removal of the emigrants from their local lifeworlds. In this, it was
comparable to separations such as those entailed by participation in long-term
warfare, army service, and death. The earliest immigration songs indeed lamented the departures of relatives with the built-in expectation that they would
never return, as they emigrating family members were seen on their way to
potoĭbichnyĭ svit, which literally means "the world on the other side."[28]

The "Song about Brazil," one of the most commonly cited immigration
songs, is a great example of a song of departure.[29] I offer my translation here. I
have divided the text into five distinct parts, each preceded by a title I have
made up. Italicized in the text are tropes of departure and farewell:

Introduction

And in that year, the year of eighteen ninety five
The song from Brazil arrived, and we should pay attention to it.
In Brazil they give away land, forests, mountains, and rocks,
And in Halychyna people are crying—we are wasted here.
The [immigration] agents started disseminating false information
And stirring up people in Halychyna:
"In Brazil the land is vast, there is no suffering there,
Neighbors live a kilometer apart from each other."

Travel Story A

So the people *began packing up* to go to the foreign lands
And *bidding farewell* to their families and friends:
"*Forgive us, our brothers and sisters*, as we depart from you.

If we will make it out there, we will recall you in good faith.
Forgive us, our father and mother, don't cry over our departure
If we will make it out there, we will write you.
Forgive us, our dear neighbors and your esteemed thresholds,
Our clean feet will not be crossing them again.
Stay well everybody, we are leaving you
And will greet you only in the Valley of Josaphat."[30]

Travel Story B

As the widow heard all this, she started thinking
And with her small children she *started her journey.*
They *arrived at the edge of the village*—there is a church there by the road.
Her small children are weeping loudly: "Mother, let us [say farewell] to God."
They *passed the cemetery*—there is a fresh grave there.
Her small children are weeping loudly: "Mother, let us [say farewell] to our father."
They *reached the grave*—they fell down on it.
Embracing the grave, they bemoaned with much sorrow:
"Our mother sold away our house
And she is taking us to foreign lands—don't let her, dear father."
They left the grave behind, and *climbed on the train.*
The children *mourned their dear homeland*:
"*We are sorry to leave you, stars,* you shone upon us.
We are also sorry to leave you, the trails, which we walked over and over.
We are sorry to leave you, the sun, the moon, you shone upon us.
We are sorry to leave you, our sacred land, you fed us for a long time.
We are sorry to leave the forests that decorated our springs.
We are sorry to leave the birds that sang us their songs."

They *arrived at the sea* and *boarded the ship.*
The powerful storm had started and all fainted from fear.
The *arrived at the dry land* and wrote to us.

Travel Story C

The righteous Christians were sorry to leave their lands behind.
Far well, dearest Ukraine,
We *have abandoned you, our dearest relatives*
Far well, dearest Ukraine,
I *have abandoned you, my dear house*!
I *have abandoned you, my dear house,*
You raised me when I was a child.
Think, brother, *when we departed*—
We shook each other's hands as if saying just goodnight.
If only you would have known, my dear brother, how painful it is for us to be here.

We *traveled across the sea* for twenty-eight days:
If only you would have known, my dear brother, how it is to travel in the ocean.
There are no birds anywhere one looks.
If only you would have known, my dear brother . . . (how sorrowful it is here).
If one did see a bird, one would call him "a neighbor."

I will describe you, my brothers, the adventures of mine.
How the sun burned us while we traveled through those horrible waters.
The sun burned us so hard, as if it was the fire from hell.
And every one was lying dead on that ship.
And when someone died—he was not buried.
They would tie up a large rock to his back and like that would put him in the water.

As you brothers sleep in your homes—the sun here is already shining upon us for four
    hours.
And as the terrible tornado struck us at midnight—many a ship sunk in those waters.

Summative Observations

This is sincere truth, what I am telling you.
If you don't believe me, ask God.
Listen, dear brothers, to my sermon:
Don't leave your homes for these terrible troubles.
We may return to you our dear brothers, but only with God's will,
And under his protection.

Brazil is a joyful country, one can live alright there.
Yet one will not hear the word of God there, nor the sermon.
The [immigration] agents tricked us, saying "The priests will come with you."
And we are left here as if motherless children.
In Brazil, they don't know God.
On Sundays, without the bells ringing, they sit down to drink coffee.
In Halychyna, the good people are looking after themselves.
By praying, reading sacraments, and preparing for His Kingdom.

Brazil is a joyful country, one can live alright there.
Maybe it would be good for us as well, if only we can make it through.
Maybe it would be good for us, if only we can make it through.
If not we, perhaps our children will see the better days.
We should be patient and wait until that time.

Was not it better back home, to eat brine without bread?
Our wives did not want to whitewash their ovens.
Now they have to start the fire on a bare land.
Our children did not want to clean their homes,
Now they have to get used to wooden shacks.

And those who want to sing this Brazilian song
Should sit still in their homes and not leave them.

Give us, God, health and strength to live in peace
So we can share this Brazilian song with others for as long as we can.

What is happening, narratively speaking, in these earliest emigrant songs of departure? At the syntagmatic level, the songs offer a chronologically progressive narrative account of the emigration process.[31] Back in 1902 in a discussion of "novel" folk songs (*pisenni novotvory*) concerning emigration, Volodymyr Hnatiuk pointed to the fact that practically all important aspects of the labor migration of the late 1800s are reflected in these songs. The songs touch on the reasons for emigration—the lack of land, hardships, high taxes, fights, lack of opportunity to make living, political demoralization, persecution by local authorities—and at the same time express hope of freedom in the new world, especially political freedom and overall a better future.[32] Following the narratives of departure songs we can register all stages of travel, from the preparation for the departure (considering emigration, selling one's property, bidding farewell to the family, community, and country) to the departure itself (going to the train station, taking a train, arriving at the port, boarding the ship, leaving the

Figure 1.2. Ocean liner SS *Cap Polonio* enters the docks. The postcard was received by the family of Maryntsiunia Smal', village of Hrytsevolia, from her father in Canada in the 1920s. Author's collection.

port, surviving sea travel), and finally arriving in the new world (landing in the new world and, in the Canadian context, transferring to the train and traveling to the homestead). In this, immigration folklore can be seen as a documentary genre, accurately representing the order of actions and making specific references to geography, urban points of transfer, names of agents, and destinations.

Compared to other songs of departure already in circulation in the Ukrainian folk tradition at the time, the early immigration songs describe a distinctly new reality of travel that involved journeying immense distances and crossing the ocean. The distances between home and the new destinations were such that the motif of crossing waters—being one of the fundamental motifs of ritual lore concerning death—features much more prominently in these songs than in earlier separation folk narratives. That the challenges of traveling these profound distances were indeed significant is attested by Joseph Oleskiw in his famous 1895 pamphlet, *Pro Vil'ni Zemli*. Reflecting on the conditions of the Ukrainian immigration to South America, Oleskiw describes just what the journey that the average emigrant to Brazil undertook in the 1890s was like:

> The saddest aspect of emigrating to Brazil is the loss of life or health. Beginning with the sea travel from the Italian shores to the Brazilian ones that lasts three weeks, one suffers bitterly. It is a bloody path. Those who are not accustomed to sea traveling will endure seasickness resulting in strong and unusually painful nausea. No one is spared this. It would not be so bad on its own. But imagine several hundred people jammed, like herrings in a barrel, in a tight space under the deck, where the bunk beds are stuck in several rows, one on top of the other, and were it is near impossible to get through them. Imagine all those hundreds of travelers falling seasick at once. Imagine also they have to travel like this for three weeks through the sweltering heat of the equatorial zone. Imagine the stench that develops in that human barn, the lack of air, and the shocking levels of discharge everywhere. No one will be able to remain healthy in such surroundings. All whither, fall sick, and the weakest and the youngest perish.[33]

It is probably not surprising that such experiences are well referenced in departure songs:

On the sea, there is hardship.
No one cares about people.
If one dies, he is not buried.
Two sailors hold a bag,
Tie a piece of metal to him.
Once they tie it, they throw him,
My dear mother, into the sea.

And the ship will sound its horn sorrowly.
And all kinds of fish will take his body.[34]

Oh my dear God, I try very hard.
How can I board that ship
If those who die (on it) are not buried by the priests
But thrown over the board by the sailors?[35]

On the ship, on the ship, priests do not perform the funeral service.
If someone dies, if someone dies, he is thrown into the sea.
His bones are floating around,
And his white body, his white body, is eaten by the fish.[36]

It would be reasonable to assume that at the end of the nineteenth century, despite the fact that the folk psychology of Ukrainians had been strongly marked by ritual and oral tradition, in their daily lives people were perfectly able to delineate between the everyday and the ritual. The irony of emigration, though, was that its reality, so out of the ordinary and of such profound scope (the great distances, the many boundary crossings, the dangerous journey over the ocean, the travel into the frontiers of the new world, and so on) in the folk imagination did indeed approximate the world of ritual and folk belief, and so it is not surprising that on the morphological level, early immigration songs mimicked the existing repertoire of narrative formulas used to describe departure and separation.

And yet these songs were at the same time quite novel in their story development. My understanding of the morphological organization of these songs is inspired by Vladimir Propp and his treatment of narrative organization of traditional Russian folktales. In his fundamental *Morphology of the Folktale*, he argues that the most important organizing principle of a traditional folktale is what he called its "function." "Function" in his study refers to a particular act performed by the character and defined from the point of view of its significance in relation to the action.[37] While Propp's analysis concerns only Russian fairy tales, his framework of interpretation is certainly applicable to other narrative contexts and situations, as attested by many of his followers and critics. For his purposes, Propp defined the whole set of actions (about thirty) that the characters of the fairy tale may undertake in the course of the tale. Propp asserts that the number of these functions is limited and their order of appearance in the story will always be the same, though not all functions necessarily appear in every fairy tale.

Emigrant departure songs are also framed by certain functions defined by the very genre of the departure song. As they appear in various collections of the twentieth century, these songs are for the most part of a "fluid" nature; they may both include parts from other similar narratives and exclude segments of their own, known from other variants of the same song. As such, they affirm the Foucauldian idea that narrative disjunctures, ruptures, and discontinuities are equally telling elements of a narrative as those that emphasize coherence and order.

Let's return to the text of the Brazil song. In the Brazil song, as with other similar departure songs, there are several storylines and distinct actors—the villagers at large in travel story A, a widow with her children in travel story B, and the narrator himself in travel story C. The presence of the narrator also brings to the foreground the audience to whom the narrator addresses his observations on the immigration experience ("the brothers"). All three narrative travelers are indeed variant instantiations of the same narrative category of a traveler. All three set off from their homes, all three bid extended farewell to people and home. The first traveler says goodbyes to brothers and sisters, fathers and mothers, then to the next close social circle, that of neighbors, then to everybody in the village. The second traveler and her children do likewise. While traveling through the village, they bid farewell to the village church, to the deceased father's grave. When leaving the country on the train, they bid farewell to their homeland and every element of nature that they associate with homeland (the stars, the trails, the sun, the moon, the land, the forests, the birds). The third traveler bids his farewell to his country, to his family home/house, and to his brother.

This abundance of farewells in departure songs speaks of primacy of the narrative function of farewell bidding in this genre of songs. In these songs all phases of departure (from home, from the neighborhood, from the village, from the country) are accompanied by a corresponding farewell (to closest family members, the neighbors, the villagers, the country). In other words, there is no departure from home without a *ritual* farewell to its occupants or its constituents. Bidding farewell seems to be the most important act that the protagonist of the narrative performs as an active agent. Importantly, bidding farewell oftentimes takes the form of lamenting the elements of the world being left behind.

Proppian functions are also predicated on the protagonist's interactions with other characters he or she meets on his or her journey. In fairy tales, the protagonist encounters donors, helpers, tricksters, testers and so on. These interactions are also the functions that, bound by morphological rules, deliver the expected narrative outcome—the challenges are overcome, the tricksters are outsmarted, the protagonist is reconnected with his or her family. In the departure narratives, the interaction takes place between the emigrant and his or her family and home left behind and between the emigrant and the "cumulative other" he or she encounters on this journey. In addition, fairy tale heroes are agents of change, and after their ordeals, they come, as winners, to fully control their actions, while the protagonists of departure songs, once they have said their goodbyes to the homeland, for the most part become recipients of acts inflicted on them by others (i.e., immigration agents, border officers) or by circumstance (i.e., the elements of nature).

The protagonists of departure songs are comparable to the protagonists of fairy tales for yet another reason. Both seem to venture out from their homes into the unknown lands (forests, fields, foreign lands in fairy tales; cities, other countries, the ocean, and finally the new world in departure songs). Both encounter and overcome numerous obstacles on the way to achieving their goals. Fairy tale heroes want to obtain something they were missing or lost, while emigrant protagonists are in search of the promised land or income. But yet here too there are fundamental differences between them. If the fairy tale protagonist returns to his or her home after successful ordeals out in the world, the protagonists of departure songs remain in the world, away from their home, and, narratively speaking, they never come back.

The work of Van Gennep and Victor Turner is relevant here. Van Gennep was the first to address the sense of separation that many departees would experience while in transit (from home to an unknown world) or in ritual transition (from one social status to another), while Turner elaborated further on the liminal nature of such journeys.[38] Consider, for example, a young bride undergoing a traditional Ukrainian wedding ceremony in premodern contexts. In a contemporary context, the bride usually takes an active role in planning the wedding and the celebration of her own new status as a married woman. In a traditional context, on the other hand, the bride did not participate at all in organizing the wedding, and although she was certainly at the center of the ritual, she had a very prescribed role to follow, and this role in fact stripped her of any agency of her own. During the wedding ceremony, the bride was mourned by others as if she were about to die, and she herself would mourn her departure from parents' home and from girlhood. She did not speak, and she was walked around by others (father, father of the groom, or older brother). She did not initiate any movement on her own, and as a ritual figure, she was subject to actions of others. The bride's liminal, transitional state between girlhood and womanhood, between home and nonhome, was marked by passivity, absence of agency, and a willingness to accept her lot or fate. Such absence of power and agency are fundamental aspects of liminality in rituals of initiation (the wedding being a good example of initiation rituals).

Emigration songs likewise describe a liminal state. Having left their familiar homes to begin a journey toward a new identity and a new social status, emigrants found themselves in an in-between state, between home and the unknown new world, between being established members of their communities and being socially uprooted and unattached. The imposition of such liminality on the emigrating family members in various folk texts dealing with emigration (as well as in the popular discourse of the time) was one of the important ways folk psychology of the time sought to process the emerging split of one ethnic group into its two branches, one in homeland and one in the new world.

Thus, on one level, the syntagmatic level, immigration songs are good examples of the vernacular documentation of the unfolding reality of emigration, while on another level, the paradigmatic one, these songs also reveal an ongoing folk appropriation of the new realities. These folk interpretations tapped into already existing frameworks that provided a means for understanding new realities that broke with the imagined normal course of life and were informed by local folk belief and ritual practices. As songs of departure address separation that the families experienced at the moment of departure, they present it as an unresolved problem. Considered in their totality, these narratives present the emigrant protagonist as trapped in a liminal status of neither here nor there. Those who left their homes become the people undone, the itinerant travelers, in these folk narratives; the motif of an itinerant traveler would in turn become a common feature of many postarrival immigrant songs.[39] The only locale where they would be sure to reconnect again with their relatives is the Valley of Josaphat.

These folk narratives underscoring the liminal status of emigrants have had as much impact on society as the mass migration itself. Once placed by folk psychology in this space of "neither . . . nor . . . ," the migrants, in the eyes of those who stayed behind, became shadows of themselves who lived on in the memory of the local people. The migrants, having arrived with the same folk psychology to the new "alien," or *chuzhyĭ*, world, not only shared this understanding of their liminal status but lived it out as immigrants in Canada. Ultimately, as new generations were born, the memory of such liminality would persist, but only in the folk domain rather than in public Ukrainian Canadian culture, which by contrast focused on asserting a place of power for Ukrainians in Canada and, in the second half of the twentieth century, on building a new myth about strong-willed, determined, and hardworking pioneers. This in fact explains why the highly powerful stories of departure hardly made it into the Ukrainian Canadian origin narrative.

Figure 2.1. Maryntsiunia Smal' looks at photos and letters sent from the United States and Canada by her father in the 1920s to her family in the village of Hrytsevolia, 1998. Photo by author.

2

Mediating Absence in Homeland

Dlia vas usikh, dlia titky Hannusi,
Dlia vsiiei rodyny ia ziklala virsh.

Vidlitaiut' z domu leleky
I buduiut' hnizdechka svoï,
Odni blyz'ko, a druhi daleko,
Odni doma, druhi v chuzhyni.

Poletiv v svit vid ridnykh daleko,
Vid svoieï matusi, vid nen'ky zemli.
Zbuduvav sam domivku leleka
U dalekykh kraiakh, v chuzhyni.

Porodyv vin rodynu velyku
Khoch v dalekiï chuzhiï storoni
Ta navchyv vin liubyty tu zemliu
Iaka bula vid nykh v dalyni.

Ioho ditiam, onukam, rodyni,
Stala ridna chuzhyns'ka zemlia
A dumky ïkhni lynut' i nyni
De isnuie bat'kivs'ka zemlia.

Na zemli tiï zostalos' hnizdechko
Shcho zalyshyv ïkh dido kolys'.
Na zemli tiï zrostaie korinnia
Vid iakoho my vsi povelys'.
Te korinnia mitsne i hlyboke
Rozroslosia na ridniï zemli.
Berezhut' svoiu pamiat' kriz' roky
Ridni vashi, velyki i mali.

45

Ne bida shcho zhyvem tak daleko
I shcho nas rozdiliaut' velyki shliakhy.
Nas z'iednav nezabutniĭ leleka
Na dovichne zhyttia, na viky.

For all of you, for aunt Hannusia and
All your family, I composed this poem.

Storks are leaving their homes
And are building their nests,
Some nearby, others far away,
Some at home, others in alien lands.

A stork flew into the world, far away from his kin,
From his own mother and from his motherland,
And built himself a new home
In the faraway land, in the alien place.

And with time, his family grew.
Although in the faraway lands,
He had taught his children to love the land
That was left behind and far away.

To his children and grandchildren, to his new kin,
That foreign world became their new home.
But their thoughts, even now,
Are reaching out to where their fatherland is.

In that land, a nest remains,
Left empty by their grandfather.
In that land, the roots have been growing
The same roots we all have come from.

Those roots, deep and strong,
Spread around the native land.
Through the years your kinfolk, old and young,
Have been cherishing the memory of homeland.

It's alright that we live so far away from each other
And are divided by many a great road.
We are linked through a cherished stork
For centuries and for eternity.

This poem was written by a young woman in the village of Khutir-Budyliv, Sniatyn District, Ivano-Frankivsk Oblast of Ukraine, Kalyna Berlad, who composed it with the specific purpose in mind, to send it to "all her family" in Canada. She included the poem in a letter addressed to Christine Pawluk, who lives near the town of Mundare, in east-central Alberta.[1] Back in the 1920s, the three siblings of the oldest generation of the Berlads in Khutir-Budyliv bid fare-well to their brother, who emigrated to the Mundare area. Over time, a whole new clan of Berlads sprang up in Canada, and Christine Pawluk is one of many members of this Canadian extended family. For decades the families kept in touch via letters, but as the years passed, the correspondence withered. In 1982, when Christine's mother went to Ukraine, the contact between the Berlads in Khutir-Budyliv and Christine's family in Canada was reestablished, and now letters from Ukraine arrive in Mundare on average three times a year.[2] The visit in 1982 is remembered and referred to in all letters that were sent to Mundare over the last two decades of the twentieth century.[3] One can still hear the elation that the Berlads experienced during the brief family reunion of 1982 in the beautifully crafted poetic letter Kalyna wrote to her relatives in 2000.

In another letter a few months after Kalyna had sent off her poem, Kalyna's mother inquired with the Canadian family as to their opinion of her daughter's composition. Expressing her suspicion that the poem, originally written in the Ukrainian language, remained inaccessible to the English-language-speaking kin, she proceeded to ask Christine to translate this poem into English and to make it available to everyone in the Canadian family, so they all could read it and share the bonding of kinship so poetically stated in it. Kalyna's mother felt the need to explicitly ask for the poem to be distributed among the relatives, for the family in Ukraine had not received yet any response to this poetic procla-mation of shared kinship.

Why did the Berlads in Ukraine have such a strong desire to receive a con-firmation of the kinship ties between them and all the members in Christine's extended family? What motivated Kalyna to write such a poem in a first place? Why was her mother so impatient to hear back from the Canadian family? In this chapter, I explore the reasons for the apparent anxiety that overwhelmed the Berlads from the moment they reconnected with their Canadian kin two decades ago.

In the previous chapter, I focused on new experiences of separation that Ukrainian villagers were facing at the time of their mass migration overseas by looking at immigrant songs dealing with the departure that were composed at the time. Here, I turn to the question of how those who remained in their home-lands dealt with the new reality of their family lives, now characterized by the poignant absence of many loved ones. How did individuals, families, and communities in Ukraine understand the new kinds of separation that the mass migration from homeland introduced to their lives? How did families manage the absence of their kin folk over the course of several generations?

On a broader theoretical level the question here concerns the issue and the meaning of separation itself. As in the past, partings and farewells became a highly pronounced part of local life in twentieth-century Western Ukraine, and the experience of separation was common in the lives of many. Over the course of several generations, has absence of kin been accepted as a "normal," given, aspect of life or has it been seen as something incongruent with local under-standings of kinship and community, as something to be resolved? To properly address how separation has been understood in Ukraine's communities, one not only needs to consider private family practices aimed at mediating the separation (such as cross-Atlantic letter writing, which I explore in chapter 4) but also has to consider the role of local culture and community. It is the rooted-ness of the diasporic longing for "other Ukrainians" in local lifeworlds and in the traditional makeup of the community rather than, say, in evident economic disparities between the two worlds of homeland and the diaspora in North America that explains the intensity and persistence of diasporic longing for and fascination with overseas kin as well as the belief that overseas kin have certain obligations to fulfill to those in the homeland. In addition, as the members of the earliest and largest emigration wave originated primarily from the village communities of Western Ukraine, one has to account for the social roots of the first localized representations of overseas kin in order to understand subsequent representations—to appreciate Kalyna Berlad's emotional commitment to her newly found relations in Canada and to explain the persistence of vernacular representations of longing such as the Luzhany family's "Canada" song discussed in chapter 1.

The discussion in this chapter immerses us into the rural world of twentieth-century Western Ukraine. To address the question of how the absence of kin was mediated in the communities of Western Ukrainians throughout the twentieth century, we visit the remote community of Hrytsevolia, where over the course of several summers (1998–2003) I did my ethnographic research, exploring, together with the villagers, the relationship of the villagers to the long-departed kin, as well as *zemliaky*, or covillagers.[4] It is important to note here that my inter-pretation of this community's sense of rootedness in a local lifeworld is largely based on observations made by me during the last few years of the twentieth century. Yet my immersion in their home village, along with my twenty years' worth of experience researching rural communities elsewhere in Ukraine, enabled me to see that the Hrytsevolian understanding of community is deeply traditional and owes much to folk psychology. In other words, conversations I participated in and stories I heard while in the village reflected not only the ideology of the late twentieth century but the impact of an older system of values, rooted in the history of *longue durée*.[5] Hrystevolians at the end of the twentieth century continued to see themselves as living in a tightly knit community, despite all the economical and political pressures that pushed many of them outside of it. One can speculate that the commitment of previous generations of Hrytse-volians to community was similar and perhaps even stronger.

Let me briefly touch on the twentieth-century history of Hrytsevolian com-munity. The choice of Hrytsevolia as my field site was dictated by, among other things, my desire to work in a smaller rather than large rural community that was not near an urban center and that was populated by ethnic Ukrainians rather than by people from different ethnicities. I was also seeking a community that displayed a certain genealogical rootedness and continuity, as I wanted to be able to track down people with memories of pre-Soviet life in the village. After all, many rural communities in the former USSR were subject to popula-tion reshuffling by the Soviet authorities, and this policy affected many villages and towns in Western Ukraine. Hrytsevolia seemed to be fit the profile I was seeking quite well. In the 1990s, its community consisted of 165 active house-holds with about 570 adults.[6] Surrounded by forest on three sides (figure 2.2),

Figure 2.2. The village of Hrytsevolia, 1999. Photo by author.

the village was connected to the rest of the world by one paved road as well as a number of small forest roads, each of which led to equally small neighboring communities. Although the 110 kilometers between the village and Lviv, the largest nearest urban center and the historic capital of Halychyna, may seem like a short distance to the Canadians, in reality, a trip to Lviv in 1998 was a full-day affair for most Hrytsevolians, as, having no transportation of their own, they had to rely on a public bus that ran once a day. The majority of Hrytsevolians at the time were members of the Ukrainian Orthodox Church, though later I learned that there was also a Protestant minority. About twenty households, all ethnic Ukrainian and local, belonged to the Stundist Order, a particular type of the Ukrainian Baptist Church that had made its way into the village in the 1930s.

It may appear that the local lifeworld of Hrystevolia has been self-contained and uninterrupted over the long course of time, but this would be a false impression. The collective memory of the villagers recalls Hrytsevolia's complex involvement in the ebbing global flows of modernity, those of power, capital, ideas, and people, that coursed through the region throughout the late nineteenth and twentieth centuries. In the twentieth century alone, Hrytsevolia was ruled by at least seven states. Before World War One the village was a part of Austro-Hungarian Empire. During this war, the village was temporarily brought into the orbit of tsarist Russia. The Western Ukrainian People's Republic briefly ruled the region in 1918, and the village fell under its jurisdiction. From 1921 until 1939 Hrytsevolia was a part of Poland. In 1939, the Soviet Union took over the region and the area became a part of the Soviet Ukraine. Between 1939 and 1944, Hrytsevolia frequently changed hands, falling under either Soviet or Nazi German jurisdiction. In 1944, the Soviets had control again and went on to rule the region for about fifty years. In 1991 Hrystevolia became a part of the independent Ukrainian state. The topography of the region speaks powerfully to the changing borders and turbulent history of Hrytsevolia. Neighboring villages bear the names of Nimets'ka Mytnytsia (German Customs), Pol's'ka Mytnytsia (Polish Customs), and Avstriïs'ka Mytnytsia (Austrian Customs).

Many of these border changes were a product of the extended political and military conflicts that marked the last century. During both world wars, the villagers often found themselves at the center of military battles. The frontlines literally cut across the village during both wars.[7] A cemetery in the nearby forest, with, according to the villagers, eighteen "Austrian graves," is a powerful reminder of the havoc caused in this locality by the First World War. The frontlines of the Second World War also cut across the village on several occasions, leaving it flattened to the ground. Only thirty scattered buildings out of two hundred households that were in the village before the war (including a few houses, several barns, and some small storage facilities) remained standing after the last retreat of the Nazi army.[8] In the five years after the Soviet army regained control over the village in 1944, the Soviet authorities killed, arrested, and exiled those in the village who were fighting against the Soviet takeover.[9] The village council registrar books state that by 1948 the villagers reclaimed 130 households, which means that more than one-third of the families that had been living there never made it back to the village.[10] In 1949, those remaining alive after the turbulent decade of fighting were subjected to forced collectivization and enrolled in a newly created collective farm named after an early Soviet leader Felix Dzerzhinsky, the first head of the Soviet secret police feared for its torture and persecution tactics. The subsequent decades of Soviet rule witnessed the formation and firm establishment of a distinct Soviet lifestyle in all spheres of village life, with villagers employed either on the collective farm (mostly women) or in local state enterprises such as the mechanical brigades or forestry (mostly men). At the time of my stays in the village, the last two Soviet decades, the 1970s and the 1980s, were remembered by the older generation as economically stable, relatively prosperous, and comfortable times.

The post-Soviet era brought further structural transformations to the local world of Hrytsevolia. In 1992, the *kolhosp* was reorganized into an agricultural cooperative, and former collective farmers each received about two hectares of once collectively owned land.[11] Most of this land was still rented by the cooperative, and the villagers continued on with their lives in a way similar to that under the USSR. As with the rest of the state-run sectors of Ukraine's economy, the members of the cooperative were rarely paid their small salaries on time. Throughout the 1990s, a decade of slow and ineffective reforms in the agrarian sector of Ukraine's economy, the cooperative continued to generate little cash flow and was reimbursing its members for labor in kind and irregularly.[12] Hrytsevolian families worked on the private strips of land that provided them with about 80 percent of the produce the family would consume during the year.[13] Horses became a pricey commodity, as villagers rarely could afford a car, much less a tractor. All in all, for many, life became far more challenging than it had been during the last two or three decades when they enjoyed a stable Soviet lifestyle and centrally coordinated economy.

Given this turbulent history, it is not surprising that the Hrytsevolian community saw many departures throughout the twentieth century. It also saw many returns but those, statistically, were fewer. The villagers began leaving their community in the 1880s and 1890s, first going to Brazil and Argentina.[14]

Between the 1880s and 1914, many left for Canada and the United States. After the First World War, in the 1920s and the 1930s, others followed to join their kin across the ocean. Some villagers traveled back and forth between the two worlds. They worked and lived overseas and financially supported their families back in Hrytsevolia. After a few years, they would come back to the village for a short visit and then go back to Canada or the States, until the next visit. In many ways this pattern of going back and forth is reminiscent of other kinds of seasonal work that used to be communally undertaken by the men in the village, who would go in brigades to do forestry work nearby or to other agricultural regions of the former USSR, especially in the south. Such a high level of mobility between Hrytsevolia and the Americas was possible only until 1939, when the Soviet Union annexed Hrystevolia to the Soviet Ukraine and banned contact between the villagers and their relatives overseas.

There were circumstances besides emigration that forced Hrystevolians to depart for the outside world. During both world wars, the villagers were recruited into the ruling armies that in their pursuit of the enemy marched across much of Europe. Those who returned home from the First World War brought with them stories of Italy, Austria, and other places.[15] During the Nazi occupation in the Second World War, many young villagers were taken to Germany as *Ostarbeiters*, and after the war they emigrated to the United States and Canada. Once the Soviet Union regained control over the region in 1944, those less compliant with the new political establishment were shot and their families were exiled to Russia's north or Siberia. Later on, in more peaceful times, there would be other kinds of departures as well. Family members would move to marry, to pursue postsecondary education, and after graduation, to work elsewhere, as the place of employment was assigned to a person by a special state commission upon graduation. Soon after Ukraine's independence, as a result of worsened economic conditions, many villagers started looking for employment outside of the village, first mainly as contract workers in the construction industry within Ukraine and Russia. With the arrival of the twenty-first century, following their compatriots in search of work and cash, they began emigrating to other countries as well.

All and all, the life of the Hrytsevolians in the twentieth century appears to have been dominated by departures, partings, and separations that were not necessarily always matched by a subsequent reunion. This, in turn, resonates with Stafford's thesis on partings and separations that I discussed chapter 1. Partings and separations became commonplace for Hrytsevolians, a dominant characteristic of this community's development. Thus, when it comes to the question of how the villagers have been dealing with the emigration of their kin into the world outside of their village, one needs to place those departures in a broader context of villagers' wide experience with separation from kin and the failure of kin to return brought about by the village's direct participation in the global and regional history of the twentieth century.

As discussed earlier, one of the claims made by Stafford in his discussion of the place of separation and partings in traditional cultures is the assertion that because these experiences are so obvious and dominant, it is erroneous to expect, that separation can be fully resolved, that the departed will be brought back and the re-unions, however real or virtual, will be played out. One needs to consider the presence of separation in a culture in a different light, as a particular parameter of people's lives, a cultural constraint that is always in the background of people's actions. Stafford's thesis applies well to the case of Hrytsevolia, yet working in the community, I was nevertheless struck by an implicit yet powerful cultural drive to either eliminate the constraint of separation or at least work around it, as if to prevent the disassembling of the puzzle that represented the community's togetherness and to prevent individual pieces of the puzzle from getting lost.

Despite all these challenges and continuous fluctuations in the membership of the local community that the villagers experienced in the twentieth century, in the second part of the twentieth century those who departed overseas as emigrants occupied a special place in the villagers' minds and networks of relations. This, of course, is because their disappearance from the local lifeworld did not result in their complete erasure from the local social charts. With the arrival of the Soviet rule to the village in 1939 and then again in 1944 the ties between those overseas and those behind the newly drawn "iron curtain" were cut. The villagers began to rely on other means of maintaining a connection to their kin overseas than direct encounters, such as storytelling, folklore, rituals, and imagination.[16]

The Hrytsevolian case of mediating the absence of the overseas kin serves us as an example of how, in local communities of the old country, the kin and covillagers that went abroad, beginning with those who left at the turn of the twentieth century, have never ceased to be seen as "present" in local life. Although over time they became a part of the past and of a different universe of "*zemliaky* and kin elsewhere," the overseas folks continued to be seen as members of the local kin groups and community and as branches of the same kinship tree as local kinship trees, even with new generations coming of age. As a result, the overseas kin became constructed in highly dichotomous terms of departed/ remaining, here/there, and present/missing. On the one hand, the persistence of this seemingly conflicted picture has its roots in traditional understandings of the community. On the other, it was also informed by newly formed folk practices, however traditional at their core, including oral lore (stories, beliefs, and reminiscences concerning the overseas kin) and new rituals that mediated the departures and helped to resolve the ambiguity of kin's actual absence and ritual presence.

The Meaning of Community

Vernacular private interpretations of separation experiences, a main focus of this monograph, above all concern such experiences within family networks. Yet given the powerful presence of folk psychology in many contemporary Ukrainian communities, it is important to explore how separation is construed within the framework of a community. The sense of community in twentieth-century Hrystevolia was deeply rooted in the workings of traditional culture, despite the village's direct participation in global affairs. Being a community that can be described as a closely knit *Gemeinschaft* type, in which everyone knows everyone else, and where members of the community are regularly engaged with each other in more than one way, much of the community life, as well as life of an individual in it, is governed by a very important consideration—how people are related to each other.[17] In fact, the question of relatedness very much defines locals' understandings of who is part of the community and who is not. Thus to be a member of the village community one should have ties to local family networks. This equation comes to the foreground in how the villagers, especially elders, commonly greet people they do not recognize, asking, "Chyia ty?," literally meaning "Whose are you?" or "What family are you part of?"

Undoubtedly, kinship plays most definite role in determining who is "in" and who is "out," who is a member of the local community and who is not. But in a closely knit community, which Hrytsevolia remained even by the end of the twentieth century, other relationships, approximating the one of kinship, also played a defining role in people's lives, whether these lives unfolded locally or elsewhere, all contributing to the evasive but nevertheless always tangible divide that separates those who are "in" from those who are not. The following extracts taken directly from my field diary speak powerfully about Hrytsevolians' sense of community, their understanding of outsiders, their need to know all in their community as justification of their membership in it. The insider/outsider divide comes to the foreground in all the circumstances the extracts recount and plays itself out in a variety of ways, depending on a changing context, acting at the same time as means of reestablishing the existing meanings of the community again and again.

Pride in Knowing Everybody in the Village

NADIA TRACH: We have 564 people [living in Hrytsevolia].

NATALIA KHANENKO-FRIESEN: How do you know the exact number?

MYROSIA TRACH (Nadia's niece) [*laughs*]: Every night she counts them in her head.

NT: Because I know all people here, from one house to another. There are not many of us here. We have 140 [postal] numbers.

NKF And you count how many people are in each home, from house to house?

NT: From house to house, how many people there are in each of them, how many died. As far as I remember, 285 people have died. It is about who the family has in the house. For example, there are seven of us here. There are seven souls in the neighbor's home. Now, we have fourteen people in total already. Then, in that home there are five, there there are four. There there are two, there there is only one person. So I go, from home to home, from home to home, from home to home. Until I fall asleep. That's how I count.[18]

Shame in Not Knowing Everybody in the Village

It is the last day of school here, and the local school hosts an annual concert. It is an important event, and half the village gathers in the school auditorium. I am seated with the youngest generation of the Bakus'ko girls, Svitlana and Maria, and their girlfriends. Eighteen-year-old Svitlana chatters with her girlfriends and says that she is worried because she cannot recognize some children on the stage. She does not know "whose" they are [*chyï vony*]. She tells her girlfriend that not knowing to what families the children belong bothers her. Later on, she will be inquiring with her mother about who is who.[19]

Greetings in the Village

People here greet each other with "Slava Bohu," or "Glory to God," and the answer is "Slava naviky," or "Glory forever." This is a local greeting practice and serves as another means of testing out whether you are part of the local lifeworld or not, whether you know how to greet locally or not. Svitlana says she was taught to greet people this way in her childhood, despite the fact they could be strangers. Greeting everybody, whether one knows them or not, is a traditional local sociolinguistic practice, speaking strongly to traditional understandings of the community and local expectations that a stranger may not be a stranger after all, as she or he could be an extension of some local kinship network. Better be safe and say hi to all, than to be impolite to one of ours.[20]

"Whose Are You?" ("Chyia Ty?")

The boundary between insiders and outsiders is well maintained here. I strongly feel it while in the village. The first test whether you belong or not is memorable. When, an outsider, I walked through the village for the first time, everybody I encountered stared at me from afar. They looked into my eyes directly, prolonging the eye contact studying my face with their eyes, while their minds try to place me within local networks. "Ty chyia?," or "Whose are you, what family do you belong to?" They would ask this question immediately after I would greet them with "Slava Bohu." When they failed to identify me as "whose," that is, were unable to determine which family I might belong to, the next question some of them would ask me was "What are you selling, *zhinochko* [young lady]?"[21]

"Whose Are You?" ("Chyia Ty"?)

I am returning from Baba Maryntsiunia's, who promised me that there would be other women [*babas*] hanging out with her in the afternoon after church, but as it happened there was no one except her own family. So I did not stay. On the way home I follow the local rule on greetings and shout out the short and accentuated "Slava Bohu" to everybody I meet. A group of women sit on the bench in front of someone's house, on the street outside. I greet them, they greet me. Then I meet Stepanykha, who I know from last year and who was part of my group interviews then. I greet her as well. She responds, "Slava Naviky." She says that I look familiar and immediately proceeds with the next question, "Ty chyia?" By now, I know that this question/response is very common among the representatives of older generations when they meet with young villagers. I saw the young kids being asked the same question by the elderly as well. It is important to belong to a local kinship network if one wants to claim the membership in this community.[22]

On Madiary Residents as Outsiders

Slavko [the father of my host family] describes to me the village and its various *kutky*, or literally, village corners or neighborhoods. Hrytsevolia has quite a few *kutky*. Each is a community of its own. Each has its own name. "Here in Hrytsevolia," he told me, we had Hungarian families. They were from Madiarshchyna [Hungary]. So in this *kutok*, the people are called Madiary [Hungarians]." Later I would be told that generations ago, in one household in this *kutok*, there was a woman who married a Hungarian who moved into with the family. That family's offspring was known in the village for generations to come as the Hungarians.[23]

On Madiary Residents as Outsiders

As of 1989, the village of Hrytsevolia had 165 households and 579 inhabitants. The village is located on the banks of the river Styr. The parts of the village have their own names—Kovali, Hrytsyky, Pichkari, Lypky, Mokliak, Sovryshchyna, Vyhin, Lypky, Dubyna, and Madiary, the last being named as such because one man served in the Austrian army during the World War One, and while in Yugoslavia he married a Hungarian woman. So the name of this part of the village derives from this history.

It took only one person to be an outsider, for the whole neighborhood to be named after a nationality.[24]

Stundists as Outsiders

NKF: Babo Maryntsiuniu, where did the Stundists come from?
MARIA SMAL': Who knows. From Lviv may be.
NKF: When did the Stundist faith come to the village?
MS: They came in 1939.
NKF: And how did they end up here?
MS: How do I know? From somewhere. I have no idea.
NKF: Are there many of them here in the village?
MS: Quite a lot. See, my neighbors are also *Shtundy*.
NKF: Do they have their own church?
MS: They have their church, of course. Over there, across the street, they have their house [of prayer]. The family moved out to America, and they moved

into the house. Those who moved out were also Shtundy. So they gave their home to those who stayed so it could be used as a house of prayer. They are very punctual when it comes to service.

NKF Are there many of them in America?

MS: Oh, there are many of them around the world. People here say that our Stundists came from America. People say that they are from America.[25]

Stundists as Outsiders

NKF: So, where are the Stundists from?

BABA GENKA: First we had none here. Those Shtundy, they showed up here while the village was under Poland [za Pol'shchi]. Somewhere closer to the end of the Polish rule. They came somewhere from abroad. Somewhere in 1936, something like that. Back then, one man showed up in the village from Kustyn, to work here, and he had enlisted the others. In those times, they were wearing such haircuts, cut "na bubny." Then it could be that they came from Volyn. Somewhere from abroad.[26]

Stundists as Outsiders

From the conversation with the local elderly woman: "The Shtundy, when they get old, they all lose their minds and become senile or they become blind. Look at the faces of 'ours' [non-Stundists]. 'Our' faces are all lit up, our eyes are sparking, and their faces are all gloomy and they just always look down [demonstrates how the Stundists look down]. Look, look, see? Over there, there are two of them are walking. You can see their eyes from afar and what they are like."[27]

Married into the Community, Still an Outsider

KATERYNA KROKHMAL': I go to the church. People do approach me to speak to me while I am in the church. But I don't have many coming over here [home], only my neighbors, Myrosia, for example.

Kateryna Krokhmal' (born 1912) moved to Hrytsevolia in the 1930s. A few times she complained to me that she does not have much to write to her sister in Canada, since "she lives in a different village" (that is, not in her native village). She would say that her relatives and neighbors in Zavydche, the village she is from, have probably died, and she does not really know who is alive there. I can't stop thinking about this comment. It speaks strongly to local under-standings of who is a part of the community and who is not. Kateryna remained an outsider, despite the fact that she lived in the village for the most of her life [her two children have moved out of the village]. She told me that she really does not know people in Hrytsevolia. And she has been living in this village since the day of her marrying into its community some sixty years ago!²⁸

On the Meaning of *Zemliaky*

Stepan Stets', a neighbor of the Bakus'kos family, shares his story of traveling to Germany to visit his aunt, who, after the war, as a former Ostarbeiter, married a German. This story was shared with me during my visit to Stepan's house-hold. His children were part of this conversation. It was not the first time Stepan shared this story with others, as the girls were contributing with smiles, encour-aging nods and even details:

ss: So, soon we arrive at that train station [in Germany]. We are disembarking from the train, and it finally dawns on me what this thing is like, the *zahranytsia*, the world abroad.

nkf: Yes, I imagine you probably did not know German.

ss: Not only do I not know the language, I don't know where to go! We dis-cussed on the phone with my aunt [*titka*] that once I arrived at the train station, I would call them from the payphone, and then they would come and pick me up from the station. So I stay there and look around, all the people are humming away in their language [*bel'kotiat'*], they are all there without hats, I am the only one standing there in my tall fur hat. Well, "the first time abroad"—that's what the scene is to be called. I am looking and looking around and I am noticing that among all those Germans there is a guy that has the same hat as mine. I come closer to him, we look at each other. I ask him, "Where are you from [*vy otkuda*]?" He says, "From Dnipropetrovsk." And he asks me, "And where are you from?" "I am from Lviv," I say. "We are *zemliaky*," I say.

And the time was 1990. No one really traveled yet abroad in those times. So among all those Germans on the platform there was only one non-German, this guy from Dnipropetrovsk. I think it was God helping me in my travels. "Well," I tell him, "we are *zemliaky*, help me out, brother [*davaĭ, bratan, vyruchaĭ*]." "So you know their language [*po-ĭkhn'omu*], don't you?," I ask him. And I already saw him talking to them in their language.

"Go, and ask them where one can call," I tell him. So he goes. He comes back and tells me everything. So, it is with his help that I managed to call our aunt. It was the uncle who picked up the phone. He told us how to transfer to another train, which would bring us to the little town where they lived. He told us that then his son would come and pick me up. The guy [from Dnipropetrovsk] translated.[29]

On Overlapping Kinship Ties

Baba Genka tells me something that I never knew or was told before, that Slavko, my host, and Bohdan, my primary Hrytsevolia contact in Canada, are relatives. Moreover, they are not just related, they are twice related, because Genka's mother and Bohdan's father are from the same family, *ridni*:

NKF: Are they *ridni*, related like brother and sister?

BG: Yes, my mother and Bohdan's mother are cousins [*dvoiuridni*], and here we say they are *stryiachni*. There, Bohdan and Slavko went somewhere to the wedding, those marrying were also our *ridni*.

NKF: While in Canada?

BG: Sure, in Canada. The Vanchuks, they are also from our village. But they are stingy. Kept telling us that Bohdan would come to stay with them, but it was a different relative that invited him to come to Canada, what was his name . . . [*tries to recollect the name*]?[30]

On Overlapping Kinship Ties

I often hear here "we are related on both sides" ["porodychalysia z dvokh bokiv"]. Baba Hanka, speaking of her relatives in the *kutok*, states: "My mother and their father are brother and sister. And my father and their mother are *pershostryiachni* [second cousins]."[31]

It Takes a Village to Raise a Child

The school concert is over and we are lingering in the school front yard. There are still many people around us, the concert was attended by practically half the village. Two toddlers appear from somewhere, walking across the village center toward the school. They get attention of at least four different women who have just come out from the school. The women start scolding the children for being underdressed for the weather [it was a cool evening], and then tell the children to go home to dress up warmly. The children oblige.[32]

For a Hrytsevolian born and raised in the village, the local lifeworld could be represented by a metaphor of an onion bulb, with its many layers of flesh standing for the layers of social relations within the community. The closest layer to the core of the bulb, the self, would be the relations within the immediate family, the next layers would represent the relations among the extended kin (from more intimate to more distant relations), which could include the relations with those who are tied to the family through godparenting and who are called *kumy*, or through marriage and who are called *svaty*.[33] Further out from that core would be the relations between the household and the neighbors. Then would follow the layers representing the relations between the individual and the members of his or her part of the village or *kutok*, then the relations with *zemliaky*, who play a very important role when an individual finds himself or herself outside of the community. At different times, the layers, each representing a kind of "once-removed" tie, would appear in a different order than the one I have presented them here. Depending on one's circumstances, relations with the neighbors or with the in-laws could be more important than the relations with kin living in a different community. The relationship with *zemliaky* may not be even recognized as such until a person encounters a *zemliak* while elsewhere.

Importantly, it is oftentimes difficult to draw a clear line between those who are just neighbors and *zemliaky* and those who are the members of one's extended kin. In Hrytsevolia, many people find themselves in overlapping relationships. One can be related to another person in a multitude of ways. Sisters can be godmothers to their nieces and nephews. One's siblings could be also third cousins, once or twice removed. The same two individuals can be related by blood as well as by the ties of marriage (in the same or preceding generations). As a result of such an intermeshed social space of kinship defined by a multitude of social relationships rooted in various genealogical (vertical) histories, it is not surprising the people living in a place like Hrytsevolia might have very different community experiences than the members of a rural community in another socially mobile context (say, a North American rural community subject to waves of economic booms and busts). Even though Hrytsevolia, like so many other communities in Western Ukraine, was subject to the most dramatic events of Eastern European twentieth-century history and even though the community lost many a villager to these events and to the larger world, at the very end of that century it remained a community that embraced traditional conceptions of what is kin, who can be kin, what is community, and who can and cannot be part of it.

Thus, when a person left the village for the Americas as an emigrant, his or her departure was perceived as to having an impact not only on the immediate family but on the community as a whole, constituted by these overlapping social and family networks of which the individual was a part. Thus, departures, separations, and subsequent absences were as much communal affairs as the affairs of a family. In symbolic terms, their importance to community life can be compared to that of newborns. Consider here the claim advanced by the renowned scholar of ritual Albert Baĭburin. Baĭburin, a researcher of Slavic folklore, points out that the birth-related rituals in many rural Slavic communities including Ukrainian ones often used to feature large-scale family and community celebrations during which a special kind of porridge, or *kasha*, would be served.[34] The children of those who attend (often representing the whole community) the celebration would get a portion of this *kasha* during the meal. If the children were not brought along, the parents would be given some kasha to take home for them. At stake here, Baĭburin claims, is the ritual redistribution of personal luck that was held as communal symbolic property. With each newborn, the number of children increased, and this communally held luck needed to be redistributed, and hence a large communal celebration was held during which this luck got redistributed among all village children (or kin children) by their partaking in the meal. One can likewise think of eating special funeral porridge (*kutia*) as the same ritual practice directed at redistributing the commonly held luck among the living members of the community whose membership just decreased due to death. Departures overseas, by extension, also called for the communal luck to be negotiated and redistributed, again, due to the change in membership. It is not surprising, given this consideration and the multilayered overlapping of kinship, friendship, and *zemliatstvo*, that all the departures and the absences that ensued from them had had lingering effects on local folk psychology as well as on the community.

Mediating Absence

Rural communities responded to the absence of the emigrated kin in three distinct ways over time. First, in the first half of the twentieth century when the emigration was still ongoing, villagers interpreted and placed these departures in the context of other long-term departures known in their community. Second, with the final establishment of the Soviet rule in 1944, villagers kept the departed overseas kin present in private lives, conversations, and longings, even as physical contact with those in the diaspora was cut off by the authorities. Third, after the state ideological control began to loosen its grip on local cultures by the end of the 1960s and the overseas relatives occasionally came back for a visit, villagers developed new rituals of homecoming to deal with the ambivalent status of the absentee relative and to offer some resolution to the anxiety such a status induced.

Dealing with Departures

In Hrytsevolia, like everywhere else in Western Ukraine, departures overseas were a familiar part of local life from the 1880s to the beginning of World War Two in 1939. In many cases, these departures were temporary. *Zarobitky* (or working for money outside the village) overseas was a continuation of other established local practices of extended laboring outside of the village, such as *v naïmy*, which was an arrangement whereby younger siblings would go work in wealthier neighboring villages for the summer:[35]

> MARIA SMAL': My father first went for *zarobitky* [in 1925,] when I was very young. He was there for seven years for the first time. Then he came home.
>
> NKF: Did you recognize him?
>
> MS: Oh, how could I? Of course not. He came home just for a month, for his vacation. He spent a month with us and then went back to Canada. I was afraid of him, in our house we had no men, just my *baba*, my mother and I. So I was quite scared of my dad, and it was only after he spent some time with us that I got used to him. Then he went back to Canada. And again, seven years later he returned. It was just before the Russians came [in 1939]. He could not go back to Canada anymore, so he stayed with us.[36]

Such undertakings were local responses to ongoing transformations in global flows of capital, the global economy, and the labor market. Yet within the lifeworld of a small rural community whose members for the most part continued to embrace local values and ethics, global interactions were not necessarily understood in the most clear fashion. In order to be comprehended by the locals, these new global experiences had to be mediated locally; they had to fit into the existing currents of meaning that normally circulated in the locality at the time. Understandably, villagers made sense of the very first departures by drawing on their own repertoire of local knowledge. Local meanings for these departures were already at hand in the villages. Ukrainian rural communities of the Austro-Hungarian empire, for example, were already accustomed to giving away their youth as military conscripts. The twenty-five years of absence from the village and the family that it entailed amounted at the community level to "social death," imposed on the family by the forces of fate, that is, by outside forces that could not be controlled. The recruits' most productive period of their lives would be spent outside of the community. Serving away from home, they were oftentimes not able to marry, and if they were already married, their contribution to the household would be minimal. Add here the shorter lifespan and higher probability of perishing away while in military service. New departures, this time overseas, also took the villagers far away, across expansive waters, and into what locally oftentimes was perceived as an unknown world. At the moment of separation, the villagers believed the migrant would no longer be a part of the local lifeworld in any form. It was only later, when letters and remittances eventually reached the village, overseas kin occasionally visited their families, that the status of being "socially dead" initially assigned to the emigrants would be questioned.

It is not surprising, writes Valeriia Eremina, the Russian scholar of Slavic folklore who draws on folklore from Central and Eastern Ukraine to explore the meaning of death in Slavic culture, that the forms of lamenting for departing conscripts—and I would add, the rites of farewell bidding—were modeled after the funeral rituals.[37] Processions for the deceased (figure 2.3), conscripts, and emigrants shared the same sequence of actions, the same morphology and ritual structure. They would begin by first stopping for a moment at the threshold of the house, so the deceased or departed could bid farewell to his or her home. Then the procession would pause at the gates to the household's yard as well as at the village borders, so that the deceased or departed could bid farewell to his or her homestead and native village. Folk songs born during the period of mass emigration contain much information about farewell bidding for those departing overseas, revealing its ritual nature and its similarity to the rites of separation with recruits and the deceased. In chapter 1, the Brazil song presented us with a detailed poetic rendering of farewell bidding that the departing overseas engaged in. Rituals of emigrant departure have also been described in memoirs, in literature, and folklore, as well as referenced in local stories of Hrystevolians.[38]

Throughout the rest of the twentieth century in Hrytsevolia, despite the Soviet control of local interactions with those abroad, there were occasional departures overseas, a few individuals leaving to reunite with immediate family members abroad. Despite the dramatic social change of the local lifeworld in

Figure 2.3. Bidding farewell to the deceased relative, village of Hrytsevolia, 1960s. Photo courtesy of Hanna Pyvovarchuk, Hrytsevolia.

those times, these departures were often handled in quite traditional ways, confirming the influence that tradition and folk psychology continued to exercise on the Hrytsevolian community. Nadia Trach, one of my primary respondents in Hrytsevolia, describes the departure of her relatives to Canada in 1976:

> My [older] sister was leaving in 1976 with her children. Our *dido* [grandfather] had been in Canada since 1937. My niece, her daughter, was always saying "ty" when addressing me, although I am her aunt.[39] There is little difference in our ages, and we were always on *ty* terms. We went together, the whole family, to Moscow to bid farewell to them. [. . .][40] We spent two weeks in Moscow waiting for tickets [. . .] and then one day, that was the day they were finally leaving, [my niece] comes to me and starts talking using "vy." I stared at her and stared. Then I asked her, "Did you fall off a tree?! We are on *ty* terms!" Then she says to me, "I am going to 'chuzhbyna,' the alien world, and I won't see you, my dear aunt, again. So my mother said to me that I should address you proper way now, like an aunt. That's how it was.[41]

This incident speaks strongly to the ritual compression of time that had to happen in the very moment of departure so the proper kin relationship between an aunt and a niece could be established before the separation would threaten the vitality of this kinship tie. In the very moment of parting, a young girl had to instantly grow up to become a proper aunt to her departing niece. The plural personal pronoun "vy" used by the niece in addressing her aunt was meant to signify the respect one had to pay to elders. It also signaled the instantaneous change in the relationship between the two parting girls. dictated by the ritual structure that framed the interaction in the moment of separation. To mitigate the pain of separation and preserve the kinship tie, the parties in the above inci-dent intuitively turned to this ritual, capitalizing on its distinct ability to alter the flow of real time. Compare this ritual to other traditional rituals of separation, such as funeral rites performed for a deceased maiden or an unmarried young man, in which physiological time is likewise accelerated in order to compen-sate for the unfairness of premature death. During the funeral ritual for an un-married girl, for example, the deceased would be dressed up as a young bride and the funeral rite might include features of a wedding.[42] This ritual accelera-tion was meant to allow, even if merely symbolically, for a deceased to live longer and to obtain the status of fully realized (that is, married) human being. It also provided the community and the family with a symbolic means of dealing with untimely death. Likewise, the ritual in 1976 parting of Nadia and her niece was intended to ameliorate the anxiety induced by the departures overseas and to deal with the separation. The instant progression in status, from playmates to an aunt and a niece, and the reenactment of the aunt/niece relationship were the ritual response to this symbolic death.

Mediating Absence

After the establishment of the Soviet rule in Western Ukraine, the overseas kin became far more inaccessible to the villagers. The correspondence and remit-tances, the reminders of their existence in the world outside, were also signifi-cantly scaled down and at times actively surveilled. These sparse contributions to local relationship networks were augmented in the village by local practices of remembrance, through storytelling, conversations, and various private and group reminiscences about those abroad. These local practices of remembrance were informed by tradition and folk psychology.

A dual conceptualization of the world in terms of home or homeland (safe and known) versus non-home, the outside (dangerous and unknown), has long governed the lives of Hrytsevolians.[43] The fear of the outside, even if symbolic rather than real, was constantly reenacted in local rituals and spoken of in con-versations during my time there. One popular ritual for confronting the fear of the unknown is *posydity na dorohu*, that is, sitting down before the departure and staying silent for several seconds to ensure the traveler(s) will have the best of luck while traveling outside of his/her home, and it is still performed today in many Ukrainian families. It was commonly performed in the village if one was to venture further than the usual, known and proximal, destinations. Laying a cross on the traveler (*pokhrestyty*) before she or he departed was another means of protecting the departees from the harms of the outside that I witnessed when I was in Hrytsevolia. In my host family, when the older daughter was catching the morning bus to go to Lviv for a week to attend her university classes, her grandmother would cross her as she was rushing out of the house.

The outside, the "nonhome," is a vast and oftentimes undifferentiated terrain. It may begin at the boundary of the country, as was the case for Stepan Stets' when he traveled to Germany and encountered there a *zemliak* from Dnipropetrovsk. But far more commonly it begins at the outskirts of the village. Kateryna Krokhmal' (born 1912) once proudly listed to me all her travelings: "I have been traveling quite a lot in my life. I have been to Lviv. I have been to Ternopil, I have been to Radekhiv, Berestechko, . . ." (she continued on with the names of other local villages nearby that she had been to). Her sense of outside literally extends only few kilometers outside of Hrytsevolia.[44]

While in principle the boundary between home and nonhome is not absolute and has been reimagined in different contexts and situations, in general it distinguishes between a physical locality that is the province of the familiar and the secure and the outside that is seen as dangerous and unknown. Though the modern times certainly suggested new and different meanings of home to Hrytsevolians, its old meanings as safe, known, our own, and that which is rooted in the native land persevered, and the understanding of the outside as strange, foreign, and mysterious, were preserved in local oral lore, stories, and actions. The furthest corners of this vast domain of the "outside" often remained undifferentiated in the minds of the local people—it was the least known, least understood, and most feared. The emigrants leaving for the Americas ventured out to reach those furthest extensions of the "outside," of the nonhome, and an important part of their journey was crossing the ocean.

On How to Travel across the Waters

This is my second extended visit with Maryntsiunia. We talk about her father who worked in Canada for fourteen years before coming back in 1939. Maryntsiunia speaks of how he traveled overseas. This is not the first time she has told me this story. Though it comes in a form of a dialogue, it has already been formalized into a particular story:

MS: Ah, my *tato* [dad] was on the sea for three weeks. Tied up. They said, if people went by the sea in the summer time, the sea was calmer. And once *Tato* went in the spring, in April, so there was lots of ice, lots of everything. All were rolling around.

NKF: Was it that the people were tied up? Or what?

MS: People, people were tied up. Everyone had his bunk, his seat, and everything was tied up to it and that's it.

NKF: So no one would be rolling around?

MS: Imagine, to be on the sea for three weeks. And when he came back to us, my *tato* said, "I will take you with me." I was not even able to grasp it, where I would sit there? Why I would ever go onto the ship? So I could be thrown into the sea? [*laughs*] My bladder would explode from fear! I can't go near the river here, I am so afraid of water. I don't want to be near water. If I needed to cross a small stream, I probably could, but to board the ship— never ever! I can't even go to a dock by the river, I can't![45]

In the traditional lore of many cultures, the motif of crossing a river or sea is associated, among other things, with the transition from life to death. Incidentally, this was not the first time that I heard Hrytsevolians, especially women, stating their fear of water, like Maryntsiunia did in her story. I'd also heard that some wives, back in the 1920s, chose not to follow their husbands out of all-encompassing fear of crossing the vast waters of the Atlantic. According to Maryntsiunia, her mother for example, refused to follow her husband specifically for these reasons.[46]

Vernacular understandings of overseas kin emerged at the intersection of these traditional beliefs that projected the world outside as dangerous and unknown and that conceived of crossing the seas as traveling toward death. Departed kin came to be seen not only as having exited the world of the familiar and familial but also as trotting inevitably toward the terrain of death. Immigrant songs, composed in the moment of emigration, projected the travelers as both liminal and stranded in the unknown domains of the world outside, for example in the Valley of Josaphat, as in the Brazil song discussed in previous chapter. After the Second World War, however, when the two groups of Ukrainians grew further apart, local folklore in Hrytsevolia and elsewhere in Ukraine redefined the overseas kin by transporting them, metaphorically speaking, from the Valley of Death, into the domain of "netherland," described in local texts and narratives as a parallel world, not unlike the parallel universes that exist for many toddlers, who often see themselves as being surrounded by the creatures of the fairy world in their daily lives. This universe remains intangible, undifferentiated (Canada's cities of Ottawa, Yorkton, or Canora being understood as a part of "Amerika"), inaccessible, unknown, and as far away as indeed North America was for many Soviet citizens after the Second World War.[47] Perhaps that is why, the Luzhany song, a product of recent folklore, profiled in the first chapter, presents us with no specific and tangible descriptions of the song's protagonist, his or her environs, relations, looks, and so forth.

The ambivalence of these traditional understandings of departed kin as both absent from and present within local networks of relations was not lost on villagers. While the departures of the dead and of conscripts were perceived as absolute, irreversible, and imposed on the family by the external forces of fate, travels overseas, though in the moment of the departure seen as absolute and irreversible, were understood to be the result of the individual's will (when men were involved) or of a family decision (when women were involved) and seen as potentially beneficial for the families staying behind. Many of those who went overseas in the early 1900s returned to their homes. With them came stories, new understandings of their lives in the new world, and material confirmations of its existence. Maryntsiunia Smal' grew up in the 1920s and 1930s without her father, like many other children in the area, for he was off to Canada for *zarobitky*. "When he came back in 1932, I was seven years old. I was told this was my father. So, I said 'Father' to him. I didn't know him, I never saw him."[48] Like other overseas kin, Maryntsiunia's father sent his earnings (*fasuvaly*) back to Hrytsevolia. "Dad was sending us some money. My mother bought new land. When he came back he bought horses too. He brought other things, too. I remember nice shiny shoes, shoes from Canada."

Cultural practices of the new world were also making their way back to the village. Upon his final return, Maryntsiunia's father built a house that became an item of local curiosity and is referred in the village, even today, as *kanads'ka khata*, or the Canadian house (figure 2.4). Maryntsiunia shared with me that her father "built this house like many other ones he built in Canada while he was there working as a construction worker." It was, she exclaimed, "such a strange house!"[49] Indeed, this house structurally is very different from those built locally, and the village elders told me how much laughter it caused when it was being built.

The stories those who returned and those who visited temporarily told entered local discourse as new folk narratives about the overseas kin and their Ukrainian "otherland." Recycled both within and outside the families, they contributed to the local folklore, each time updating local imaginings of overseas kin and their world. Many have crystallized into distinct folk narrative items. In Hrytsevolia, I happened to hear the same story of Maria's father's

Figure 2.4. The "Canadian House" built in the 1930s in the village of Hrytsevolia, 1998. Photo by author.

arrival twice. Maria shared it with me first in 1998 and then happily retold it the next year. Twice she presented me with the same narrative and twice she placed an intonational emphasis on the same particular moment in the story. Her storytelling techniques and her use of the present tense suggest that the episode she described has become a part of the family and village folklore:

> One day I was in the house. Someone comes by. He asks me, where is your father? I tell him, in Canada. Then he asks me another question. Where is you mother now? She is in the field, I say. He asks me a third question. When will she be back from the field? I say to him, when she gets hungry. Then she will come back. So, my mother comes. And I tell her, Mom, some kind of a man is here. My mother comes to the man, takes his hat off . . . [pauses], looks at his head, and they just start kissing and kissing . . . [pauses and makes eye contact]. See, my mother took the hat off to see whether the man was bald. And he was bald. So, he was toĭ samyĭ, the same one. That was my father.[50]

Throughout the twentieth century, mediating the absence of the kin was a village-wide and not just family preoccupation. Socially constructed, these mediations heavily borrowed from local rituals and folklore associated with

other critical departures the community regularly experienced, such as conscription to army and death. While pertaining to families, they were informed
by the ways community was understood and were tied to its membership responsibilities, governed by archetypal structures as home/otherland and structured
by the universal metaphor of traveling across water as dying.

At the beginning of this chapter I asked whether over the course of several
generations the absence of kin who had emigrated had been accepted as a
"normal," a given aspect of local life, or whether it came to been seen as incongruent with local understandings of kinship and community, as a problem to be
resolved. The answer to this question is complicated. If we subscribe to Stafford's
idea that the separation constraint is a universally present feature of human life
in any culture, then the separation that accompanied emigration can be indeed
considered as having been normalized. Yet we need to differentiate this kind of
separation from other sorts of separation experienced by the villagers throughout the century. The departures overseas resulted in the formation of another
kin group abroad and not, as in the case of death or conscription, in the loss of
the departed kin. Thus with time, separation ceased to be a private matter pertaining only to one historical moment and to horizontal relationships (those
with peers in the community), but grew to become the corporate experience
involving vertical relationships (those with kin in subsequent generations).

All in all, overseas kin, defined broadly and including *zemliaky*, came to
occupy an ambivalent position in the local lifeworld, a position of simultaneous
presence and absence, characterized by their ongoing absence from real, here-
and-now relations of the villagers and their sustained, if symbolic, presence in a
traditionally conceived world of kinship, *zemliatstvo*, and the village community.
To employ the lenses of ritual analysis once more, given the limited communication between homeland and the departed after the Second World War, and
thanks to the strength of traditional culture in the village, in Hrytsevolia the
departed firmly entered the domain of myth, legend, and ritual, coming to
constitute an important symbolic horizon in the local life in village. And while
within the domain of real life, separations are not necessarily mediated, in the
symbolic domain, mediation is actively pursued, albeit intuitively, implicitly,
and not always knowingly or reflectively.

Within the framework of ritual, separations require resolutions, and this
brings us back to Van Gennep and Victor Turner, who see separation as a
temporal phase in the ritual progression of time, status, and so forth. In the
context of our discussion here, the concluding step in the chain of ritual events
of departure and absence or separation would be return. The last step in this
sequence is the subject of our discussion in chapter 6 on homecoming.

Figure 3.1. The front cover of *Kalendar Al'manakh Novoho Shliakhu*, edited by Juriĭ Karmanin (Toronto: Novyĭ Shliakh, 1995). The caption says, "We are the children of the same nation." Courtesy of Novyĭ Shliakh.

3

///////////////////////////////////////

Constructing Longing in Diaspora

One day I went to visit with Mary Dorosh, an active member of a local women's committee, town of Mundare, East Central Alberta.[1] Here are my field notes about the visit, dated May 30, 2001:

> I knock at the door. I am at Mary's after a year of absence. The kitchen is full of family, her son, Jerry, his wife, Alice, and their children. "Come in," Mary says, greeting me at the door of her home. "Let me introduce you." And to her family, she says, "This is Natalia, she is . . ." I interrupt her: "Doing research here." "Yes," Mary picks up and moves this comment of mine into the background. "Yes, and you know, she is from Ukraine!" This remark provokes some curiosity among the younger Doroshes. Lunchtime. Coffee is served. Mary, an amazing cook, puts a delicious apple pie on the table. Conversation moves back and forth from the topic of this year's harvest to my year of absence and to Jerry's new contract as a teacher in a neighboring town.

NKF: And, Mary, you know last spring I went to Hrytsevolia?
MARY DOROSH: Oh, did you?!
NKF: And some people there actually remembered the Doroshes from Mundare.
MD: Is that true?
JERRY DOROSH: What is this, Hryts . . . ?
MD: This is the village where John came from.[2]
JD: I see. Is this a big village?
NKF: Not too big, there are about five hundred people there.
JD: Ah, the same size as Mundare then.
NKF: It is quite isolated, too, there is one road to the village, through a beautiful forest . . .
JD: And what is the nearest town there?

73

NKF: It is just one hour's drive from Lviv.

JD: . . . ?

NKF: Lviv, a large city, nearby. The village is in Lvivs'ka oblast'.

JD: Is this near the Black sea?

NKF: No, it is in Western—

MD: Jerry, this is where most of Ukrainians here came from.

JD: I see.

MD: I'd love to go there one day, only I am afraid I am too old.

After her son and his wife left, we continued our talk about town affairs and other issues. At some point we returned to the topic of Hrytsevolia. I hadn't yet shared with Mary much about my stay there, when she launched into a disquisition.

MD: You know *they say*, that I will be quite disappointed if I go there. But I don't think so. May be my children would be disappointed if they went. They have not lived through what we have lived through here. We didn't have running water, there was an outhouse in our home. My mom had *piac* and we baked a lot. My children didn't know those conditions, in which I lived. No electricity, no heating. We needed to provide wood for our heating. May be if they go to Ukraine, they would be disappointed. But I know all this. We had it all here.

Four Years Earlier, October 17, 1997

MD: My aunt came out, and a cousin [from Ukraine] had come to visit. When my mom was still alive. That was years ago [*pauses*]. My ambition was to go back [*pauses*], to go there, not go back, but . . .[3]

NKF: Were you born in Canada?

MD: Yes. I was born and raised in Mundare, actually [. . .] I have lived here all my life. So, you know, people here in the area, some went back. My mother-in-law, she went back years and years ago. It was very much [*pauses*], you see, she was very cautious.[4]

When I arrived at the University of Saskatchewan in 2001, I started teaching a course in Ukrainian Canadian culture to a group of local students, most of whom were active members in the local Ukrainian community of Saskatoon. Together we discussed not only the wide range of cultural practices of Ukrainians in Canada from art, literature, music, and media to folklore but we also explored Ukrainian Canadian culture in the context of Ukrainian Canadians' relationship with their ethnic homeland. For the most part, the students taking the course were in their early twenties. Many were active in well-established, reputable, and successful ethnic cultural organizations such as choirs and dance groups. Some of my most active students of Ukrainian background were third- or fourth-generation Ukrainian Canadians. When the day came for us to examine academic reflections within the field of diaspora studies on the nature of diaspora/homeland relations and imaginings of those in each realm, Roxana, a member of Lastiwka Choir, brought into the class a poster that advertised the fundraising campaign that the choir had recently initiated in support of their upcoming tour of Ukraine. Across the white space of the ad there were dark letters that read "Lastiwka Choir—Back to the Homeland." It was Roxana herself who raised the question why exactly Ukraine had been labeled on the poster as a "homeland." For her, she shared, as well as for many other young members of the choir, the statement was an oxymoron: "Our homeland is Canada, of course; we were born and raised here, our families have roots *here*," she stated confidently. This discrepancy between the lived homeland (Canada) and the one pronounced to be the homeland (Ukraine) in the fundraising materials of the choir was not lost on my students, born and raised in Canada as Canadian Ukrainians. Together we engaged in a lively discussion about this discrepancy while trying to unwrap the meanings of Ukraine in the Ukrainian Canadian context and explore the reasons for the continued hold of these meanings.

The discussion in this chapter takes up the question raised by Roxana and brings us back to the twentieth-century diaspora where the notion of Ukraine as the "homeland" of Ukrainian Canadians was established, acted on, maintained, and reconstructed over time again and again. As it has been touched on in the introduction to this book, this idea has its roots in the institutional and political discourses of those Ukrainian Canadians who over the course of the twentieth century worked hard to become a culturally prominent and politically active community in Canada. Ukrainian Canadians' differing attitudes toward Soviet rule in Ukraine stimulated much debate about Ukraine throughout the twentieth century and kept the issue on the front burner for many active (*svidomi*) members of the Ukrainian Canadian community. Yet when one examines the political construction of homeland in the diaspora among Ukrainian Canadians, it becomes clear that political discourse heavily borrowed from folk psychology and its vernacular manifestations. Thus, in this chapter while exploring the ways in which Ukrainian Canadians address their longing for the

ancestral homeland, I focus on the vernacular, as it provides powerful metaphoric tools for decreasing the distance between the two worlds.

Having just read the previous chapter where we looked at Ukraine-based
conceptualizations of the overseas kin, the reader might ask a question why this
chapter is not focusing on a similar question—how Ukrainian Canadians in
the twentieth century understood and imagined their kinfolk left behind in
Ukraine. The reason why I am not turning to a truly parallel exploration, at least
not yet, is because it is important to focus first on homeland in general, as longing for the Ukrainian "diasporic other" expresses different meanings on each
end of the diaspora-homeland binomial. In the twentieth century in Western
Ukraine, for example, sentiments regarding the diaspora above all concerned
the departed relatives, the specific individuals and their networks of relations.
Vernacular reflections in Ukrainian villages on their own "others" (who grew
in number over time, across a few generations and across the community)
rarely elaborated on the physical domain of "Ukrainian otherlands," that is,
communities and countries where the departed settled, and never focused on
organized Ukrainian diasporas, their organizations, political movements, cultural productions, and so on. This is not surprising as the new worlds were not
seen as home and remained beyond imagination in the "old country." As a
result, in Ukraine the focus of the diasporic imagination was on *people* and, moreover, on *specific individuals* and their kinship networks in the diaspora.

At the other end of the binomial, in twentieth-century western Canada, the
longing for and imaginings of the overseas kin and the old country among
Ukrainians born and raised in Canada followed two distinct paths and with
time grew apart. While longing for homeland found articulation in many
Ukrainian Canadian practices, longing for overseas kin had moved into the
background, remaining dormant until the global transformations of the late
1980s provided new opportunities to travel back to the homeland. Conceptions
of the old country overall are thus far more intimately tied to the spatial domain
of homeland than to kinfolk there.

It is not surprising that the vernacular trope of *staryĭ kraĭ*, the old country,
pointing to an uncertain place far away in time and space, an ambivalent domain
of the family's past, remains in circulation among Ukrainian Canadians today.
The vagueness of the idea of the old country makes it a useful tool in vernacular
understandings of Ukraine as ethnic homeland. While political constructions of
homeland in the public discourse of the twentieth-century Ukrainian Canadian
community produced a very particular image of the motherland, vernacular
understandings of Ukraine came with time to occupy a pronounced place in
Ukrainian Canadians' personal memory, which also had an impact on the way

they imagined their diasporic "others." Ukrainian Canadians of course continued to maintain their real, virtual, or imagined relationships and connections with the relatives in the old country. I discuss this topic later.

In addition to exploring the longings of Ukrainian Canadians for the old world, this chapter also picks up the thread of preceding chapters, exploring the impact of the vernacular on diasporic imagination of Ukrainians in modern and late-modern contexts. The diasporic dimension of Ukrainian culture, while still relatively new in the early twentieth century, grew to become an important part of the folk psychology of both groups of Ukrainians, those in Ukraine and in the diaspora.[5] In the second chapter on mediating absence in Ukraine I demonstrated how diasporic longing continued to affect the local lifeworlds in the homeland from whence the immigrants departed. Although this chapter addresses the matter of diaspora's longings for homeland, it also pays tribute to the role that vernacular diasporic consciousness plays in Ukrainian Canadian identity projects. Within the field of diaspora studies, many scholars have observed that longing for homeland in diasporas is indeed a global phenomenon.[6] Many have noticed that communities in diasporas, separated from their homelands by distance, politics, and time, tend to conceive of their homelands in romanticized terms. This was especially the case before the explosive revolution in communication technologies of the 1990s. Ukrainian Canadians have been no exception, building all manner of memorials to their ethnic homeland they have left behind. One need only page through the numerous publications produced by community organizations (be they the newspapers, annual calendars, magazines, etc.) to see how often these publications turn to Ukraine and its citizens. While researchers of other cultures have already produced some accounts of diasporic imaginings of homeland, the book has yet to be written on political uses of "Ukraine the homeland" in the lives of the organized *svidomi* Ukrainian Canadians.[7]

For some, there will be little difference between the way they personally imagine the homeland and the way it is represented in the official public discourse. Consider, for example, the life story of Yaroslav Fedorkevich, a post–Second World War DP immigrant, which I heard in 1998. He made a point to regularly watch the TV news from Ukraine (this was when the internet did not exist and when one had to know where to get VHS tapes with news pirated from Ukraine and then pay for their conversion into a North American VHS format).[8] For others, like Mary Dorosh, whose parents came to Canada prior to Second World War, and especially for her children, the old country long ago ceased to exist as a definite entity, having become a foggy zone of personal and family memory, and contemporary Ukraine has never grown to fill that vacated spot in her heart. And then there would be others like Natalka Husar, an artist of an international caliber, whose personal and professional selves grew to be defined by the never-healing sense of split and by the never-ending call of the old country.[9]

If one attempted to map that uncharted terrain of personal and family memories that never made it into the well-polished public narratives, one would be hard pressed to neatly categorize the various meanings the old country holds for Ukrainian Canadians. Further, perhaps the idea of undertaking such a categorization is questionable in the light of growing recognition of the crisis of representation that has been so intensely debated in social sciences and humanities. Hence, instead of offering a list of all possible kinds of such personal memories, I turn here to their manifestation in various public discourses, national and local.[10]

I begin with a brief general discussion of Ukraine and its relevance to the Ukrainian Canadian culture, outlining the political uses of nostalgia for homeland in the Ukrainian Canadian community. Here I touch on the role that folk psychology has played in the process of the political reclaiming of Ukraine as a homeland for the organized Ukrainian community in Canada. Ritual, employed in the celebrations of key community events organized by pronationalist camp, in particular has been effective in facilitating the interpolation of political interpretations of Ukraine into the private worlds of many individual Ukrainian Canadians.

To move beyond this background of political appropriation of Ukraine as homeland, I turn away from the national palette of the Ukrainian Canadian community and revisit my ethnographic work in the small rural community in east central Alberta, a community considered by many to be as Ukrainian as it gets in Canada.[11] This community, of course, also has its own public discourse, very local, yet very telling, on the role and place the old country ought to play in the lives of those many Ukrainian Canadians who may not directly participate in established Ukrainian organizations, both nationalist and procommunist. Yet local public discourse, be it about current community life or about the local past, is actively shaped by local Ukrainians, who have been the dominant ethnic group in the community, by their values, anxieties, and desires.

These values, anxieties and desires that contribute to and represent the folk psychology of the Ukrainian Canadians in general routinely enter the plane of community life in the form of narratives, which have woven themselves into various local public events, exhibits, performances, and texts ever since the period of the first mass emigration. Initially, at the end of the nineteenth and the beginning of the twentieth century, the separation of kin and the splitting up of communities were especially actively profiled in the folklore and culture of both worlds, the old and the new. In Canada, with new generations of Ukrainians coming of age, with the ongoing modernization of life and its growing dependence on a wide range of new communication technologies as vehicles for information and knowledge transfer, with community building and the establishment of political public discourse, the vernacular longing for homeland was thrust from the domain of folklore and from the private lives of individuals into the world of literacy and the domain of Ukrainian Canadian public life. That is why in discussing the continuity of vernacular or folk means of cultural maintenance in the modern and late-modern period, it is important to consider texts and contexts other than traditional folklore.

Homeland in Ukrainian Canadian Politics

It is nearly impossible to pursue the question of the vernacular without considering the ideological currents that circulated in the Ukrainian Canadian cultural milieu over the twentieth century. In the context of Ukrainian Canadian organized life, the political aspirations of the so called pronationalist camp played an important role in forging a rather powerful and lasting set of ideas about Ukraine that lingered on and seeped into the daily lives of many members of this ethnic group. The very fact that Ukrainian immigration to Canada occurred at a critical point in the nation-building process of both Canada and Ukrainian nation-building processes was pivotal in the evolution of Ukrainian Canadian attitudes toward their ethnic homeland.[12] The majority of the first immigrants arriving in Canada at the end of the nineteenth century were neither fully engaged in the political debates of the day in their home regions nor deeply preoccupied with nationalist ideas of the Ukrainian intelligentsia. Many of these villagers turned emigrants had not obtained a full primary education, and few nurtured patriotic feelings for the Ukrainian territory that would become the state of Soviet Ukraine in 1922 (with Western Ukraine added in 1939).[13] Predominantly peasants, their sense of homeland often did not go beyond their own local villages, communities, and districts.

On the eve of the twentieth century, when mass migration was at a peak, the Ukrainian intelligentsia from urban centers of Western Ukraine began arriving in Canada as well, bringing with them a variety of political and ideological outlooks on the matter of Ukrainian nationhood. Although the appearance of the intelligentsia on the North American continent directly contributed to the birth of the wide spectrum of political and ideological orientations within

the Ukrainian Canadian and Ukrainian American communities, the impact of
Ukrainian nationalist ideology on average Ukrainians before the First World
War was minimal.[14] The intelligentsia were too small in numbers to successfully
reach out to recently arrived immigrant villagers, who were scattered around
the vast prairies and focused on how to survive in the new land.

The quest for the Ukrainian nationhood among nationalists both at home
and abroad was further spurred on by the First World War in Europe. As the
Russian and Austro-Hungarian empires crumbled in 1917–18, Frances Swyripa
claims, Ukrainians acquired a new sense of themselves as a people and soon
translated that sense into a bid for political independence.[15] Yet the end of
the First World War did not bring the establishment of the fully independent
Ukrainian state that the Ukrainian nationalists had hoped for. And social
democrats, wearing various political hats, celebrated the formation of the
Ukrainian Soviet Socialist Republic, a federated member of the Union of Soviet Socialist Republics. These developments in Europe expedited the further
strengthening of the organized Ukrainian community in Canada. Not surprisingly, they also firmly placed the issue of a homeland on the front burner,
and Ukraine's independence from the USSR became of highest concern to
Ukrainian nationalists in the diaspora for years to come.

Occasionally, Ukrainian nationalists attempted to bring the debate on an
independent and sovereign Ukraine into mainstream Canadian politics.[16] As
political uncertainty grew in Europe in the late 1930s, Ukrainians once again
began putting their hopes in the rearrangement of East European borders.
After the Second World War, when Ukraine once again did not emerge as an
independent and sovereign state, the Ukrainian question remained unresolved
in the Ukrainian Canadian community. "With the exception of a pro-Soviet
minority," Swyripa reflects, "the organized community has been united in
support of an independent, non-communist Ukrainian state, although disagree-
ments on the nature of the future Ukrainian state and Ukrainian Canadian
involvement in its realization have frequently hindered cooperation for the
great and common good."[17] Both socialist and nationalist ideologies gained
their momentum in various Ukrainian Canadian communities, thanks also to
growing networks of reading clubs, drama circles, and various community halls
where the community activists held lectures, public readings, and discussions.[18] Yet, given the format and the structure of these events, neither lectures
nor readings attracted large audiences, even in Winnipeg, which had the
largest and most politically active Ukrainian community. Instead, asserts Orest
Martynowych, the concerts, that "combined speeches, songs, recitations, humorous monologues and appeals on behalf of numerous causes were far more

effective in communicating ideas, values and useful advice to unlettered peasant immigrants."[19]

Scholars in anthropology and sociology agree that ritual and ceremony can serve as important conductors of political ideologies across large populations.[20] Over the course of its history, the organized Ukrainian Canadian community created its own political and cultural ceremonies that not only marked important anniversaries in the life of the community but also routinely appealed to its members to commit themselves to their ethnic homeland and to work toward its independence. Without doubt, many dramatic developments in Ukraine (Holodomor, or the man-made famine of 1933, Soviet repressions of the 1930s, political persecution of the Ukrainian intelligentsia in the 1970s, among others) stimulated strong reaction in the diaspora, highlighting in each instance the important attachment its members had developed to their ethnic homeland. But it is the routinely repeated formalized community ceremonies highlighting selected aspects and prominent figures of Ukrainian history that were held in many towns and villages in Canada that most effectively catered to nonpolitical Ukrainians, instilling a profound sense of moral obligation to the ethnic homeland through the particular imagery of it that these ceremonies appealed to. In these ceremonies Ukraine was projected as engaged in a perennial struggle for a better future and the Ukrainians in Europe were represented as brothers and sisters unable to escape the tyranny of the Soviet rule.[21] Ceremonies celebrating Taras Shevchenko (March 9), the reunification of Ukraine (November 22), and the proclamation of Ukraine's independence (January 22) became key cultural events in the life of the organized ethnic community.

The first ceremony, Shevchenko Day, emerged as a national commemoration within the first two decades of the arrival of the first sizable group of immigrants. Martynowych gives us the following account:

> In many districts the first concerts were held in 1911, the fiftieth anniversary of Shevchenko's death, or in 1914, the centennial of his birth. Such concerts usually began with a speech or brief lecture in which the teacher or another local notable presented biographical information about the celebrated individual and exhorted the audience to follow the person's ideals. Songs and recitations reinforced the exhortations and stirred the audience's national pride.[22]

Through their recitation of Shevchenko's politically charged poetry from the middle of the nineteenth century, the young performers would task the members of the audience to embrace their national identity, to pay tribute to the homeland and to commit themselves to its liberation. As musical performance was an essential part of such gatherings, the ceremonies often concluded with everybody in the audience and on stage singing one or both unofficial Ukrainian national anthems that called for the unwavering commitment to Ukraine's liberation. Here is a verse from Ivan Franko's "Ne Pora" ("The Time Is Past"):

> It is time, it is time, it is time,
> To refuse to serve Russian and Pole,
> For an end is at hand, to the past and its crime.
> Our Ukraine claims your life and your soul.[23]

Shevchenko Day celebrations organized by various readings clubs and cultural societies gained momentum especially in the year of 1914 that marked the centennial of the poet's birth. The Shevchenko Day celebrations that year became an important catalyst in the unification of various Canadian Ukrainians in the ethnic community in Winnipeg while also serving the important purpose of further solidifying and normalizing the ritual itself. The organizing committee included representatives of pronationalist organizations and proposed that a main feature of the celebration in Winnipeg should be a concert that would promote the close ties between those in Canada and those in the Ukrainian lands of Europe:

> We will forget the sea that separates us from our brothers in Ukraine, from our beloved Ukraine. We'll send our hearts back to where soon will be waving the sea of wheat and where our oppressed brothers wait for the moment to pay the aliens back for their longtime injustice and persecution.[24]

The opening speech delivered at the concert proclaimed the unification of all Ukrainian Canadians as a significant achievement of the Ukrainian Canadian community under the national leadership. Shevchenko's poems as well as other Ukrainian poetry were recited by local youth, songs and folk music were performed, and a lecture on Shevchenko was presented as a part of the celebrations. The concert was followed by a street procession that attracted a large group of Ukrainians. Telegrams were sent to the organizing committee from other cities in solidarity, and the event was widely reported by a number of Ukrainian newspapers.[25]

Yet a ritual ceremony cannot be considered as fully established unless it takes over a particular spot in the calendar. The 1914 Shevchenko event, for example, was linked to and held around the date on which serfdom in tsarist Russia was abolished in 1861, where Shevchenko lived. The organizing committee explained the choice by referring to the lifelong struggle of the poet, himself a former serf, against Russian tsarism. In the late 1920s, however, a trend emerged to hold the celebrations on the poet's birthday, March 9.[26]

Shevchenko Day was the first pan-national Ukrainian Canadian public event; Independence Day (January 22) and Den' Zluky (November 22) were added to this calendar of important national dates nearly a decade later. Both events concerned political developments in Ukrainian lands in Europe. In 1918 and 1919, Ukrainians proclaimed the existence of a Ukrainian state, even if it only survived for a very brief period in both cases. Both events had a fixed place on the calendar, which were eventually commemorated in Canada on the same dates. All three commemorations became important annual public events for Ukrainian Canadians, first in the pronationalist political camp and then, with the gradual weakening of the socialist camp in the second part of the twentieth century, in the Ukrainian Canadian community in general. The Ukrainian Canadian newspaper *Ukraïns'kyĭ Holos* (founded in 1910) regularly reported on such festivities held across Canada. By the 1970s, according to my review of *Ukraïns'kyĭ Holos* issues published between 1910 and 1986, there were more articles concerning these three important political commemorative public and the nature of the events had changed. These articles not only provided reports on ceremonies held in various cities and towns but also offered in-depth reflections on Shevchenko, his place as a prophet and leader in the Ukrainian independence movement, on the oppressive state of Ukraine under the USSR, and on the implications of proclamations of an independent Ukraine.[27]

A shared feature of these public ceremonies was their explicit and persistent preoccupation with homeland. Ukraine's metaphorical presence in acts undertaken and in speeches delivered during public meetings on all three occasions advanced it into a position of supreme importance to the Ukrainian Canadian community. By the 1970s, the ceremonies and the concerts were framed by a well-established ritual scaffolding, with its symbolic codings, performative nature, prescribed actions, and ritual language. The ritual framework and the message the ritual conveyed routinely reinforced a sense of obligation and duty toward Ukraine among Canadian Ukrainians, repeatedly inviting them to fight for a better future for Ukraine and for the liberation of "brothers and sisters suffering under Soviet tyranny."[28] The cyclicity of these events (held in March, November, and January) ensured year-round exposure of many members of the community to both the idea of homeland and discursive clothes in which it was presented.

The powerful and near holy image of the motherland in public rituals was insured by the use of highly ritualized speech and singing. Both, according to Maurice Bloch, a renowned anthropologist and a scholar of ritual and a specialist in traditional Merina ritual of Madagascar, singularly promote the transcendental powers of ritual and implant particular ritual-generated meanings in the culture and population.[29] Analyzing Merina circumcision ceremonies, Bloch asks how ritual makes their statements appear powerful and holy. The answer is through the use of uniquely ritualized speech and song. Like in Merina ceremonies, the three public commemorations we have been looking at powerfully communicated a particular image of Ukraine because all three used highly ritualized language, relying on formal oratory, repetition, and singing, three of most important vehicles for conveying messages. In all public commemorations concerning Ukraine, speeches were delivered with the help of preselected and limited vocabulary, the speakers relied on established formulaic and intoned patterns of speech, and singing was an important component. Bloch successfully demonstrates that the use of formalized speech and singing increases the authority of ritual messages and the potential for social control. This is because all ritual participants accept without questioning the formalization of language, and so what the ritual communicates becomes the *only* true and only possible message, the truth itself.

A highly moral image of the motherland constructed in the ritual was utilized in speeches, actions, and art in such a fashion as to emphasize the imperative for everyone to serve it. Ukraine was depicted as *daleka/doroha* and *ridna*, Ukraine's people as sufferers under the alien rule, and Ukrainians in Canada as brothers that were deeply concerned with the destiny of their brothers overseas.[30] Ukraine was regarded by those in the diaspora as a beloved mother and its people as siblings. The caption "we are the children of the same nation" on the opening image in this chapter, also a cover image for a Ukrainian Canadian periodical *New Pathway,* projects this idea very well. Conceived as female like many other countries in different languages, Ukraine was always struggling for her freedom.[31] The lasting impact of Soviet communist rule on Ukraine in the twentieth century was likewise felt in the Ukrainian Canadian community. In speeches and ceremonies, Ukraine continued to be seen as poor but proud, talented but deprived of opportunity to shine, strong but sickened by constant battles with external enemies for her freedom, rich in resources but exploited by the occupiers, rich in her people but compromised by having lost her best children to repression and emigration and so on. Another cover from the same annual almanac published by *New Pathway* in 1983 commemorating the fiftieth anniversary of the mass man-made famine in Ukraine that took millions of lives in 1932–33 captures well this idea of Ukraine (see figure 3.2).

Certainly there were many other occasions outside of these three annual ceremonies during which Ukrainian Canadians vicariously engaged with their

Figure 3.2. The front cover of *Kalendar Al'manakh Novoho Shliakhu* (Toronto: Novyĭ Shliakh, 1983), commemorating Holodomor of 1932–33. Drawing by M. Mykhalevych. Courtesy of Novyĭ Shliakh.

remote homeland that was hidden behind the iron curtain and therefore in-accessible. But it is the ritual framework of such annual commemorations, with its power to disseminate the oftentimes unspoken meanings of symbols and ideas employed in the ritual and to initiate the participants into a new mental state, that ultimately brought about important changes in how Ukraine came to be most commonly understood in the Ukrainian Canadian community prior to the 1990s.

There is another important outcome of these commemorations worth mentioning here. With time, Ukrainian Canadians' ethnic homelands were all united into a newly reimagined homeland, one for all, stretching between the western, eastern, northern and southern borders of Soviet Ukraine.[32] Creating one common homeland for different groups of people who had understood themselves to be Galician, Bukovinian, Volynian, and Hutsul helped unite these people under one national umbrella. Homeland thus encapsulated one shared identity for all in this diaspora community, and the diaspora's powerful symbolic dependency on it helped invent a community without a locality.

Outside of the Mainstream

With Ukraine construed as an explicit and potent symbol of Ukrainian Cana-dian identity, public longing for it grew throughout the twentieth century. At the same time, Ukrainian Canadians continued to nurture private nostalgia for the homeland. Such longing sustained and seeped into various Ukrainian Canadian cultural practices, including those outside of the domain of poli-tics. In these contexts, the diasporic consciousness persevered across genera-tions, even as it changed in intensity, content, and character, just as it did in the political discourse of Ukrainian Canadians. Reused in a constructive way, it reemerged in various actions, texts, and narratives of later generations, revealing within these practices the lingering of diasporic memory in otherwise quite local Canadian contexts. Focusing on the small prairie town of Mundare located in the heart of the so-called Ukrainian bloc in the province of Alberta, I turn here to explore how twentieth-century Ukrainian Canadians on the prairies constructed and construed their new home against the metaphorical back-ground of the old country and seek to explain what these constructions achieve in local settings.

I chose to focus on the community of Mundare for a number of reasons. First, it was the site of my extended ethnographic immersion in the late 1990s, where I explored the meanings of local Ukrainianness in a transnational context while preparing to write my doctoral thesis on the topic.[33] It was in this town that I met Mary Dorosh, my dear friend and primary consultant for this project, whose ideas about the ancestral homeland triggered my interest in exploring personal longings for the old country. "Old country," a nearly universal term, was prevalent in Mundarites' personal reminiscences about their past, suggesting how potent and all-encompassing this notion that lacks precise definition is, even as understandings of the concept varied. In the context of so many personal encounters with so many different town folk representing a variety of generations, occupations, income, age, I came to understand that the term "old country" above all refers to private conceptions of the ancestral "otherland," localized in one's personal memory and associated with a remote geographic setting. Among members of the Ukrainian Canadian community in Mundare, I learned that "Ukraine," conversationally, is not necessarily interchangeable with "old country." I also noticed a familiar linguistic slippage into the phrase "going back" when people discussed the idea of visiting the old country. All in all, the private imaginings of the old country in among Ukrainian Canadians whose ancestors settled the prairies in Western Canada at the turn of the twentieth century were not consonant with the public image of Ukraine cultivated in Ukrainian Canadian mainstream culture.

This dissonance came into view with the introduction of representations of Ukraine in Mundare's public space. Back in 2000, a mural consisting of several paintings appeared on the wall of the National Hall of the local Ukrainian Greek Catholic parish in Mundare. The word "national" in the name of the venue points to it being an important part of local Ukrainian, rather than Canadian, history and of the local Ukrainian social scene. The central painting in the mural (see figure 3.3) does not focus on local scenes as the other paintings do but instead depicts four enigmatic figures, three male ones and one female. The young woman, wearing only an embroidered traditional long shirt, is reclining casually and reading a book.[34] Whether the underdressed reclining female with unmade hair is meant to symbolize Ukraine or the people (narod) in need of emancipation and enlightenment is subject to interpretation. While the three male figures are real historic figures, one can assume that given the symbolic placement of the female figure below them and her contrasting characteristics, she is not a real historic figure. At the end of the twentieth century, unlike back in the 1920s when the original image was displayed as a photo in the hall, practically no one in the community knew who the figures in the painting were or what they might mean. Most commonly, perhaps repeating what others had said before, the townfolk in my conversations with them referred to all the figures in the painting as poets, not dwelling on details or the visual

Figure 3.3. The central painting in the set of exterior wall murals in the National Hall of the Ukrainian Greek Catholic Parish of St. Peter and Paul, Mundare, Alberta, 2000. Photo by author.

symbolism that made room for other interpretations as well. Their commentary on the painting revealed a significant gap between official Ukrainian Canadian public discourse and its established representations of Ukraine and local understanding of Ukraine.

While Mundare's public representations of Ukraine over the course of the twentieth century somewhat receded into the background of the town's social life, private imaginings of the old country persisted. And since there has always been mutual cross-feeding of private and public discourses, these private imaginings eventually successfully worked their way back into local public narratives.

When I saw Mundare for the first time, the town struck me as both unique and ordinary. Mundare's uniqueness lies in the fact that the town is known to be one of the earliest Ukrainian settlements in Canada. It started as a hamlet on the prairies in the early 1900s, and the surrounding area known as Beaver Creek saw the arrival of the first Ukrainian immigrants—Bukovinians, Galicians, and Ruthenians—in the 1890s. Railway construction set in motion the economic development of Mundare.[35] In light of the high concentration of the homesteading Ukrainian settlers, the area was chosen by the Greek Catholic Church as a home base for its extended mission in the new world, and the representatives of two monastic orders, Order of St. Basil the Great and Sisters Servants of Mary Immaculate, were sent there as early as the turn of the twentieth century.[36] The presence of these two monastic orders representing the by now global religion of Ukrainian Greek Catholics deeply affected the sense of Ukrainianness in this community, making it a special case when it comes to the question of what role interactions between the diaspora and the homeland can play in local contexts.[37]

The local lifeworld evolved throughout the twentieth century, informed by a variety of social processes that were unfolding globally, nationally, and locally. The Great Depression of 1930s deeply affected the local economy, as elsewhere on the Canadian prairies. Later, local historians and the authors of books commemorating family reunions would speak about how the hardships that the families had to endure strengthened local social institutes of family, neighborhood, and *zemliatsvo*. During the Second World War, Mundare youth actively enlisted in the Canadian Army to fight in Europe. In 1941, Mundare once again found itself the center of Ukrainian Canadian life when the national celebrations of the fiftieth anniversary of Ukrainian immigration to Canada were held there.[38] After the war years, Mundare's growth accelerated. The technological innovations of the late 1950s and 1960s brought changes and new experiences to this locality. Having become more affordable, telephone lines and electricity came to many private farms. New homes were built with modern facilities; the outhouse and reliance on wells for water became a thing of the past. Television was spreading rapidly. The railway lost its importance as the link between Mundare and other communities, and auto vehicles that would take one anywhere one wanted to go became the main means of transportation. On a cultural front, several bands, known beyond the locality and consisting predominantly of Ukrainians, a drama circle, and a choir were active in the community.[39] "Weddings were large, not like today. We used to feed 500 or even a thousand people at once! Those were times, I remember, when in the summer and the fall we used to have weddings every week in the hall, can you imagine!"[40]

With accelerated changes in the lifestyle of the community also came a feeling of rupture, and loss, all marking the beginning of a new stage in the

Mundare lifeworld, in which the community was confronted with new challenges that put its continuity, vitality and Ukrainianness in question as never before.[41] Significantly, at this time the generation of first settlers who had lived through harsh conditions of pioneer times and who had laid the foundations of the Mundare community was dying out. The generation of their children was aging as well. Various commemorative projects were launched to respond to these challenges. In 1980, the community produced its own local history book. In the 1990s, local families began publishing their own family histories and genealogies. Local culture and community was the focus of the Basilian Fathers Museum, which was established in 1949 and moved into its current modern facility in 1991. The turn of the twenty-first century has been marked by even further intensified production of local memorials, such as murals, monuments, memorial plaques, and more family history books. Mundarites often refer to these multiple representations as evidence of their Ukrainianness.

All these at their core vernacular local reflections on the past attest to a fundamentally new kind of cultural knowledge production that began to emerge sometime in the 1970s. On the one hand, these projects were the outcome of collective action undertaken by the community activists. But on the other hand, the merging of new technologies of knowledge sharing with long lived local vernacular values resulted in the production of qualitatively new kinds of community narratives. These community narratives are deeply local (like the stories in the Mundare history books), as they involve local reminiscences of the past, but they are also surprisingly universal, as is evidenced by the fact that many other similar projects were produced on the prairies around the same time, indicating that not only Mundare experienced a tear in the fabric of its social and cultural life.

The creators of new community and family narratives faced the dilemma of selecting the beginning point for the history of their changing lifeworld. One might wonder how there could be such a dilemma—the starting points of many communities like Mundare, linked to the arrival of the first settlers to the area under question, have been well documented. Yet in many Ukrainian Canadian communities this search for origins resulted in symbolically journeying across the ocean to the homelands of their ancestors. It has long been common for writers of local histories and family histories to go beyond the years of settlement and to seek the roots of local lifeworlds in the history of the old country. Intriguingly, though, the old country did not emerge in these texts only as the place of origin of the writers and their communities. References to it reentered the narratives at many other junctures, contributing to narrative representations of local lifeworlds on the Canadian prairies.

The narrative organization of *Memories of Mundare*, a local history book, illustrates my point about how the old country enters understandings and representations of the new world. The book employs narrative means and techniques to produce on its pages a particular image of this locality and its Ukrainianness. Published in 1980, the book was a product of a special editorial committee, whose membership was drawn from local citizens who were in good standing and active in the community. *Memories of Mundare* offers the reader a sequence of several hundred stories, representing, in a rather complex way, the workings and overlaying of public and private memories of Mundare's past, many of which go back to Ukraine.

Mundare's community life and town history are recounted in this book in its first nine chapters, which totals 170 pages. The last chapter, "Family Biographies," occupies almost 400 pages and includes 297 individual family histories. Descriptions of various organizations presented in the first nine parts of the book emphasize the virtues of the community at large. In this "public" story the emphasis is placed on the community's spirituality, which is described as unique, the benefits that accrue from this spirituality, that is, material success, adherence to Ukrainian traditions, which is also viewed as part of this spiritual virtue, and upward mobility and the education instrumental to its successful pursuit, both of which are also presented as part of the collective virtue of this community. The individual family stories in the remaining part of the book revolve around several topics that structure the narrative. There are brief references to the challenging life in the old country and more elaborate stories about rooting themselves in Mundare area early pioneer hardships, successes achieved through hard work and strong faith, growth of the family, and finally the prosperity and good community standing earned through hard work.

The family narratives vary widely. Some authors merely state facts, describing family progress in terms of marriages, children, and their education ("Paul and Katherine were blessed with thirty-five grandchildren") or in terms of wealth, acres and acquired farm machinery, as for example, in the story of John and Katherine Bilyk.[42] In some cases, like the Lysyk's story, the story is supplied in just twenty short sentences:

William was born to Sam and Marie Lysyk in February of 1915 on a farm in Mundare. He attended Vladimir School till he turned eighteen. He then left school to help his parents on the farm. [. . .] In 1941, he met Elizabeth Bohaychuk, daughter of Mike and Mary Bohaychuk. [. . .] They lived on the farm, SW-1-54-17-W4, in a small two-room frame house, which was later plastered. [. . .] Their son Sam was born in 1944 and William D. in 1950. In the spring of 1951,

William bought a half-ton truck and by the fall he had acquired half a quarter of land. He kept farming with horses till 1953, when he bought his first tractor and equipment.[43]

Many other stories are more developed. Authors provide descriptions and specific reminiscences about the past. The most diligent writers devote much attention to the early years of their families. In their stories the depiction of their progenitors' hard beginnings are quite elaborate:

> On July 25, 1901, they reached the land that was to be their home, one mile east of Mundare. They chose a place on the south side of a heavy stand of trees, on the side of a hill to build a home. The heavy bush was looked upon as a blessing, to supply firewood and logs for buildings for years to come. The heavy growth of hay was a promising sight after years on the "morgy" land in Ukraine. Little did they realize the hours of heavy labor in store for them before the heavy roots from these giants gave way to farm land. The roots were no match to their meagre tools and many of them had to be grubbed by hand. The heavy logs cut from the trees made walls for the houses and barns and the holes were plastered with a mixture of clay and dry grass.[44]

In addition to providing a collective portrait of this community, the family stories offer a unique portrayal of the authors' own local lifeworld. Although I have been using the term "lifeworld," I have left it mainly undefined.[45] In defining "local lifeworld" I rely on conceptualizations of the social world advanced by Alfred Schutz, Austrian phenomenologist and social scientist.[46] Schutz argues for a phenomenological understanding of the social world, the latter being understood as based on various kinds of social relationships, an approach that is not new in the social sciences. But Schutz also sees it as constructed and projected in our minds through our own social experiences of it. He asserts that our social experiences make up the expanded social world.[47] This social world is constituted in a highly complicated network of dimensions, relations, and modes of knowledge. Schutz distinguishes between various experiences of this expansive social world, such as between a *directly* experienced social reality and the reality lying beyond our direct personal experiences. The reality that I experience directly consists of those people with whom I am directly involved, "my fellow men," as Schutz puts it.[48] It also consists of those with whom I may become involved. They are my contemporaries. But there are other realities, other social worlds that I cannot experience directly. These are the world of my predecessors and the world of my successors. Thus, our expansive social world consists of these four "realms," or worlds of experience.[49]

A central point here is that directly experienced social reality is not conceivable without the experiences of other worlds that appear as other dimensions of the world immediate to me. Following Schutz, I understand the local lifeworld to be a realm of directly experienced social reality that depends on preceding social realities and succeeding social realities peopled by predecessors and successors, even though these cannot be directly experienced. Both a (social) past and a (social) future are crucial constituents of one's experience of one's present social reality of one's community and locality. But they are not directly experienced, and therefore the narrative representations, that preserve the past for the sake of the future are vital ways of constituting the present. In the case of Mundare, this is doubly reinforced by the generational dimension of kinship, as the predecessors and successors are one's ancestors and descendants.

Memories is a vivid illustration of the importance of the world of predecessors and successors for Mundarites' experience of their ongoing life, as well as how these past and future worlds are constitutive—and thus potentially restorative in a time of rupture—of the local lifeworld in the present. In fact, the book is written about ancestors for descendants. The statement of purpose cited in the book, to preserve our past for the future of our children, is recycled in all segments of the book.

The interconnectedness of the social realities of the world of predecessors and the local lifeworld is achieved in the text not only through the assertion of genealogical and generational continuity and order but also through the use of spatial metaphors as well as through recurring juxtapositions of "here" to "there" ("here," meaning Mundare or Canada, and "there," meaning Ukraine).[50] Such juxtaposing frames the reader's very first encounter with the book. Simply opening the book and looking at the front and back covers and their insides immerses the reader into both worlds. On the inside front cover is detailed map of Lamont County, where Mundare is situated, while the back inside cover features a map of Ukraine. Such a choice of cartographic imagery firmly links the two locations, turning them into one symbiotic domain of home, as the beginning of the new home and its lifeworld is extended to the domain of the old country of local Ukrainians.[51] When one has an option to place a map on a page, the obvious choice is to fit the map into as much space as one has on the page. While such choice is logical, in the case of the two maps in *Memories of Mundare*, it also has a specific effect on the casual reader, as the maps presenting the places of here and there significantly differ in scale. The

map of Ukraine is of far smaller scale than the map of the county, and if one
has little familiarity with Ukraine's geography (think of Mary Dorosh's son,
for example, mentioned in the fieldnotes at the beginning of this chapter), one
can come away with the impression the two worlds the maps represent are
comparable.

The difference in scale is further obscured by similar geographic terminology
presented on both maps. In his influential book *Imagined Communities*, Benedict
Anderson notes the typical habit of Europeans of drawing on the geographic
names of their homelands for the names of places in the new world. Hence the
world now has both Hampshire and New Hampshire, York and New York,
Orleans and New Orleans and many other twinned toponyms. Anderson under-
lines that this method of naming allowed locations in the new world to be
imagined as the extension of a particular location in the old world.[52] This naming
of the new lands with the geographic names of the old homeland was likewise a
widespread practice of Ukrainians who emigrated to Canada and the United
States.[53] In the Mundare area, the adjective "new" was rarely added in front of
geographic names brought from the "old country." In the so-called Ukrainian
bloc of Alberta, for example, Brody, and Kolomea (the names of two towns in
Western Ukraine, Galicia) labeled what was seen as "undomesticated" space.[54]
Such a presentation of the two worlds, the one here, the one there, as super-
imposed, suggests that the new home on the prairies was to become a true new
home, a substitute for the home left behind rather than its extension, and attests
to the complex manner in which the locality in the new world has been thought
of and imagined by its own residents. The common toponyms, no matter how
distinct the two worlds are that share them, enhances the reader's perception of
deep relationship between the old country and the new home in the Canadian
West. It also serves as a powerful visual metaphor for the highly ambivalent
meanings of home(land) that have emerged in Mundare over many generations.

It is not only in its toponyms that the old country emerges in the descriptions of the local lifeworld. Other kinds of narrative oscillation between the
world of here and that of there that are employed in the representation of the
Mundare lifeworld in *Memories* include oscillations between spatial characteristics
of the two worlds. It has been noted by other scholars that spatial metaphors,
both verbal and visual, are habitually employed in the narration of personal life-
stories, memoirs, and autobiographies. Vieda Skultans, British social anthropologist, analyzing autobiographical narratives of post-Soviet Latvians, notes how
firmly personal memories of Latvians who survived persecutions under the Soviet regime are embedded in various physical landscapes.[55] Others, especially
cognitive psychologists, have emphasized that the imagery of autobiographical

memories is encoded in a person's lived space and time.[56] This practice of framing of one's memories in personal reminiscences using spatial terms and metaphors is a fundamental aspect of human memory and human remembering, and so it is not surprising that collective memories tend to be encoded with similar metaphors. *Memories of Mundare* opens with the following poem authored by a local poet, which illustrates this point quite well:

> Then once again we will recall
> The things we loved so well . . .
> The shady lanes where we would stroll
> As evening shadows fell.
>
> The park, the church, the school, the store,
> The friendly folks back home,
> The sunny creeks, the meadows, and
> The hills we used to roam.
>
> These memories are something which
> My heart will always store . . .
> And joys and happiness they bring
> Are mine forevermore.[57]

Memories of Mundare, however, goes beyond enlisting the spatial contents of the past of this locality in its depictions of the local lifeworld. In their efforts to demonstrate the virtues of the new world, the writers refer to the spaces and landscapes of both homelands, the old and the new. For farmers, the land is the most meaningful referent, almost to the degree of being sacred, as their livelihood is dependent on it. As such, it is often the focal point of such cross-referencing:

> The [Mundare] region is part of the Aspen Parkland, which is a phenomenon of that part of the Steppes of Ukraine known as Halychyna from which most of the Mundare pioneers came. . . .
>
> The terrain is not level but varies with gently undulating countryside in which trees and tangled shrubbery mingled with the cultivated fields. Everywhere, too, are sloughs and marshes and creeks but no rivers as there are in Halychyna. . . .
>
> The Ukrainian homesteaders knew that underneath the fescue grasses and aspen trees was rich black soil like at "home"; therefore, they searched for homesteads in the heavily-wooden areas. . . .
>
> How right they were! Visitors from other parts of North America, and even from such rich farm areas as those around Calmar and Nisku, marvel at the blackness of these "Chernozem Soils."[58]

In addition to comparing the land here and there, articulate contributors to *Memories of Mundare*, contextualize their personal memories about their parents' and grandparents' households, drawing both on their lived experience and on family lore and local public memories of the old country:

> The gardens are a delight with their well-kept green lawns, trees, and a profusion of colour when the geraniums, dahlias, delphiniums, asters, marigolds, petunias, begonias and other flowers are in full blossom. The Ukrainians love bright colors in their embroidery, in their Easter egg writing, and in their costumes. Poor as they were in the "old" country, they all had small plots of colorful sunflowers, poppies, larkspur and others. Almost every weeping woman took a handful of flower seeds when she left her dear homeland to venture out into the unknown.[59]

Beautification of the new land is another means of justifying the forefathers' choice to leave the old land for the new:

> Settling in the Podola district, at the north end of Beaverhill Lake, Prokip was happy because Beaverhill Creek cut through one corner of his homestead. So plentiful were the fish in it that on one occasion he took a wagonload to the church at Seniuk's for his neighbors who did not have the luxury of their own creek. Living close to the lake, with its millions of waterfowl that filled the twilight hours with a clamor that will never be heard again, he had big and little game close to hand, a well-stocked creek and plenty of sloughs everywhere.[60]

The author completes his account of settlement with a reference to "there," that is to Ukraine, in order to accentuate the rightness of the grandfather's choice to come to this new land: "This was something like the life he had seen in the Ukraine except that here it was for his own enjoyment, not that of a titled count or duke."[61] All in all, these oscillations between the here and the there in public and personal narratives create a new lived geography that patches together the past and the present, two lands and two cultures.

This tendency to metaphorically go back to the old country while describing the new one is further evidenced in Mundare's subsequent public and personal history projects and writings. Family historians, for example, utilize this technique quite regularly in family history books and even expand on it. Typically, family historians include entire chapters now on the old country (with technological advances and the internet, it has become quite easy to replicate the authoritative writings of scholars or other analysts in otherwise quite vernacular projects of family history writing).

Memories of Mundare, being one example of this practice, gives us a good exposure to the workings of local public and personal memory at the time of the book's creation, in the 1970s, a time of rapid lifestyle changes in the local lifeworld. One important consideration in this regard (and supporting my thesis on the perseverance of the vernacular longings for the old country) is that the community history book both encapsulated in its narrative family lore that the authors, typically descendants of the first settlers or their children, had learned orally and at the same time, having committed this oral tradition to print, undermined its further circulation. It is not surprising that oftentimes when I would approach local people in hopes of interviewing them about their own personal pasts and memories, their common response was that I should read the book, as "everything is already written there." Moreover, if interviews proceeded without such a suggestion being made, what I would often be told appeared to be a close retelling of the information already stated in the book or in a family history book. The publication of *Memories* may have indeed undermined the future "natural" flow of family lore and personal memories about the past in this community. At the same time, the book's presentation of Mundare's lifeworld, now fixed in writing, serves us as a window and a gateway into the workings of local diasporic memory.

Vernacular memories, imaginings, and values found their way into many public narratives of Ukrainian Canadians, both those documenting mainstream Ukrainian Canadian identity and those describing local manifestations of Canadian Ukrainianness. As a part of this process, vernacular longings for homeland actively contributed to, and were in fact responsible for, a set of lingering conceptions of the old country that proliferated in the twentieth century before they were challenged by resumed contact between the homeland and the diaspora after 1991. Private longings for homeland gave rise to a powerful public symbol of Ukrainian Canadian identity and also defined local lifeworlds. The example of the community of Mundare illustrates the latter quite well.

The question the reader might be asking now is so what? My answer is the following. Vernacular longings for homeland and its various manifestations in Ukrainian Canadian public discourses became an important background against which other practices of sustaining imagined or real relations with the old country unfolded throughout the twentieth century. These practices include transcontinental letter writing, family history and genealogy research, and eventually homecoming. Let's turn to those now.

Figure 4.1. Personal letter from Ukraine, 1960s. Wakarchuk Letters, Personal Sources Archive, Prairie Centre for the Study of Ukrainian Heritage, St. Thomas More College, University of Saskatchewan. Courtesy of Paraskeva Semenuik, Yorkton.

4

////////////////////////////

Enveloping Distance

$\mathcal{T}$he anxieties and nostalgia for homeland that distance between Canada and the old country introduced into the lives of many Ukrainian Canadians played themselves out in a variety of ways throughout the twentieth century. They seeped into the domain of public life—into discourses of homesickness, into public rituals and ceremonies, into debates on homeland, the Ukrainian nation, and its future, into fine literature and the arts, and even into local Canadian geography. In the domain of vernacular culture, folklore scholars, as discussed in chapter 1, have documented in the early period of Ukrainian Canadian history a vast body of folklore that lamented the insurmountable distance between an immigrant and his or her small homeland. Vernacular poetry written by ordinary folk and recent immigrants in the early twentieth century and later personal memoirs turned into a full-fledged practice of Ukrainian ethnic self-reflectivity, reflecting on the distance between Canadian and Ukrainian worlds in a number of ways.[1] In the last quarter of the twentieth century, local histories produced in various Ukrainian Canadian communities paid tribute to the old country in their narratives. In the last decade of the same century, family histories, written for centennial celebrations in the 1990s and beyond, recounted the homeland and kin there, oftentimes in both ideological and personal terms.

This distance between homeland and diaspora was experienced and lived most intimately through personal correspondence that quietly accompanied the formation of Ukrainian Canadian ethnicity in early twentieth century as well as its subsequent flourishing. If so-called immigrant folklore asserted that the two sides of the separated families would only meet again in the Valley of Josaphat, it is the letters, and the alternative lettered universe that they created, that came to serve as the intimate meeting ground of the separated. Exploring another aspect of the vernacular roots of imagining "other Ukrainians" in both the diaspora and the homeland, this chapter turns to personal correspondence, revealing how it contributed to these imaginings. As I show here, with time and ritualization of letter writing practice, personal family letters came to serve as effective vernacular tools of diasporic imagination of "other Ukrainians." Let's start with a few examples of letters and letter-focused exchanges from my field notebook.

The letter below, written by a Ukrainian villager to his brother in Canada, exemplifies typical rural letters from homeland.

Davydivtsi, Ukraine, 1964

Dear Badika Wasyl:

I send you and *lylika*, your children and grandchildren my best regards. I bring to your attention that we are all in relatively good health, and we are wishing you even better health. I am writing to inform you that I received your last letter, and I received the two dollars, for which I am very grateful to you. I exchanged them for eighty kopecks each. Altogether I got one ruble and sixty kopecks; for that one can buy two kilograms of white flour, or one kilogram of meat. The dollars are valued very cheaply here. I heard from those who receive parcels with *fustky* [head kerchiefs] that a small *turpan* [kerchief] that costs two dollars in Canada fetches here thirty rubles and that shawls go for seventy to eighty rubles. Therefore, I ask you, dear Badiko Vasyl' not to send us dollars, as those saints are making fun of these dollars here. If you would have an opportunity, send us a parcel with those *turpans*, but don't put down the high value on the envelope, because they will charge us a lot then.

I am writing you, *badika*, to tell you that our new life [*povodzhenia*] here is the same. We have become accustomed to it by now. We hope that soon it will be easier, like those who are sick hope for an improvement, but the others say, it will be better only in the hole [grave], when, instead of spitting on one's knee, one will be spitting on one's beard. We are now used to life without our field and our gardens. Now, if we can get used to living without the jobs, it will be just perfect. Here, they are introducing a lot of mechanical and automated work, so the manual work has changed. This past summer I worked on the construction site, but in the winter I worked around the house. Unfortunately, there is not much to do. There was little hay, not enough for silage, and there is no *labuza*, unless I dig under the snow. It saddens me to look at our cow, I am sorry to sell it, but there is nothing to feed it with.[2]

I visited recently the family of Paraskitsa; they are all healthy. Their son Vasyl' works on tractor, son-in-law Mytro and Frozina are looking after the children, Maria's husband, Mykolaĭ, is working with cattle, the youngest son Oles'ka is also working on a tractor, and his wife works at the woodcutting factory. And the Paraskitsas live with them. I gave them your address, and they will write a letter and will send you *fortyhrafiĭ* [pictures]. They will send you pictures later, they don't have them ready, and because it is winter now, they cannot go to the city. The winter here is not the one like further in the west, where the temperatures are mild. It started in December but has no inclination to finish at this time. I would like to ask you, *badika*, to tell me whether you have an orchard and sheep on your farm. I am wishing you good health, and everything else— good life and satisfaction from your children and grandchildren. All the best.[3]

And here are a few extracts from my field notes I took during research trips that highlight the importance of correspondence to both, those in the homeland and those who emigrated:

Kyiv, Ukraine, October 7, 1989

"We were told we would be sent to Siberia if we wrote to them, so when letters stopped coming, we were afraid to write to them," she said, speaking through tears. Liuba, a woman in her fifties, had just arrived at my apartment in downtown Kyiv, having taken the first available train from her village in Volyn (Western Ukraine) some four hundred kilometers away. I had never met her before and had no idea who was buzzing my doorbell. She came to my home, and into my life, in response to a letter I wrote on behalf of an American friend of mine inquiring, with little hope or expectation, about lost relatives. I had sent the letter just a week ago to a small village in the Volyn region, addressed in an unusual manner, to the relatives of Hryts' Berdyk. In it I simply stated that the Bradleys of Florida were looking for someone named Hryts' Berdyk and if Hryts' or someone from his family received the letter, please respond to the address below. The address was mine. Liuba tells me that she departed as soon as she received my short letter. The idea that she might meet the American side of her family, or even an intermediary who knew them, led her to pack up canned homemade meat, bacon, or *salo*, smoked turkey (all those precious foods that were now all but unavailable in my semi-hungry city struck by all kinds of food shortages!) and then rush to Kyiv. Liuba stayed with my mother and me for two days in our tiny downtown apartment before managing to get a ticket back to her village. What an unexpected response to my short letter, but a very moving and telling one. One letter only and the woman sprung to action.[4]

Hrytsevolia, Ukraine, May 10, 1999

Nadia Trach and I are visiting Baba Krokhmalykha, her neighbor. As a good neighbor, Nadia, in her early forties, mother of three, keeps an eye on Kateryna Krokhmal', born in 1912 and known to all as Krokhmalykha. Both rely on each other, and their means of existence seem to be minimal. A year ago, I did an interview with Baba Krokhmalykha, and now I am hoping to follow up on the stories we shared earlier. This time, Baba Krokhmalykha shares with me her bitter recollections of postwar injustice when Soviet rule returned to Hrytsevolia, a topic once outlawed in Soviet Ukraine. Nadia interrupts us and says, "Maybe you should not record this." I oblige and stop the tape recorder. Once the story is over, Nadia proceeds to explain her request. "Once upon a time," she tells me, "me and my family were making an audiotape with the greetings from the whole village to pass on to the relatives in Canada. The audio letter. We recorded everyone and everything we could [*chysto vs'o*]. Our grandmother spoke into the tape recorder, the neighbors did, even the priest recorded his blessings on it. But when we were passing on the tape with the recorded village greetings through people to take it across the border, the border officers took the tape to check it out. They said that transporting the audiotapes was not allowed. Then later, the relatives from Canada wrote and told us that when they put the tape into the tape player, the only thing they heard on it was white noise."[5]

Mundare, Canada, October 4, 2011

October 2, 2011. The Basilian Museum in Mundare is buzzing with people; Karen Lemiski, the director, is hosting another exhibit opening to which I have been invited as a guest speaker to reflect on the role of women in this community. I am thrilled to be back in the community where I spent years researching local Ukrainian practices in the transnational context for my graduate work. Most of all, I am excited to be reconnected with the ladies who over the course of my fieldwork became to me far more than just my key informants. Christine Pawluk and I revisit our days together. We pose for pictures, we chat, we laugh away, happily reconnected. I thank Christine again for sharing her family letters she received from Ukraine in the 1990s and tell her that I used some of those letters in my writing. And it seems that we are back again in the same shared space of memories of our time together, delving again into an old conversation about letters that her family exchanged with Ukraine. You know, Natalka," Christine tells me, "I remember when I was still a child, my mother receiving the letters from her family in Ukraine. I remember how she read them, withdrawn from everything around her. We always wondered what was in those letters. I also remember my mother never writing back. You know what she told me? That it was dangerous for her family in Ukraine to receive letters from her.[6]

Ternopil, Ukraine, October 26, 2011

Olena, Ihor, and myself are sitting in Zoloti Dukaty, a lovely coffee shop in downtown Ternopil, discussing the prospects of new research project I hoping to set up here in Ternopil. Both Olena and Ihor are professors in mid-career at the Ternopil Pedagogical University, and in the recent past we shared many wonderful experiences running the university summer semester for Canadian students in Ternopil. I am back now to set up a research team that will be searching for and documenting personal letters sent to local families from Canada and abroad. Zoloti Dukaty's coffee is delicious, and the conversation is even better, as we have not reconnected for a while as group. While I am out-lining the goals of the project, Ihor, with his amazing ability to turn nearly any information into a good story, immediately begins sharing with us his own family saga about the relatives abroad. The brother of his father left for Canada in the early 1930s. He did come back once, Ihor says, in the 1970s. The meeting with his village folks took place by the walls of the Hotel Ternopil. Obviously, no one went to the village. It was not allowed then. Soon after this visit, his father decided that he wanted to invite his brother to come to Ternopil for a real visit and stay with them for a month in the village. He was running around, from one office to another, trying to *vybyty* [obtain] all proper documents for the invitation. He prepared all kinds of papers, which he got from all kinds of offices, but in the end the KGB did not approve the invitation.[7]

The years went by, continues Ihor. Time came for the father's sons to apply to the university and then enter the workforce. The oldest son was suddenly denied the permission to work at the military plant. And at that time, jobs in military industrial sector were highly prestigious and well paid, Ihor reminds us. It was a very good job that the boy could not have, because, as it turned out, of his father's "connections abroad." A record had been made somewhere in the KGB that the boy's father maintained a "connection abroad" and had even dared to invite his own brother for a month-long visit. A few more years went by. It was now time for the second son to enter the university. This time, before the university entry examinations, the father went directly to a local office of the KGB, to ask the folks there to remove from the record the note about his "connections abroad" and to stop harassing his sons. The KGB office was of course a small regional one. "Everybody knows everybody in our neck of the woods," says Ihor. So they promised to erase the entry about the "connections" and not to chase the sons anymore.

At this juncture in his story, Ihor stops for a few seconds, as if pondering something. When he resumes talking, his voice and intonation have changed. In a distinct storytelling fashion of his, his voice slightly lowered and his words better accentuated, he begins sharing with us a story of how when his father was writing letters to Canada he would feel lost in that "space of letter writing." "I remember, how, when the time to write a letter came, my father would get uncomfortable, would sit by the table, feeling and looking lost," Ihor started. He then shifted into the present tense: "Another minute goes by. He stares at the paper. He turns to my mother and asks her pleadingly, 'So, *zhinko* [wife], what should I write about?' 'Well,' she answers, 'thank them first for the parcel.' But the parcel had arrived some two years ago," Ihor chuckles, "and my father has already thanked my uncle three or four times for it in previous letters! 'Well, you can thank him again,' she further insists. And so it was for my father, Ihor continued. He simply did not know what to do with these letters, what to write in them."[8]

Corresponding with Natalka Husar, a renowned American/Canadian contemporary artist of Ukrainian origin, about her prospective visit to my university to give a lecture, we soon found ourselves deeply engaged in a vivid discussion about letters from the old country. The topic surfaced when Natalka found out that our center has been developing an archival collection of old country letters. Natalka had used the theme of old country letters, *lysty z kraiu*, in her art on and off throughout whole her life. In her usual fashion, Natalka would attach an image from the vast art collection of her own works to her emails, and for a short while she attached the images of paintings and other art works that profiled in one way or another an old country letter. The letter in these works was embedded into the painting, as if it were a character in the story, sitting as an open sheet on the side table, laying still in the envelope under the vase on the shelve, dancing away in the air, or constituting an art object itself, as in the case of the real-size ceramic rendition of a letter removed halfway out of an envelope, the envelope glued to the flat surface of the frame (see the image on the cover of this book).

A year later, on a beautiful afternoon in May, I found myself in Natalka's home in Toronto. We agreed to look at the letters that Natalka herself received from Ukraine over the course of her life and art career and that she still had in her possession. A collector of life's miscellany, an ethnographer of the abandoned, and an archivist of the discarded treasures from someone else's life, she has in her home many a trivial object that once upon a time got transformed into art, merely by her touch and thought. The old country letters that came into Natalka's life did not escape that fate. Browsing through those letters, I became fully aware that their old yellowish envelopes, with all kinds of stories and images trapped in them, long ago become an important dimension of Natalka's art and life. Her mother, after escaping war-torn Ukraine during the Second World War, corresponded with her family in Ukraine throughout the rest of her life, and her other family members and family friends likewise corresponded with Ukraine. Natalka herself wrote many letters to Ukraine. To top up my rendezvous with her letters, Natalka brings out from storage a piece of ceramic art she created in 1977. I am happy to see the live version of the ceramic letter from the old country I so admired from a distance. "I made up the text myself," Natalka is telling me. "You know, I made it like the typical text of these letters, 'Good day, dea—. . . thank you very m—. . . it has been raining, but the summer. . . . Stepan's daughter. . . . To school, Nykola is also . . . the institute of biochemistry . . .'" (see the image on the cover of this book). And then she disappeared into the basement again. "It was meant to be a diptych," she continued, laying out on the table another ceramic object, a life-size replica of a 1970s large yellow envelope of Canadian make, partially displaying its ceramic contents, replicas of items that were commonly sent from Canada to the families in Ukraine, such as chewing gum, pens and pencils and the omnipresent *khustka*, or *khustyna*, the head kerchief.[9] In the domain of everyday culture, the kerchief had become a most potent vernacular symbol of the lettered/parceled relationship that both groups of Ukrainians found themselves in for as long as they had been separated. The *khustka* not only played significant role in traditional culture, especially of women. In the Soviet era, which were cash-deprived times, especially in rural settings, it also acquired significant monetary value, being worth much more in in Ukraine than what it cost to buy in Canada. As such, it became a coveted item obtainable only from the parcels of the overseas relatives.

Natalka Husar's 1977 diptych, little known to the lovers of her art or to Ukrainian Canadians, captures the very essence of what had become of transnational family correspondence by the mid-twentieth century. Representing the two-way traffic of correspondence, the life-size diptych underscores the persisting distance between the two worlds, encoding its complex character in well-known verbal, visual, and material formulas and metaphors of the disconnected kinship.

How is this distance organized, communicated, and dealt with in letters and in letter writing? How did it contribute to diasporic imaginings of transatlantic kin? To contextualize the search for the answers to these questions, I first briefly discuss the place of transatlantic family correspondence in Ukrainian Canadian culture and the attention it has received in Ukrainian Canadian historiography and scholarship thus far. Then I present my approach to the study of transatlantic family correspondence, which I see as a cultural *corporate* practice, providing the framework for the subsequent discussion of how the distance between the two writing camps is sustained through both letters as texts and social practice. Afterward, I look into one particular example of transnational correspondence and consider how this correspondence constructs and maintains distance between the writers, turning to the question of liminality.

The Public Life of a Family Letter

During the initial tide of Ukrainian emigration to Canada (1891–1914), in addition to being an informational lifeline between the immigrants and their families overseas, the letters, addressed to close relatives and friends, routinely served as public means for passing on information about immigration to others. They were read out loud during gatherings at neighbors' houses and passed around the village and among the members of extended family. Many were also published in magazines and newspapers of a time, including *Kanadiis'kyĭ Farmer* and *Ukraïns'kyĭ Holos* in Canada and *Rus'ka Rada*, *Ukraïns'kyĭ Emigrant*, *Bukovina*, and others in Ukraine. It is not surprising that back in the era of preelectronic communication, the personal letter was a powerful tool of cultural production. On the one hand, the letter as an informational vehicle that carried messages across the vast expanse of the Atlantic firmly entered the folk imagination of Ukrainian villagers. In the traditional lore of premodern Ukrainians, it was the coocoo bird, which was the news carrier, bringing news from various unreachable domains of the "outer" world, be it the land of death, the other shore of the Danube, or some other unknown terrain. By the turn of the twentieth century, the letter had taken over this function in many folksongs of the so-called immigrant cycle, connecting the world beyond the Atlantic and the families in the homeland.[10]

Ukrainian Canadian popular culture of that time also embraced the personal letter as an important element, as exemplified by the early twentieth-century Canadian Ukrainian pop culture icon Shtif Tabachniuk. A character created by Winnipeg-based artist Yakiv Maidanyk, Vuiko Shtif, or Uncle Shtif, appeared

— 142 —

Штіф пише лист до жінки.

До стола сідаю, за пюро лапаю, до тебе моя мила письмо укладаю. Іди листоньку, бо я йти не можу, прийдеш до порога, поклониш си Богу.

Христос сі раждає.

Кохана жено, моя кубіто.

Доношу тобі, що моє поводзене орайт сказати. Ми дістали на зиму лейдоф з шапи, але на Марч знов буде джаб. Сьвяткую нині, бо Хрісмис маєм. Ей жоно, Яв дохо, коби те сюда примуфувати, то то пєкно. Миnі ліпше як ксєндзови в краю, та де, де ксєндз в краю має такий ґуд тайм як я в Канаді? Ади вче-

Figure 4.2. Vuiko Shtif writing a letter to his wife. Published in Yakiv Maidanyk (under Shtif Tabachnyk), *Kaliendar Sh. Tabachniuka* (Winnipeg: n.p., 1918).

in a series of cartoons, feuilletons, and other media. The eternal wanderer and a "simple" man, Uncle Shtif was immensely popular among Ukrainian immigrants in Canada. Transplanted from the old country and never fully rooted in the new one, Shtif, like many of his countrymen, wrote letters to his wife whom he had left behind, to the amusement of many admirers of Maidanyk's sharp and biting sense of humor (see figure 4.2).[11] Early Ukrainian Canadian poetry, considered to be an example of Ukrainian oral folk art in Canada, also reflected the popularity of letters.[12]

With time, the public role of letters diminished. The gap between the families on both sides of the Atlantic kept growing. With new families springing up in the new homeland, the meaning of family and kin among Ukrainians in Canada gradually changed as well, as the focus shifted away from the old country kin and to newly formed family networks in Canada. Letters between the old country and new branches of family in Canada nevertheless continued to be exchanged throughout the rest of the twentieth century, although over time, these exchanges ceased to play a prominent role in the public life of Ukrainian Canadian communities. They were now circulated only in private spheres of Ukrainian Canadians. Natalka Husar's turn to personal correspondence as an art form attests to the fact that the letters to and from Ukraine, which in the second part of twentieth century continued quietly stitching together the ripped mesh of transnational kinship ties, have by now become culturally and discursively invisible in the official Ukrainian culture and in scholarship.

Despite the public role of letters in the early years of the Ukrainian Canadian community, neither the community nor academic institutions of the day saw the immigrant correspondence as worthy of research and archiving, unless they were letters to established organizations or dignitaries, who retained their records, as was the case with letters from immigrants sent to Metropolitan Sheptytsky in the early 1900s to which he responded.[13] In subsequent years, the homeland/immigrant letters profiled in the public media at the turn of the twentieth century inspired just two scholars to reflect on the phenomenon of transnational letter writing.[14] In the late 1960s, Robert Klymasz published an article on the immigrant letter as a productive motif in early modern Ukrainian folk culture,[15] and some two decades later.[16] Oleksandr Sych produced a small collection of forty-two immigrant letters and folk verses, reprints of letters originally profiled in selected Ukrainian media at the turn of the twentieth century, nearly simultaneously in Canada and Ukraine. In his introduction, Sych does not go beyond the historical context in which these letters were written, nor does he examine the letters themselves; instead, he treats them only as illustrative material supporting his overview of the early Ukrainian mass migration overseas.

In the archival world, some efforts have been recently made to publicize existing collections of correspondences, either by using existing collections in research or by analyzing the collections themselves. In today's Ukraine, Volodymyr Marchuk, an archivist based in the city of Rivne, uses the letters sent by Ukrainian immigrants to Paraguay in the 1930s and held in the Rivne State Archives as a source of information in his examination of the migrants' daily lives after they arrived and settled in Paraguay.[17] In North America, selected family correspondence between Ukraine and the United States has been digitized and placed online via the Immigration History Research Center at the University of Minnesota, as a part of the pilot archival project on letter digitization recently initiated by the center.[18]

All in all, aside from these above sporadic explorations of the topic and the occasional use of the immigrant letter as reference material in historical studies of Ukrainian communities around the globe, no sustained scholarly attention has been paid to Ukrainian immigrant letter writing, despite the fact that the practice continued on throughout the twentieth century and beyond.[19]

The limited scholarly investigation of twentieth-century Ukrainian and specifically Ukrainian Canadian immigrant/homeland letter writing is puzzling. While political control in Ukraine suppressed public discourse and scholarly enquiry into letter writing, Ukrainian Canadian scholarship was free to pursue the study of letters. It is especially puzzling since international scholarship on the immigrant letter has steadily grown since the early twentieth century, ever since the publication of the seminal work on the immigrant letter, William I. Thomas and Florian Znaniecki's *The Polish Peasant in Europe and America*.[20] This book, a classic, offers insight into the sociocultural change Polish immigrants and their families behind underwent during their mass migration to North America. The twentieth century witnessed the production of many extended collections of letters.[21] In the last third of the twentieth century, beginning with Charlotte Erickson's pathbreaking *Invisible Immigrants*, excellent critical analysis of the immigrant letter began to emerge.[22] Scholars working in various contexts and disciplines began actively reflecting on private homeland/immigrant correspondences written by the Dutch, the Germans, the Italians, the Irish, the Norwegians, the Finnish, and many other groups.[23]

In my article on the phenomenon of transnational family correspondence in the Ukrainian Canadian context, I attempt to bridge this gap in scholarship and offer my interpretation of this kind of letter writing, situating this phenomenon in broader sociocultural developments of the twentieth century and in the international historiography of letters.[24] Based on the examination of letters collections that I built for the Personal Sources Archives at the Prairie Centre for the Study of Ukrainian Heritage, the article argues for a conception of transnational letter writing as a vernacular practice of modernity.[25]

Defining Ukrainian Transatlantic Letter Writing

Given the unique historical circumstances in which family correspondence unfolded, the letters exchanged between Ukrainian families on both sides of the

Atlantic in the twentieth century as well as the very practice of letter writing among Ukrainians, require a customized approach to their study. Like other scholars who have researched immigrant letters as culture-specific vernacular documents of either written orality or oral literacy, I consider this cultural phenomenon of transatlantic letter writing to be a *vernacular* phenomenon and a social practice, which came to life and has been maintained by many so-called ordinary individuals and unfolds in the domain of the noninstitutional culture of the everyday.[26] However, unlike many researchers, who in their examination of transatlantic family correspondence predominantly focus on specifically *immigrant* letters or correspondence between the immigrants themselves and their families and friends back in the homeland, I see Ukrainian transatlantic letter writing as a long-lived vernacular practice sustained not only by the immigrant generation but also by subsequent generations. As this correspondence continued throughout the century, it went through many phases of development and acquired many features of a tradition, having been steeped in ritual, folklore, and folk psychology.[27] The phenomenon of letter writing, though it is usually traced through individual letters, is best understood as a social practice, rooted in and sustained not only by individual agency but a certain kind of collective agency generated outside of individual will and within particular groups of individuals. This understanding of letter writing as social practice is instrumental to my understanding of how the Ukrainian letters I have examined both nourish and attempt to shorten the distance between the homeland and the diaspora.

Typically, researchers studying letter exchanges between immigrants and their homelands, tend to focus on personal immigrant correspondence, that is, on the exchanges that took place between individual agents of letter writing in the period that followed the migration. It is because of this focus that labels such as "immigrant letters" and "immigrant correspondence" tend to get used, labels that many acknowledge to be imperfect terms that fail to describe the whole complexity of such letter exchanges. Researchers often acknowledge the importance of kinship agendas advanced through letter exchanges and they point out that extended correspondences include many writers and last many years, but it is the individuals who are recognized by the scholars as the agents of letter writing.[28] It is true that the correspondence depended on the will and desire of individual writers to keep it going. Still, considering it in its totality and keeping in mind that its roots are neither in the diaspora nor the homeland but in that intangible domain of the diaspora-homeland binomial, allows one to identify a different kind of agency that kept this correspondence alive over the course of the twentieth century history against all odds.

To put it simply, correspondence was maintained not only between individuals but between the extended families on both sides of the Atlantic. In the context of Ukrainian transatlantic letter exchanges of the twentieth century, individuals entered and left the correspondence but the correspondence continued, albeit between the new and different members of both families. Thus, letter writing, when continued through generations, became a cultural practice of corporate nature (under an anthropological understanding of kinship as an earliest example of a corporate social organization). So, when we recognize that transatlantic letter writing takes place not just between the individuals in one historical moment or the other but between kin groups with the life span of a century, we understand that the two kinship groups involved in the letter exchange are the corporate agents of correspondence.[29] In this context, at any given moment, the distance an individual writer experiences vis-à-vis his or her correspondent is not just a distance between him or her and the correspondent but between the two kin groups they represent, as well as between the two lived realities they inhabit.

As a corporate social practice, Ukrainian transnational family correspondence over time has undergone at least three distinct phases. The earliest transatlantic letter exchanges were carried out by the immediate families who were subject to what became long-term or permanent separation. This correspondence was brought about by the departure of select family members abroad and therefore can be properly labeled as immigrant correspondence. With their writing style firmly rooted in the folk psychology of the day, letters written and exchanged in the earlier times of immigration, containing know-how and much detail about the immigration process, served, as I have already noted, both personal and public purposes.

In the second habitual phase, the letter writers were often the same people who had started corresponding with the overseas relatives in the first place. Yet their social roles as family members (as children, siblings, parents, grandparents, aunts/uncles, and great aunts and uncles, etc.), as well as the expectations they had with respect to kinship relations in local and transatlantic contexts had changed. Correspondence in this phase became a highly ritualized undertaking; letters were sent at sparse intervals (a couple of times per year), often taking the form of Christmas and Easter greetings (making letter writing itself even more ritually constructed). Letters became highly repetitive and formulaic and contained, as a rule, minimum information about the local lifeworld. Diligently registered deaths and births of the family members and thanks for parcels received would constitute the core of the message, the elaborate formulas for greeting, expressing gratitude, and bidding good byes all serving as supporting scaffolding that gave each letter the same structure. Maintained for years at such sparse intervals, this correspondence would dwindle with time, especially once the initial writers passed away.

In many cases the eventual ending of the family correspondence was also directly informed by developments in the homeland (in Soviet Ukraine and other adjacent countries where the writers lived). By far the largest contributing factor to the dwindling of the correspondence was the political regime in the former USSR and its censorship of family correspondence with overseas relatives. More than once the local Soviet authorities broke the letter chain by threatening the writers with various repercussions, according to many informants of mine in Western Ukrainian villages where I conducted fieldwork and as evidenced by the testimonies that open this chapter.[30]

Beginning in the 1980s, perestroika and then the collapse of the Soviet Union in 1991 injected new life into transatlantic letter writing, as the descendants of the original migrants, after a long period of silence, started seeking each other out. The writers who engaged in transatlantic letter writing in this period, however, possessing little to no knowledge of each other, participated in very different letter writing projects than their forebears, introducing a new phase in transnational correspondence between Ukrainians across the Atlantic.[31] With the end of the cold war and eventual political changes in Europe in the 1980s, Ukrainian Canadians began visiting their long-forgotten homelands and renewing their family connections with their distant relatives in Ukraine. Capitalizing on renewed family ties, representatives of the homeland families started visiting Canada and eventually immigrating there. Transatlantic letters continue even now to sustain the fragile bridge between the two worlds, now far more open and familiar to each other than before. Since this phase continues to unfold until this day, it is not yet comprehended by researchers as an important cultural practice of late modernity. This lack of recognition will most likely give way to a keen academic interest once the tradition of letter writing dies out at the hands of new technologies of communication based on instant electronic exchange.

I stated in the introductory discussion here that the letters are usually written with the purpose of connecting the two worlds of the writers. In many people's minds, that's what they are all about. Let me take a closer look into this claim and ask a different question. Is the connection achieved in the end? Turning to one example of the family correspondence, I explore how the distance between the two incongruent worlds is maintained through the practice of letter writing.

The Wakarchuk Letters

The Wakarchuk letters are an excellent example of a typical family correspondence that connected many Ukrainians in Canada and Ukraine throughout the twentieth century. Like much other correspondence, this series saw various phases of its development. Consisting of 122 letters written between 1924 and 1993, the collection was donated to our archives in 2010 by Pauline Semenuik from Yorkton, Saskatchewan. While the letters in this series are now housed in our archive, Pauline and her brother continue corresponding with family members in Ukraine. Therefore, our holdings represent only a part of a nearly ninety-year-old correspondence that continues on. The core of this collection consists of letters written by Stefan Wakarchuk, of Davydivtsi, Chernivtsi Oblast, to his brother Wasyl Wakarchuk of Yorkton, Saskatchewan, although other family members occasionally enter the letter exchange as well. Out of all our holdings, the Wakarchuk correspondence is unique because it is primarily maintained by a male writer in the homeland (see figure 4.3).[32]

Wasyl's story of making it in Canada is a typical one of its time. Upon his arrival in Canada in 1913, fifteen-year-old Wasyl got a job at the coal dock in Fort William, Ontario, where he spent the first two years of his stay in Canada. In 1915 he traveled to Saskatchewan and remained there, working as a hired hand on various farms until 1924, when he acquired his own land and married his wife, Zenovia.[33] One can presume that Wasyl began corresponding with his family in Davydivtsi soon after his arrival in Canada. Wasyl was the only one of his immediate family who came to Canada—it is most likely that the events in Europe (e.g., World War I), prevented other members of his immediate family from joining him. Left behind in Davydivtsi were his parents and four younger siblings, who all remained in the village throughout their lives and bore children of their own, some of whom have joined in the family correspondence in its most recent phase (from the 1980s). It is not surprising, therefore, that, since Wasyl had no other immediate relatives in Canada, staying in touch with his family throughout his life was important to him.

One of the earliest letters in this series is from Wasyl's mother, who briefly reports on the state of the family in 1928. The letters from later years are with the next of kin, a younger brother named Heorhii, who in his letters offers regular updates on family affairs, the weather, and the general health of everyone in the family. Stefan comes into the picture in 1949 with a letter dated of December 11, 1949, in which he mildly scolds his brother for not having written recently. From this letter one can assume that the two had been writing to each

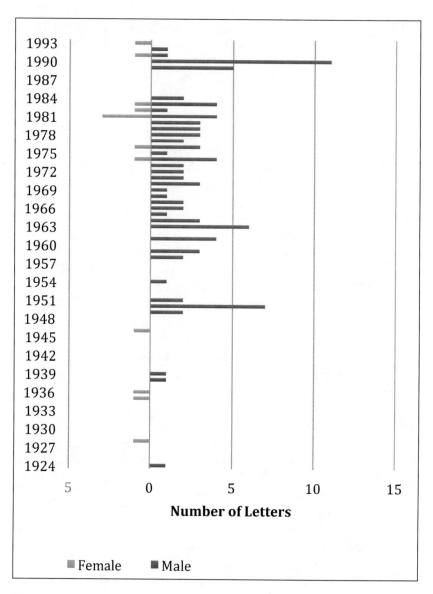

Figure 4.3. Wakarchuk correspondence by year and gender of writers. Between 1924 and 1993, 122 letters were exchanged between the communities of Hanley, Veregin, and Yorkton (Saskatchewan, Canada); Davydivtsi and Chernivtsi (Ukraine); and Lugci (Romania).

other earlier; the gap in the correspondence can be explained by a number of circumstances, including the fact that the late forties and 1949 in particular was a turbulent time in Western Ukraine.[34]

Stefan, who became the primary correspondent with Wasyl, was Wasyl's junior by fourteen years. Stefan was the youngest child in the family, and it is possible that the responsibility for maintaining contact with the oldest brother was delegated to him in accordance to some local unwritten custom. Or perhaps the reason Stefan actively pursued the correspondence with his oldest Canadian brother had something to do with the fact that the two hardly knew each other as individuals, given their age difference and the physical distance between them.

The two corresponded with each other and other overseas relatives until the end of their days. Wasyl died in 1985 and Stefan in 1991. In 1987, Stefan resumed his letter writing, addressing his letters to Wasyl's children; his last letter was dated 1989. Thus, the letters from Stefan to Canada in our collection span forty years (1949–89). Separated for more than seventy years, the brothers' only connection to each other were their letters, augmented by a very brief encounter in 1973 when Wasyl went to the USSR as an official tourist on the Intourist tour.[35]

The Letters' World

This long-lived family exchange strikes the researcher as a moving testimony to the burdens of long-term separation and longing for family. The letter-based relationship between the two brothers and their families, spanning nearly a century, is compressed into a few hundred pages; most of the letters are composed in a surprisingly uniform way despite the low frequency with which they were written. In these letters, the details of Stefan's life are preselected, filtered and compressed in space and time, to fit the letters' few pages, and these "editing" processes, informed by the very framework of transnational letter writing, ultimately produced a unique "lettered" reality of Wasyl's old-country kin in Davydivtsi.[36]

Created via the ritual of letter writing over the course of many years and perfected especially during the habitual phase of correspondence, the lettered reality of the old-country kin does not seem to change much from year to year, from letter to letter. This sense of stable continuity is dictated by the very genre of the habitual transatlantic family correspondence, which has even stronger roots, it seems, in the vernacular culture than the initial immigrant correspondence.

Scholars who have studied immigrant correspondence routinely acknowledge
its vernacular nature. Jennifer Atterbery understands immigrant letters as folk
expression, Orm Overland sees them as written folk literature, and Linda Degh
analyzes them in terms of folk literacy, to mention just a few examples.[37] With
time, the vernacular underpinnings of letter writing strengthened, contributing
to the further ritualization of letter writing and to the highly scripted nature of
letters themselves.

Like many other family letters from Ukraine, Stefan's letters to Wasyl
resemble each other in their organization, brevity, narrative techniques, use of
local expressions, stance, and mood. They tend to be elusive, offering the researcher not many answers but spurring many further questions. The writing
of each letter typically follows a well-established belletrist tradition in Davydivtsi
and a script. Stefan, it seems, hardly ever deviated from this way of writing over
the forty years, despite the fact that he lived a relatively long life that also took
him outside of Davydivtsi. In the 1950s the letters from Stefan arrived from
Romania. In 1958, he returned back to his home village, which had been collectivized following the annexation of Western Ukraine to the USSR in 1939.
After his return to his home village, the letters began to look even more alike. In
each letter, Stefan offers ritualistic greetings ("I bow to honor you"), assurances
of health, and wishes of even better health to Wasyl and his family and then
follows with short reports about current weather conditions and the harvest
(dry or wet, poor or bad). Though many hints are offered from letter to letter
regarding the difficulties of village life that the annexation to Soviet Ukraine
brought, few specific references are made to the ongoing sociocultural changes
that Davydivtsi had undergone over the thirty years that Stefan lived there. It is
as if the war, underground guerilla fighting, the collectivization of private family
farms, and the exile of villagers to Siberia had little effect on him and his relationship with his brother. The letters are full of these and other gaps that effectively
blocked the flow of information about the actual state of affairs in the village.

The following is one of many letters from Stefan to Wasyl that, relying on
formulaic writing and local expressions (which I have italicized), effectively re-
lays a coded message about the realities of the life in the village (see figure 4.4):

September 15, 1963

Dear Badika Wasyl—

I send my best regards, to you, *badiko* and to you *lyliko*, and to your children,
and to your grandchildren.[38] I bring to your attention that we are all, thanks to
God's will, healthy, and we wish all of you even better health. And I am writing

Дат. 15. IX. 68. р Вакарчук Стефан
Давидівці

Дорогі Вадіко Василю і ви
милько, і вашим дітьми і
онукам, Христос Воскрес....
Вклоняємося усі разом що
вас Ел. і жінка моя і наші
діти і онуки, і Вадіка Юрій
і Сестри Марія і Параска
і їхе діти і онуки,
Я доношу вам до відома
що ми тут ісі разом
знаходимся посередньому
здорові, А вам усім разом
ще кращого здоровя
желаям від нас і від Г. Бога
Я нашим поводженя так ни
согірше як звикло із старім
краю, Зима прійшла так
нисогірша була. А весна ни
дуже потішала нас із разу
біла посушлива а ціли
днями ипало троши сніку
і сильні приморозки,

to you, dear Badika Wasyl, to tell you that I also received your letter and photo-graphs [*fortyhrafïï*] and the parcel, for which we all thank you, *lylika*, and your children very much; [we are grateful] that you took the trouble and sent us your photographs and the parcel, in which there was everything that you sent us. The trousers are a good fit and the shirts are suitable. The parcel came a month later than the letter.

Our life [*povodzhenia*] is as usual in the old country, and in [this] new life, one has to write briefly, but understand well. *It is as happy here as at the cemetery*, and *we are as well fed as on Good Friday*. It is because this year we had a great drought from God Almighty. And from those district priests [*zems'ki svia-shchenyky*] there is only burned ground, so we are left very "rich." It's like a son brags that his father is very rich—*he has three barns* [stodoly]: *in one there is a flail* [tsip], *and in the other one there is sheaf* [snip], *and in the third one a mouse* [mysh] *who came in looking for a grain*. That is how we continue on with our life, moving forward like crawfish.[39]

And I ask you, Badiko Wasyl', if you have a chance to see Stephan's Andriy's Vasyl', his father asks him to write a few words one day. And with this, I have nothing else to write you, but I send all of you a thousand greetings.

Stay well. Please write back.[40]

In this letter, despite its brevity, Stefan, adhering to local belletrist tradition, manages to communicate to his brother with the help of metaphor and folkloric expression the general state of life in the village. Davydivtsi, like other villages, was collectivized after the annexation of Western Ukrainian lands to Soviet Ukraine, and those who disagreed with the new political powers were exiled, their properties confiscated, and the most rebellious members of the family shot. The practice of religion was suppressed as was the entrepreneurial spirit of the shrewd villagers. The reference to the district priests would have been understood by insiders as a reference to the local Soviet authorities from the district center who were responsible for collectivization and then for the manage-ment of the local collective farms. From letter to letter, Stefan makes convo-luted references to the year of 1957, which one presumes to be the year in which his household was collectivized and his family lost their field to a collective farm, in statements like "it has been six [seven, eight . . .] years since we have had no fields. . . . We are now used to not having to work on our field," and so on.

Thus, due to political control, little real information is communicated about the life in Davydivtsi. The lettered reality of Davydivtsi life is therefore "twice removed" from Wasyl's reality in Canada. The first kind of distancing is achieved by the general means of genre, through all the editorial techniques Stefan draws on. The second kind of distancing is accomplished with the help of purposely and highly metaphorical writing that relies on ironic comparisons such as "moving forward like crawfish," "as happy here as at the cemetery," and so on.

Stefan's letters contain little personal information about him or his family, though they mention important milestones such as births, deaths, marriages, and illnesses of family members in the Wakarchuk clan in Ukraine. And so this correspondence went for years, until the year of 1973, when Wasyl went on a three-week Intourist tour around Ukraine, as did many others in the 1970s, in hopes of setting foot—even if for mere minutes—on the native land. Like many others who took homecoming tours in the 1970s and the 1980s, Wasyl managed to visit his village clandestinely and only for a few minutes.[41] Wasyl returned to Canada and the correspondence between the brothers continued on, surprisingly, without much change. Thus, the same short letters kept arriving to Yorkton, containing the bare-bones information deemed by the Wakarchuks in Ukraine as of interest or safe to pass on to those in Canada—concerning health, deaths, and new family arrivals, local weather, and the prospects of the upcoming harvest. It is only in mid-1980s, when the new climate of perestroika in the former USSR was being felt, that Stefan starts to include more real life information in the letters.

The last letter from Stefan received by Wasyl is dated 1984. In this letter, in addition to the usual remarks about the weather and crops, Stefan offers a list of all the children and grandchildren in the family that were born to the Wakarchuks in the twentieth century in Davydivtsi. It is possible that he was providing this list in response to the inquiry from Wasyl, who may have requested this information in his previous letter to Stefan.[42] It is symbolic that at the end of his life, and at the end of their personal correspondence, the youngest brother is reintroducing to his oldest brother in Canada all the younger generations of what used to be their own family, hoping that each new branch will resume their relationship with the kin in Canada in time. Though it was probably hard for the two brothers to envision that their correspondence would continue beyond their own time, Stefan inadvertently introduced the new potential letter writers, some of whom entered this correspondence in the 1990s, to all the future readers of his letter.[43]

In this letter, the goodbyes are both moving and telling:

I have nothing more to write you, dear *Badiko*. I wish all the best to you, and your children and your grandchildren and great-grandchildren. All of us here greet all of you there, and we are wishing you all the best in your work, and we also wish you good health.

Stay well.

Until our next sweet meeting, even if only in these letters,

Please respond, your brother Stefan.[44]

Reciting diligently through his life, from letter to letter, all the relations on both sides of the Atlantic, Stefan continued painting the ever-expanding familial landscape of the letters, the landscape always inclusive of all relations in Canada. It was habitual for him to write personalized greetings to Wasyl, his wife, their children, and later on to their grandchildren. Stefan typically offers ritualized greetings in a sequence that reflected the importance of the kin relation to him. He regularly uses kinship terminology to refer to Wasyl and his wife, namely, *badika* (here older brother) and *lylika* (here older sister). He refers to the younger relatives of his brother's family by their group term—children and grandchildren—and never by their names. Both practices serve as a good illustration of how the corporate nature of letter writing reveals itself in individual letters in habitual correspondence.

With time, Stefan began adjusting his greeting and farewell bidding formulae, addressing the Canadian family as one entity: "all of you." In his last letter to his brother, bidding goodbye, Stefan resorts once again to the collective "we" of a family that sends its regards to Canada: "*all of us here* greet *all of you there.*" As such, the letter contains the goodbyes expressed by one corporate group to another, directed at the family at large. I read these various textual practices as testaments to the perseverance of *kinship corporatism.* The greetings are executed by individual writers, yet they are also written out on behalf of their larger families, thus constructing not just personal but collective longing for the long-lost kin. They thereby serve to disclose an implicit desire to redeem the lived disconnectedness between the two brothers, who never had an opportunity to form a real relationship outside of their letters. In his letters, Stefan unintentionally acts in accordance with the corporate principles of traditional family maintenance, despite the burdens of transatlantic family disconnections.

Enveloping Distance?

In the beginning of this chapter I made a brief reference to early immigrant folklore constructions of the liminal status of migrants. The migrants in these early vernacular texts, were projected as lost wanderers who had taken off, left home, and stepped outside of the familiar and familial world. The status of liminality as presented in these folksongs was understood at the time as impossible to overcome, as the migrants were not expected to return. Liminality as conceptual theoretical framework of cultural and textual analysis has been widely utilized by scholars of literature, anthropology, myth, folklore, and religion in their interpretations of various transcendental, marginal and peripheral cultural states, practices, and narratives in various contexts.[45] One can imagine that as a state of being, liminality is lived out and experienced in space and through time. In my effort to answer the question how the distance between the two worlds of the writers has been "enveloped," or constructed, in letters, it is necessary to return to liminality and especially its relationship to space.

First, let me focus on the experience of distance between the two kin groups as lived through personal correspondence. It is first of all important to acknowledge the distance in space or the psychical distance between the writers, since, after all, they are separated by the ocean. Second, one must consider the distance between the writers' identities that also grows over the course of time. If two people continue writing each other throughout their lives, they do so in the context of their own ever-changing identities. They may change professions, for example, which may affect their own sense of who they are. They may begin writing each other as brothers or sisters, but eventually, they become also mothers or fathers, uncles and aunts, grandfathers and grandmothers, and so on. Their kinship identities bifurcate with time, and they assume new roles. If the initial kinship roles used to define the person's "whole" kin identity, with time, they become only a fraction of it. Thus, the distance between the two individuals grows along the lines of these identity changes. This distance is created and maintained through time, and letters come to be most effective tool for asserting this distance in identity. With time, the distance between the two camps of writers also becomes genealogical if the letter exchange is continued by the next generations of writers, as in the case of Wasyl's daughter Pauline Semenuik, who is nowadays actively corresponding with Wasyl's relatives in Ukraine. When the new writers of the next generation come on stage, they are further removed from each other in genealogical terms, due to kinship bifurcation. This distance is also created and maintained through time.

But in the process of letter writing that lasts decades, writers implicitly face a very different kind of a distance than either a spatial or temporal one, namely, that between the recipients' lived reality of here and now and the reality of the overseas kin as presented in the letters, especially the habitual correspondence. The world of the old-country relations as constructed and communicated in letters as texts occupies its own special place in the life of the Canadian correspondents. And the lettered reality of the family life in Canada also occupies its own position in the lives of the old country. The distance between the two groups of writers, or, from the vantage point of a letter writer, between the very real "us" and highly metaphorical "them," in this context is better understood as incongruence between the world of here and now, the lived reality of the reader, and the world presented in letters from overseas.

Dealing with this incongruence proved emotionally challenging, as witnessed by the stories I cited from my field notes at the beginning of this chapter. The lettered world presented in family letters sent from each group of writers is a barren landscape in terms of its spatial content and dimensions. As illustrated by the Wakarchuk letters and other correspondences I have consulted, rather than fully elaborated, the contents and the meanings of the lettered physical landscapes are only vaguely outlined, through the presentation of bare-bones information about weather, crops, household undertakings, and so on. The abridged nature of these accounts can, on one hand, be attributed to the ideological control of the correspondence by the Soviet authorities throughout the most of the twentieth century. At the same time, however, the alternative universe of letters communicated a complicated social web of family relations that kept adopting, through time, new nodes and new members into the family transnational network the letters maintained. The obligatory references to births, deaths, and illnesses were meant to keep the recipient cognizant of the most important kinship developments (while also providing the writer with legitimate content for the letter). Mandatory reiteration of all family relations in letters from Ukraine came to serve as a foundational grid, a system of coordinates that, like scaffolding, is meant to situate the recipient of the letter in Canada within a system of social and familial coordinates, grounded in the mesh of local relationships. On the one hand, the repetition from letter to letter of presentations of this complicated familial landscape speaks to the letters' ability to connect the members on both sides of the Atlantic into one kin network, never lived out in real terms. Yet, on the other hand, in the context of growing distance between the social, familial, and generational identities of the writers, this complexity and extension of familial ties far away from the recipient's real world was both overwhelming and alienating.

All in all, the letters that routinely project their own fictional landscapes of the overseas kin and their environs served their readers on both ends of the correspondence as an entry into a parallel universe, or a plane of a different reality than their own daily reality, very much the way myths, fairy tales, religious texts, sci-fi books and escapist novels allow readers to enter and inhabit alternative universes. Because the world of letters exists on the edge of a person's real life, rather than constituting the core of it, because it does not regularly intersect with the domain of here and now, because the received letter oftentimes serves as a tool of withdrawal from here and now, even if only in the mind of the letter recipient (as in the stories offered by Ihor Ditchuk and Christine Pawluk that I quoted at the beginning of the chapter), this world ultimately presents itself as a liminal space. In the minds of many of my informants back in Ukraine, the world of letters is indeed a tangible plane where departed relatives continue to live, proliferate, and present themselves as kin to the villagers. The letters from Ukraine for the recipients in Canada also routinely opened up a window into the world of the homeland's familial "others," so different from the Canadian lifeworlds. For both camps, the more time that passed from the primary separation of the kin, the more incongruent the world of the others became vis-à-vis the lived reality of the here and now.

There is a difference, though, between the lettered universes and other alternative realities created by myths, fairy tales, and modern popular culture. The alternative reality of letters had no entertaining function (like fairy tales), no educational function (like myths and religious narratives), nor did it offer an uplifting escape from the reality (like escapist literature). In addition, unlike myths, fairy tales, and other stories of parallel universes shared across cultures or subcultures, the world of letters in the Ukrainian letter writing of the mid-twentieth century and later was constructed and experienced in highly private terms. The alternative universe of the letters was not shared by many in either society but only known to the writers and their families and often was not fully shared even with the family—this was the case with Wasyl and Stefan's correspondence, as Wakarchuk's children only "discovered" their father's correspondence after his death.

Thus, experienced privately, the letter writing (and letter reading) as a practice has become both a routine exercise in liminality and a third space of neither here nor there, neither now nor then, a highly intimate terrain where the writers, representing the two different domains of what used to be the same family, meet, dream, reimagine and dialogue with each other. "Until our next sweet meeting, even if only in these letters," Stefan wrote to his brother in his last letter to him, knowing by that time, that there would be no more real meetings. And just as the early immigrant folklore speaks of the liminal space as being neither/nor, neither here nor there, letter writers like Stefan and Wasyl came to see their letters as almost a tangible terrain, domain, and meeting ground where they had a chance to reconnect with their kin through the rite of writing.

The letters as physical objects that traveled across the ocean and bore the handwriting of the loved ones indeed became manifestations of that third symbolic space of writing the overseas relatives, a nonphysical space of family correspondence, virtual, but painfully present, an important and oftentimes invisible dimension of the letter recipients' lives.

The liminal space, Bakhtin argues in many of his books, is a highly dialogic space; it is the space where numerous existential possibilities are present and subject to questioning.[46] Understood in folklore and myth as the boundary space, as the world lying outside of the domain of the known, it is also a highly unpredictable space, a domain in which one has to constantly negotiate his or her chances for staying alive, such as the protagonist in a fairy tale who confronts villains at every turn on his or her journey toward his or her goal.

Yet in the context of family letter writing among Ukrainians, the world of letters, though it offered an opportunity to connect and communicate with the overseas familial others, with time ceased to be a productive space for real dialogue. Rather, the writers, on both ends of the Atlantic came to see this space as one of a highly ritualized and structured exchange, a space in which only prescribed kinds of interaction took place, in which no true (that is, real) identities could be revealed, where social bonds were maintained not between individuals and their complex personalities but between individuals representing corporate roles they played in the contexts of their mutually shared kinship. Nonetheless, while traveling to and in this third space was never emotionally easy, it was an important journey for very many people; a "corporate" journey that oftentimes could not be voluntarily ended.

And so personal correspondence continued on between Ukrainians in Canada and those in Ukraine throughout the twentieth century. A commonplace, yet a highly private one, the letter from the old country maintained its quiet place in the lives of many Ukrainian Canadians. If letter writing was directed at bridging the two worlds of diaspora and homeland, did it achieve its goal of connecting transatlantic writers and their families? By entering the liminal world of letter writing and exercising their lettered identities, were the writers able to find the way to real persons overseas? The letters did bring the agents of writing together but this does not mean that the letters enabled real contact between real people. Given the complex organization of the distance as constructed and dealt with in letter writing, the ongoing incongruence between the real lived worlds of correspondents and the lettered fictional worlds from overseas, the liminal character of letter writing itself, the safest way for the writers to proceed with long-term letter writing was with the help of formulas, stock phrases and expressions, and ritual, under the mask of a kinship-assigned identity. If this is the case, what happens when the writers indeed meet, as with Stefan and Wasyl Wakarchuk? We explore this question in chapter 6 on diaspora homecoming. First though, let's look into the question how local Ukrainians (in Canada and Ukraine) understood kin relations in their own local contexts.

Figure 5.1. The front cover of the Bayda family history book, self-published in Saskatoon in 2010. Courtesy of the Bayda family.

5

//////////////////////////

Imagining Kinship in Diaspora

*I*n my pursuit of the vernacular organization of diasporic imaginings of "other Ukrainians" thus far, I have focused on the role and place of diasporic split, absence, separation, and distance in the lives of many Ukrainians in the diaspora and homeland. Introduced into many people's lives, these modernity-informed experiences became important dimensions of the folk psychology of Ukrainians on both ends of the diaspora-homeland binomial. Central to this process has been the concepts of kin, family, kinfolk, and kin relations. Building on previous discussions and focusing on Ukrainian Canadians in western Canada, here I turn to examine how their changing notions of family and kinship, marked by the experiences of split, absence, separation, and distance informed and changed the way they understood the other Ukrainians. Of interest to us is how in the twentieth century Ukrainian Canadians have imagined both their overseas kin and their own relationship with that kin.

In the first place, though, in vernacular domains, these ideas have been informed by people's changing understandings of themselves, of who they are vis-à-vis others. That is why I turn first to the question how Ukrainian Canadians imagine their own extended families and their own genealogical continuity. Then I proceed to ask whether, when Ukrainians in Canada think of who their extended kin is, they include their overseas kin, that is, relatives in the old country? What place, if any, is assigned to the overseas family in these imaginings of one's own genealogical continuity?

*A*s these kinds of imaginings are not literally imprinted on any ready-to-view canvas, how can the researcher access them in order to reconstruct their organization and interpret their meanings? As I mentioned in the introduction, the vernacular practices of the diasporic imagination are deeply rooted in folk psychology. The critical point is that folk psychology is narrative in its nature rather than hierarchical and analytical.[1] Thus, the vernacular practices of the diasporic imagination most commonly reveal themselves in textual, visual, and other kinds of cultural narratives, produced in local settings. Two sites where we may access imaginings of genealogical continuity and relatedness are various representations as well as the actions of individuals directed at seeking status, securing resources, and building order and meaning in their lives. Hence, I focus on representations and their production.

The first site I consider is public representations of relatedness and genea-logical continuity as produced in a local Ukrainian museum in western Canada in the last years of the twentieth century. These representations highlight the workings of the cultural metaphor of generation, and I explore these workings in my discussion of the museum representations of rootedness in local Canadian soil. The second site is the modern vernacular practice of family history writing that emerged in Canada in the 1970s, informed by the rapid cultural changes that many people were experiencing on the Canadian prairies. These texts present the analyst with easy-to-access discussions of how family and kinship have been understood and indeed imagined among Ukrainian Canadians in the second half of the twentieth century. The political transformations of the late 1980s in Europe resulting in the collapse of communism in Europe triggered further changes in Ukrainian Canadian ideas of relatedness and belonging. To account for these changes, I turn to a third site, the modern practice of vernacu-lar genealogical research that by the 1990s had become a very popular under-taking, to examine how, redefining the meaning of ancestry, it yet again upset established understandings of kinship also affecting the construction of the Ukrainian "diasporic other." I explore these sites to discover in what way and why local conceptualizations of relatedness incorporated or excluded overseas kin.

As an anthropologist, I do not advance here the idea that kinship and its ties are some sort of given, that they form an external framework that exists outside of individual human actions and human thought and that governs people's lives. There is still a certain need for such view of kinship, the idea that kinship systems were the threads that held together the social fabric of pre-industrial prestate small-scale societies, which was advanced by earlier anthro-pologists, but mostly it is now just taught in introductory anthropology courses. An example of such a positivist approach to the study of relatedness in the Ukrainian Canadian context is a brief study by Zenon Pohorecky, in which he presents the terminological grid of kinship and emphasizes the continuity of the old country family organization in Canadian context.[2] Anthropological scholar-ship on kinship since the 1970s has moved from studying kinship relations in

terms of kinship grids and structures to analyzing power relations, gender relations, the role of personal agency, and practices in the lives of extended and
other kinds of families, on the production and especially reproduction, from
generation to generation, of these relations and their (im)balances. As Michael
Peletz summarizes, contemporary kinship studies emphasize the contradictions
and ambivalences that have always characterized kinship relations and interactions, whether in contemporary or premodern times.[3] I too, see much flexibility
and fluidity in how kinship ties are formulated, reformulated and utilized by
cultural agents and their groups in their efforts to advance themselves and their
visions of themselves among others. As such, I prefer to frame my discussion
not so much around traditional notions of kinship but around the idea of relatedness, as the latter suggests a less rigid approach to kinship and implies agency
and the possibility of change over time. My formulations resonate with other
contemporary scholars' reinterpretations of kinship in terms of "cultures of
relatedness."[4] Ukrainian Canadians have changed their ideas about relatedness
over time to suit their needs and the needs of their communities, and this has
been especially evident in the way they have (re)formulated their own genealogies in transnational/diasporic terms. In my subsequent discussions, it may
seem like I am focusing more on symbolic needs and group definitions of relatedness. But there is never a clear line between practical and symbolic needs, and
these labels should be understood only as heuristics that help analysts discuss
complex phenomena.

My first sustained exposure to the complex palette in Ukrainian Canadians'
conceptualizations of genealogical continuity took place during my ethnographic work in the Ukrainian bloc of east-central Alberta and the town of
Mundare. Back then, in the late 1990s, I was interested in figuring out how a
community like Mundare maintained its ethnic identity and how it defined its
own Ukrainianness.[5] Certainly, there have been many visual, gustatory, and
social markers of local Ukrainianness in this western Canadian rural community:
the Ukrainian dance, the perogies, the annual community events, and so on.
Among those "visible symbols," to borrow a well-utilized Ukrainian Canadian
scholarly metaphor, Ukrainian claims to Mundare, its history, and territory (to
the right of being seen as "masters" of this locality) were also based on two
powerful yet less explicit concepts, one being the notion of generations and the
other being the notion of family (understood as kin in its vertical and horizontal
extensions).[6] I began recognizing the workings of these concepts through my
encounters with them in a variety of social and especially public contexts, as
they had become important and powerful tools with which Ukrainians laid

their claims not only to their own family farmlands but also to Canadian soil, the Canadian West, and Canada as a nation. As highly operational tools of ethnic self-assertion in the Canadian nationhood, they therefore should be seen not as abstract symbolic categories but means by which Ukrainian Canadians maintain and promote their ethnic identity maintenance in a variety of settings ranging from institutional to vernacular.

Generation:
Searching for the Point Zero

Mundare, Alberta, October 13, 1997

October 12, 1997, Sunday evening. The Basilian Fathers Museum, after many months of preparation, launches its new permanent display *New Home in the West*, devoted to the early years of Ukrainian immigration to Canada and to the establishment of the Mundare community at the turn of the twentieth century. The liturgy devoted to the exhibit opening has just been held in Mundare's Ukrainain Greek Catholic Church of Peter and Paul, the prayers have been read, and blessings given. The bishop and the museum director, who curated the new display, are joined by other guests representing the community and various local and provincial offices. Among the invitees are the head of Education and Admission Services from the Edmonton eparchy of the Ukrainian Greek Catholic Church, the executive director of the Alberta Museum Association, and the mayor of Mundare.

But these are not the only dignitaries invited to speak on the occasion. As indicated in the program for the event, speeches are to be delivered by other presenters who were chosen to contribute to the event on the basis of their belonging to a particular generation. The pamphlet outlining the ceremony proceedings places a special emphasis on generations. Using a capital G, it first lists the generations—first, second, third, fourth, and fifth—and then gives the name of speaker under the list. Three adults, representing the second, the third, and the fourth generations, John Batiuk of Mundare, Clarence Siracky of Lamont, and Beverly Homeniuk of Willingdon, are here to contribute to the opening ceremony with their own recollections on the ways of life of their respective generations. Four children from the Siracky family, all representing the fifth generation, will play an important role in the symbolic opening of the display by ceremonially cutting the ribbon.[7]

It is common among Ukrainian Canadians to speak of themselves in terms of generations. The word "generation" has become an easy shortcut in many casual discussions of family history and ancestry, allowing all parties to quickly orient themselves in the cultural and historic niches that they fit in. When recounting their own life histories, my informants in western Canada regularly spoke of themselves as belonging to one or two generations, if their ancestors on both parental sides arrived in Canada at different historic times. As casual and commonplace as it appears to be, the trope of generation nevertheless is used by individuals and now by cultural institutions like the Basilian Fathers Museum, to position individuals and groups in a larger framework of community and history developments. In communities like Mundare, it serves as productive means of laying claims to locality, as the Ukrainians in the area, the descendants of the first settlers, seek to assert themselves in the multiethnic town as rightful citizens whose ancestors and family, understood as a clan consisting of many ascending generations, founded the community. That is why the creators of the permanent display in the Basilian Fathers Museum assigned so much importance to generations.

Yet for all its commonness, the way this trope is used in Ukrainian Canadian culture differs from how it is employed in other cultural contexts. To better understand the difference, let me briefly discuss the changes in the way the notion of generation has been used in recent history. In premodern societies, especially those marked by continuity of tradition, evoking generations was essentially a mode of time reckoning. Edward Shils claims that in such contexts generation was used to designate a distinct kinship cohort that situated the individual's life within a sequence of collective transitions.[8] Though a society might not have explicitly counted generations, generational sequence was nonetheless a widely understood concept. In modernity, the notion of generation was no longer confined to familial contexts and instead began to indicate individuals who lived through a distinct historical experience, different from the historical experiences of previous generations. Thus we understand implicitly and without explanation what is meant by the "sixties generation," "my generation," "generation X," and so on. These generational identities, associated in the society with particular historical change of national or global scale, are formed during the critical period of late adolescence/early adulthood, recognized by scholars as the most formative period in a person's life.[9] As a result, while in traditional contexts the notion of generation carries strong connotations of renewal and continuity, as each generation relives the modes of life of its predecessors, this is not the case in modern society, where it is deployed against a backdrop of standardized linear time and expedited historical change.[10] In addition, due to rapid historical change, the generations of modernity have no reason to be ordered in terms of the first, the second, and so on, as the identity of each generation is thought to be based on its own unique experiences.

In Mundare, and by extension in the Ukrainian Canadian culture, the modern notion of generation is being used in unique ways. What sets this usage apart is its strong reliance on ordering and sequentiality. Instead of implying the shared experience from generation to generation as had been done in pre-modern times, Ukrainian Canadians who invoke the idea of generation explicitly identify the ordering of generations as indicating the continuity of a particular kin-family in historical time. This has social implications on many levels. First, the ordering of generations points to a symbolic (and in reality not only symbolic) hierarchy among them, both within the families and local communities. The experiences of the earlier generations that came of age in the formative years of the Ukrainian Canadian community are usually and implicitly assigned higher symbolic value by today's families and communities. There is also a tendency to assign higher cultural status, "stronger identity," and "deeper roots" to those active members of the communities, who are of a higher, number-wise, generation. Secondly, employed in public narratives, the term "generation" speaks of shared historical experiences by each generational cohort, outside of family context and across the Ukrainian Canadian community, helping Ukrainian Canadians to carve out their own unique local and regional identities. Thirdly, the idea of generation emphasizes the role both family and kin play in communities' efforts to assert their own identity, history and continuity. As such, it carries significant cultural and at times political weight. And lastly, the ordering implies the starting point, the ground zero, of the counting of generations, before which there were no generations at all. This is a very important point for my discussion.

These distinct ways of deploying the term "generation" have deep roots in the phenomenon of ethnicity. Among various ethnic groups that emerged as an outcome of international migration in modern times, the meanings of "generation" have been modified to fit the unique parameters of ethnic cultural development. An ethnic group, having "arrived" in a new land, with time begins to establish itself in a new country, utilizing all kinds of resources including its own imagination informed by the group's folk psychology. The group becomes conscious of the fact that at some moment it *began* and that the moment of its birth was rather recent, being the historical moment of the group's arrival in the new world. As much as the group asserts its ancient roots in the homeland culture, it is important for it to celebrate its "beginning" in the new one and to cast this beginning as a pivotal point in the group's life. Placing much emphasis on that original moment of its history, mythicizing it and conceiving it as the primal event of the group's beginning, as Anthony Smith reminds us, is all about securing the group's sense of continuity, or "survival."[11]

Ukrainian Canadian community historians and activists routinely highlight in their writing and presentations the starting point of their history in Canada. In some community narratives and contexts, the point of origin is pinned to a particular year, 1891, when two Ukrainian villagers, recognized as official first immigrants, made it to Canada.[12] In others, such as academic narratives and texts informed by a scholarly take on the history, the beginnings of Ukrainian Canadian culture are usually located in the period of the first immigration wave (1891–1914), which leaves much more room for many more individuals to claim an intimate connection to the group's origin.[13]

The Basilian Fathers Museum actively participates in the construction of authoritative public representations of such beginnings.[14] Representing the fusion of both public and scholarly takes on history, its displays capture the pivotal moment of the beginnings of Ukrainian-Canadian culture. In the Basilian Fathers Museum, though, unlike in other Ukrainian Canadian museums, the grand narrative of origin has been richly illustrated by ostensibly "smaller," local and private stories of origin.[15] This merging of Ukrainian Canadian history and local history in the museum has provided further opportunities for the local Ukrainians to assert their symbolic rights to their locality as well as to their place in the history of their ethnic group in Canada. When the fifth generation, represented by the children of the Siracky clan, cut the ribbon in the ceremony of permanent display opening in 1997, they symbolically opened not only the exhibit about Ukrainian Canadian history but also one about themselves. The Siracky family was chosen, along with fifteen other local families whose beginnings date to the days of early settlement, to represent both histories, the history of Mundare and, since Mundare was the earliest Ukrainian Canadian settlement, Ukrainian Canadian history. The family has been profiled in the museum twice, in the permanent gallery and in a special exhibit devoted to it. In the special exhibit, one can find the photographs of the youngest members of the Siracky family dressed up in Ukrainian dance costumes prominently displayed on the walls.

Weaving the histories of the oldest local families into the official museum narrative of origin, the museum further endorsed the role of the metaphor of generations in local understandings of history, community relations, and hegemonies of power. By placing the Siracky story, along with fifteen other family histories, in the permanent gallery, the museum also boosted and legitimized the status of the founding family-clans in the community, pointing to the power-ful place family as a trope and a cultural code occupies in the folk psychology of Ukrainians in Canada.

"Family-Clan":
The Becoming of Canadian Kinship

Near Mundare, Alberta, March 2, 2001

It is chilly day in the countryside in the Ukrainian bloc. I am visiting Mrs. Kate Tichon on her farm, some eighty kilometers east of Edmonton. We are discussing the trip to Ukraine she went on in 1991. Mrs. Tichon and I immediately build great rapport. I am excited about our upcoming conversation. Kate went on the centennial homecoming tour in 1991 that was organized by Edmonton's East-West Travel Agency to mark the hundredth anniversary of the Ukrainian immigration to Canada, and I have been gathering stories of homecoming from those who traveled to Ukraine. Tell me about yourself, I begin. Fifteen minutes later, Kate is still running by me names after names of her relations first, on her father's side, then on her mother's side, those living in the area and those who have left, those passed away and those alive. I have long been lost in this dense forest of her relations and simply cannot pay attention anymore.[16]

A year after I wrote this entry, I coordinated an oral history project on sociocultural change among Ukrainian Canadians in Saskatchewan and Alberta. In the interviews, many individuals carefully retold me their long family histories, in response to the same request for information that I put to Kate. I had soon learned not to get lost in the web of people's family relations, as these relations appeared to be fundamentally relevant to their personal identities. Interviewing Ukrainian Canadians in western Canada with the help of the life story inter-view method has taught me to recognize that in addition to the notion of genera-tion the concept of family and family-clan has played an equally unique role in the lives of many Ukrainian Canadians, informing their personal identities, governing their understandings of belonging, maintaining local community symbolic and real hierarchies, and grounding claims to rootedness in Canada.

Both family and kinship as social institutions, of course, have occupied central role in the lives of Ukrainians throughout the history. In the early twen-tieth century, in the historical moment of the group's beginning in Canada, family and kinship dictated even the development of future communities. John

Lehr, a Canadian geographer, has observed how the geographic distribution of families during the period of the planned settlement of the Canadian frontier was based on kinship and how new immigrants oftentimes chose living next to their relatives and neighbors from the old country over living on better land but further from kin and covillagers.[17] At the turn of the twentieth century, "family" among Ukrainians usually meant an extended family, typically of three generations at most, all living in the same household. As time went by, the cultural pressures of Canadian society and ongoing modernization transformed the institute of family. For all practical purposes, by midcentury "family" began to mean parents and children only.

Yet while in practical terms family as a household "shrunk" to include only parents and children, family as a cultural concept acquired over time much symbolic weight. By the end of the century, it came to play an important role in Ukrainian Canadian culture, promoting, together with the notion of generation, rootedness and continuity of Ukrainians in Canada.

While the notion of family has been actively utilized in a variety of cultural practices and profiled in numerous representations of Ukrainian Canadians, the best elaboration it has received is in the vernacular practice of family history writing. Rooted in sociocultural changes of the second part of the twentieth century, family history writing among Ukrainian Canadians remains a little understood phenomenon, as it has received limited academic attention in Canadian scholarship. Together with memoirs and local history books, these projects have been a part of a larger movement in vernacular writing that emerged in Canada and elsewhere in the second part of the twentieth century. Offering a wealth of evidence documenting the personal and collective identity of Ukrainian Canadians and the interplay between them, these family histories provide an excellent introduction to the vernacular subjectivity of Ukrainian Canadians of that period as it pertains to such matters as kinship, family, and generation. As such, family histories have became an important cultural site to be examined, as they not only offer an ongoing reconceptualization of the Ukrainian Canadian family but also reinforce the symbolic value of family in Ukrainian Canadian culture.[18]

Because their value is predominantly local, and since they are produced in small numbers without ISBN numbers, family history books are not always easily accessible. Over the years I have gathered bibliographical information on family histories in western Canada, both in various communities of my research and various libraries. Recently, Myron Momryk, a former archivist with the National Archives of Canada, produced a bibliography of family histories.[19] These bibliographies combined allow one to estimate, however

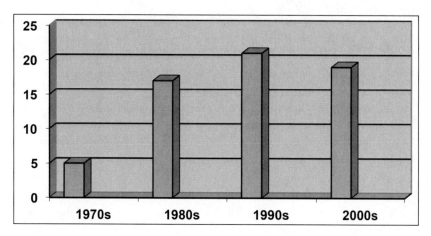

Figure 5.2. Number of Ukrainian Canadian family history books by decade: 1970s, five items; 1980s, seventeen items; 1990s, twenty-one items, 2000s: nineteen items.

approximately, the chronological dimensions and the dynamics of family history writing (figure 5.2).

As it is evident from the information that has been gathered, family history writing as a cultural phenomenon began shaping up in the 1970s.[20] This development came in the wake of profound sociocultural changes in the preceding decades in the world, Canada, and on the prairies. Stephen Cornell aptly refers to those historical times as a period of rupture.[21] In western Canada throughout the first half of the twentieth century, many Ukrainian Canadian towns on the prairies experienced a period of relative socioeconomic stability, in terms of generational continuity, technological advancement, and agricultural and business practices. With economic and technological revolutions of the 1950 and 1960s, farmers on the prairies witnessed a major shift in their living conditions. The primary feature of these changes was the post–Second World War challenge to the primacy of farming within the provincial economies of Canada's West. In the post–Second World War period, production in the agricultural sector of the western Canadian economy dropped along with the population, and government and commercial services became increasingly centralized.[22] In Alberta, for example, where Mundare is located, agriculture's share of the net value of production had fallen to less than one-third of its prewar level by 1971.[23]

These macroeconomic processes and new technologies brought changes to life on the prairies. Electricity, water, the telephone, and even television started reaching the farmers. "You know when we first got electricity? My goodness, that was only in 1964!"[24] "In our house, where I grew up, we didn't have a phone, or a TV either. When was it? Oh dear, let's say some twenty, yeah, twenty some years ago [the 1970s]. And there were many other houses like ours. Things have changed so much since then."[25] Small farms began to disappear, being swallowed up by other more entrepreneurial neighbors. Upward mobility led to out-migration to towns, cities, and other provinces. The pioneering generations of Ukrainians started to die out.

Within this context of perceived loss and rupture, personal and collective memories about the days bygone began to take shape. Scholars in psychology and anthropology have pointed out the direct correlation between tears in the fabric of social life and the accelerated mobilization of cultural activity, resulting in revitalization movements, increased personal reflectivity, and the resurgence of personal reminiscences about the disappearing past.[26] Much of this activity is oriented toward the past and aims at its reevaluation, as the breakdown in the structures of the familiar lifeworld creates a need for people to come to terms with their disappearing world. The growing distance between people's lives in the present and the traditional structures of their lifeworld with its conventional unquestioned assumptions and values elicits self-reflection. The risk of losing sight of this disappearing life incites them to narrate it, to write about it.[27]

In the Ukrainian Canadian context, after the Second World War, stories and narratives describing the "old ways" received much currency, and the old-timers were celebrated as founders, pioneers, and trailblazers. Reminiscences of the old days were published in local media, and various commemorative projects marking various anniversaries were launched. Families and communities began undertaking historical research in an effort to overcome the sense of rupture in their lived environs. In these undertakings, a particular perspective on the past began to take shape. If at the time of settlement, the challenges and hardships of pioneering were experienced locally and mostly privately, half a century later in time of increased personal and public reflectivity, their overcoming became to be understood as a public, collective achievement.

One can assume that prior to the 1970s and its accelerated circuits of reflectivity, kinship and family were simply lived, experienced, more or less without extensive conceptualization of what they meant or should be. These networks had real weight and primacy in people's lives and as such they were meaningful, but their significance remained mostly internalized and concerned individuals and their families. In times of rupture, kinship and family began to figure in the ongoing reevaluations of the past, even if they were not the primary focus, and thus came to acquire much symbolic weight in them. The utilization of family as a metaphor in public discourse ultimately promoted it as a powerful component of ethnic identity. Very much like the notion of generation, family became both a cultural symbol of personal continuity and a public means of ethnic self-maintenance. Understood and utilized in this way, it broadened, becoming a family-clan, incorporating more generations into its vertical makeup, expanding itself into a larger real and imagined networks of living relatives and ancestors.

In considering all these important developments one cannot help but notice how Canada-centered these metaphors of relatedness are. Both the notion of generation and the notion of the family-clan have tended to be applied to Canada-born kin only, and both have quietly pushed the overseas relations into the deep background of the pre-Canadian history of Ukrainian Canadians, so much so that genealogical charts at first placed these overseas relations outside of families and family-clans and then outside of Canadian Ukrainian genealogies altogether. Thus, one can claim that these concepts of family and kinship as they evolved by the late 1980s, focusing on Canada as a place of origin, have ultimately bestowed the status of the external "diasporic other" on Ukrainian Canadians' overseas relations. Let's consider how this has been achieved.

Family Histories and Families' "Others"

Owing to the historical circumstances of Ukrainian immigration to Canada, the family history books that emerged as a part of the larger phenomenon of vernacular reflectivity that also saw the resurgence of personal memoir writing and the development of community history writing peaked in 1980 and 1990s, when Ukrainian Canadians were actively preparing to celebrate the one hundredth anniversary of Ukrainian Canadian settlement in Canada.[28]

In line with other Ukrainian Canadian centennial initiatives and in connection with the town's approaching anniversary, in 2000, Dagmar Rais, the director and curator of the Basilian Fathers Museum, organized a special exhibit called *Centennial in Canada* devoted exclusively to the pioneer families in the area. By the year 2000, at least thirty local families had produced family histories, detailing the beginning of their new life in Canada at the turn of the twentieth century, a period when the Mundare area was actively being settled by immigrants from Ukrainian lands. These thirty families applied to be included in the exhibit, but since not all of the material was of even quality, the curator, as she told me, had to introduce specific requirements. A family had to have been in Canada a hundred years or more, had to have held a family reunion commemorating the centenary of its arrival, and had to have had its family history published.[29] Of the thirty families that applied, only fourteen met these requirements.[30]

Interested in local vernacular representations of Ukraine, I closely read all the family histories along with other materials accompanying the exhibit and discussed them with Dagmar. What struck me then is how similarly the local family histories represented and constructed the idea of the Ukrainian Canadian family-clan and how similarly they portrayed overseas Ukrainians—this despite the fact that the families had distinct histories and the family history writers had neither training in historical research nor experience in historical writing. In my further encounters with the Ukrainian Canadians outside of Mundare, I came across other family histories, written in the 1980s and the 1990s, that likewise presented a similar idea of Ukrainian Canadian kin.

Yet Ukrainian Canadian family histories are not uniformly written assemblages of data. They may have been authored by one or many writers, they may have been produced in a form of single narrative or be an eclectic collection of various stories, and they dwell at length on different aspects of family histories. Still, what makes them a genre of vernacular literature is their adherence to a particular internal narrative order, or, in Proppian terms, to the internal principles of plot development. Vladimir Propp, renowned Russian folklorist of the mid-twentieth century known for his morphological study of Slavic fairy tales, asserts that fairy tales as a genre are defined by the fact that their narratives unfold in accordance with a single predetermined order of actions and events, or functions, as Propp calls them, that take place in the story, notwithstanding the vast variety of storylines, characters, and settings that characterize them.[31] Ukrainian Canadian family histories also follow a predetermined order of narrative development. First, they pay tribute to their ancestors and describe the land they left behind. Then they track Ukrainian Canadian postarrival genealogies, accompanying their findings with numerous photos depicting various generations, maps, and citations from contributions by other family members. Some include stories of homecoming, describing the travels to the USSR and the hometowns of their predecessors. In using the same elements in their presentations, all histories thus follow the same progression in their narrative constructions of Ukrainian Canadian family clans.

The fourteen family histories selected for the exhibition in Mundare supply an excellent example of Ukrainian Canadian family history writing of the late twentieth century. In addition to documenting their families' centennial, the books reveal both individual agency and collective memory. Their organization, format, sequencing, and ordering of the presented material convey both explicit and covert messages, pointing to the impact public discourse had on these seemingly private projects.

When I turned to analyze the descriptions of Ukraine and Ukrainians in family history books, I first considered the most obvious and explicit presentations of the old country and its people, taking at face value carefully crafted and

ideologically informed portrayals of Ukraine and its people. In addition to
exploring their own private family pasts, all family histories devote a significant
amount of attention to describing the lands their ancestors emigrated from and
to proclaiming transnational brotherhood with Ukrainians in Ukraine; some
also dedicate a number of pages to condemning the Soviet regime that still
reigned in Ukraine at the time of writing. Such attention to the old country, its
politics, and its people was dictated by the writers' desire to position themselves
and their families at the very core of the Ukrainian Canadian history; after all,
their families are the oldest Ukrainian clans in Canada. The tables of contents,
taken from the exhibited family histories exemplify this tendency. The *Eleniak
Family Tree* (1991) offers a history of factors that led to emigration as well as an
account of Ukrainian emigration, a family tree, a section on last names in
Canada associated with the Eleniaks, a section on the Basilian fathers and the
Sisters Servants of Mary Immaculate and their celebrations of the centennial of
Ukrainians in Canada, a section on Shumka dancers and the Basilian Fathers
Museum, a chronology of events, a bibliography of books on Ukrainian Cana-
dians, and a section devoted to Ukrainian Canadian patriotism.[32] Altogether,
out of twenty chapters in this book, ten deal with the general history of Ukrainian
Canadians.

The Stetskos's family book *Fame and Despair* (2000) devotes over sixty pages,
or a third of its volume, to Ukrainian history in general, featuring sections on
Galician history (including the history of Premyshl and Halychyna), the immigration experience, Dr. Josef Oleskiw, immigration by district, the development
of parishes, and the role of Ukrainian Canadians in National Railway of Canada.
The Romaniuk family history *Z rodu v rid* ([From Generation to Generation],
1991) features similar topics, with sections on the land the family left behind
and national celebrations of Ukrainian families' centennial.

As a part of the effort to connect their family history to the history of Ukraine,
family historians inevitably convey their own image of those who remained in
the land "left behind," constructing their ties to them in terms of transnational
siblinghood. For example, the Romaniuk family history offers an extended
discussion of such transnational kinship, despite the fact that, at the time of
writing, the Romaniuk descendants were not in contact with Ukraine after
their ancestors left the old country:

> Ukrainians continued to suffer throughout World War Two and after, when
> Galicia was also brought under the Russian yolk [*sic*]. The enduring desire for
> Ukrainian independence . . . was trampled again and again, but it obviously
> never died because the 100th anniversary of first Ukrainians' departure to

Canada coincided with Ukraine's peaceful and very surprising emergence of its own nation in 1991–92 after centuries of subjugation and denial. In that century and in just a few generations, Ukrainian Canadians overcome poverty and discrimination to achieve their current status with membership in all the professions including government of this land. While they have become assimilated and many have forgotten the language and some of the customs that existed in their homeland, pride in the Ukrainian heritage is still strong. And fewer are happier than Ukrainian Canadians to know that their brothers in the "old country" have escaped from the tyranny of the USSR and now have the opportunities to enjoy the freedom we have known in Canada in the past century.[33]

Such representations of the ethnic homeland and the overseas others reflect established Ukrainian Canadian "mainstream" ideas about the group's origin and of Ukraine as suffering motherland (as documented in chapter 3). Promoted in various public presentations in the Ukrainian Canadian community, the kinship with Ukraine and Ukrainians is also been highlighted in family history books. While family histories were not produced as part of official, institutionalized Ukrainian-Canadian discourses, they readily reproduced the dominant, shared understanding of Ukrainian-Canadian history and the old country as presented in those discourses, especially in pronationalist circles. Repeated interjections of this collective subjectivity into family histories reveal that the official story of the Ukrainian Canadian beginnings, its plot and narrative organization, were readily appropriated by lay family historians.

Yet a closer look at the way family history books are structured and at the principles they draw on to advance their representations of family and kin reveals a very different understanding of the overseas relatives. As a genre, the family history books, firmly rooted in the vernacular subjectivity and folk psychology of an ethnic community, routinely undermine and contradict their authors' explicit proclamations of strong and uninterrupted kinship ties with Ukraine and its people. At their core, these histories reassert distance and deepen disconnection and undo the tie between those in the diaspora and those in the homeland. As their primary goal is to document and construct a history of a given Ukrainian family in Canada, family historians, inevitably produce specifically Ukrainian Canadian genealogies, depicting themselves as members of the Canadian family clans, excluding distant relatives in Ukraine from their family history charts and reproducing in the end the distance between themselves and their "diasporic others." This production of specifically *ethnic* genealogies, that is, genealogies rooted in the generation of the first immigrants, is a core characteristic of ethnic family history writing in the second part of the twentieth century and the primary means by which Ukrainian Canadian families effectively distance themselves from their diasporic and familial Ukrainian "others." Unlike letter writing, which sustained this distance in private, family histories effectively broadcast this genealogical distance in public.

In sum, family history writing in Ukrainian Canadian culture gave rise to a very practical definition of the Ukrainian Canadian family, understood as a family-clan consisting of several generations all rooted in Canada. That most traditional of genealogical means, arboreal metaphors, underwrite this defini-tion. One of the primary purposes of family history writing is to present a family tree, and all the books I consulted offered their own versions of the tree on their pages, and the title of the Eleniak family history makes reference to the primary symbol around which the book's narrative is advanced. The Eleniak family history's book cover also includes an image of the family tree decorated by several prominent representatives of the Eleniaks in Canada. Steven Eleniak, the man behind the book, told me that he felt he had to use this image, since at the time he was putting the book together, everyone commented on how repre-sentative the image was (figure 5.3).[34] The family tree also appears as a visual symbol as on the front page of the Koroluk family history (1999).

In all of the family history books, the tree begins with the so-called first generation of the family's name bearer and his wife. The family trees do not extend back to members of the family from the "old country," with the exception of the Moszczanski family, whose family tree goes back to fifteenth century.[35] The Moszczanskis are the exception to the common practice, as the family has a well-documented origin in the fifteenth-century Polish nobility.

Thus, there is an obvious contradiction between the explicit statements of cross-Atlantic kinship asserted in various public narratives in Ukrainian Canadian culture, including those offered up by the museum, and the family histories. In explicit statements, inspired by the ideological currents of the day, a relationship with Ukraine is posited, but in the family histories, Canadian Ukrainian family trees are rooted in Canada and by default exclude any branches that may have sprung in Ukraine. These two distinct ways of seeing kinship are informed by the two distinct domains of Ukrainian culture. The first has its roots in public discourse, the second is governed by folk psychology. The first is an outcome of collective explicit proclamations of relatedness, the second is an outcome of lived experiences, implied in local practices of related-ness that routinely excluded, out of practicality, the overseas kin from the domain of the lifeworld.

Figure 5.3. The cover of *Eleniak Family Tree*, edited by Steven P. Eleniak (Altona, Manitoba: Eleniak Heritage Society, 1991).

Family history writing has multiple purposes, but what the practice of constructing family trees that excluded branches of members in Ukraine achieved is the formalization of the ideal Ukrainian Canadian family. The ideal family was modeled in times when Ukrainian Canadians celebrated important milestones in the lives of their local communities, from the seventy-fifth anniversaries of the establishment of the provinces of Alberta and Saskatchewan in 1980 to the celebrations of the Ukrainian Canadian centennial in 1991. The family history books produced during this period laid down the foundations for the subsequent production of many other family histories by the descendants of those who arrived to Canada during the first immigration wave. Because their production was governed by the political and ideological community agendas of precentennial times, centennial family histories, explicitly asserted transnational brotherhood with Ukrainians in Ukraine, but hidden underneath the veneer of such ideologically informed proclamations of such brotherhood was a very different message that in fact conveyed disconnection.

Redefining Ancestors:
Popular Genealogy and the "Other" Ukrainians

If by the 1970–80s, Ukrainian Canadians, especially those whose families came during the first immigration wave to Canada, had learned to imagine their families as rooted in the Canadian soil with branches spreading only across the new homeland, what happened to this conception when they, like many other North Americans, embraced the new tool for family history research, popular genealogy? How did they begin to see their Ukrainian "diasporic other," the kinfolk in the old country that sprang up after their predecessors left for Canada?

Popular genealogy has profoundly changed how many people including Ukrainian Canadians see and understand their personal and family pasts.[36] The story of Janet's engagement with genealogy that I discuss in the introduction to this book vividly reminds us of the effect that popular genealogy can have on personal identity and a person's understanding of her roots, her family, and her genealogical history. Prior to embracing genealogical research and before spending numerous evenings online searching for her ancestors in various internet archival databases, Janet knew herself to be a Russian Canadian, married to a fellow Slav of Ukrainian origin. Yet as I note in the introduction, at the time of our interview, Janet told me that she was applying for Métis status, as she found out in her ancestral lines strong Métis presence of which she was never aware of prior to her genealogical research. Janet's case is only one example of a complete makeover of person's ethnic identity that the engagement with popular genealogy can bring about.

Equally, genealogical research can "rewrite" a person's understanding of his or her extended family and reposition her or him in the course of history as a member of different family groups and clans, with symbolic and at times political consequences. In other words, genealogical research of today, however commonplace and casual it may be due to its popularity and accessibility, can have far-reaching effects on individuals and their communities.

In what follows I briefly discuss the phenomenon of popular genealogical research among Ukrainian Canadians, outlining its dynamics, participating agents and activities in the context of both genealogical research in North America and other kinds of Ukrainian Canadian vernacular practices of engagement with the old country. The reason I am doing this is simply because other scholars have not yet done so and also because highlighting its development contributes to the argument I am laying out in this chapter about how Ukrainian Canadian ideas of transnational kinship have evolved over time. My primary interest here is with the impact popular genealogy has had on Ukrainian Canadian understandings of their "diasporic others." I claim that this kind of genealogical research has substantially redrafted existing relationships with the kinfolk overseas. At the same time, those relationships continue to be shaped in the domain of imagination through the construction of new family trees; these new family trees primarily serve the identity needs of families in Canada without reviving real transatlantic family ties.

Scholars who devote their academic attention to popular genealogy agree that it can mean different things to different people, and therefore it is hard to offer a single definition of it.[37] I understand popular genealogy as another modern vernacular practice that among Ukrainian Canadians has been informed by traditional family lore, storytelling, and history sharing and that speaks to both the continuity and renewal of folk psychology. In most narrow sense, modern genealogical research can be defined as the construction of family pedigrees, which involves the creation of lists of ancestors and descendants that can go back far in time.[38]

Genealogical research differs from family history books in some important ways. First, among Ukrainian Canadians, family history writing for the most part has meant the compilation of various narratives describing the living history of different branches of the extended family-clan. Family history stories may take up the lives of predecessors, but importantly they focus on the lives of all contemporaries. As such, in anthropological terms family histories, unlike

genealogical research, profile not so much the genealogical rootedness of an
individual but instead reconstruct the genealogical production of kindred (or
all living relatives related to one shared ancestor). Genealogical research oftentimes presupposes an ego whose history is being rediscovered in a chronologically reversed way. The ego in many cases corresponds with the ego of the
genealogist who undertakes the research, as is the case with Janet. Family history
writing highlights the corporate agent of genealogical history, the family itself.
It is not surprising that family history writing has been directly linked to the
centennial commemorations of individual families and that family history
books were seen as necessary dimension of Ukrainian Canadian centennial
family reunions. Yet genealogical research can be a part of family history writing,
and when it is pursued, it serves the purposes of the family history writing, to
profile the living memory of the kindred.

In the twentieth century, as a popular pastime, genealogy reached a new
high in the 1990s, when it became effectively computerized. On the one hand,
this modern vernacular search for personal heritage is informed by the premodern practice of genealogy upkeep as sustained by the nobility and landed
gentry, for example, in Europe. The retention and transmission of genealogical
knowledge among premodern European nobility and landholders was a highly
specialized activity, reserved for the privileged and educated few, and it served
the very practical purpose of defining who was entitled to the family inheritance and who was not. In premodern times, literacy was an important tool for
passing on genealogical knowledge, through charts and graphs and through
birth, marriage and death records, and it is literacy that can be seen as responsible for the formation of the habit of record keeping and genealogy upkeep.
On the other hand, in other cultural contexts around the world, including
among the common folk in premodern Europe, where the mastery of the technology of writing and reading was rudimentary or absent but the mastery of
oral tradition and the techniques of oral transmittance were high, genealogical
knowledge was passed along via oral narratives and stories rather than through
charts, drafted pedigrees, and family trees. Alex Haley in his famous book
Roots: The Saga of American Family wrote convincingly about the oral transmission
of genealogical knowledge among African Americans in the U.S. South and in
Africa.[39] All in all, in these various premodern cultural and historical contexts,
individuals, whether nobility or ordinary folks, whether tied to the place where
they were born or uprooted, were primarily engaged in genealogical upkeep.

For many ordinary people of today though, genealogical explorations into
their family pasts has meant not so much upkeep of the existing family trees as
the discovery of genealogical pedigrees from scratch, which brings the old
countries elsewhere in the world from whence many families trace their roots

into play. Contemporary Ukrainian Canadians are nowadays actively engaged in constructing such pedigrees, as prior to turning to family history in the 1970s, most did not have an elaborate understanding of the mesh and sequentiality of relations in their family pasts. The overwhelming majority of Ukrainian Canadians did not inherit genealogical charts and family trees from their parents and grandparents, being the descendants of displaced farmers, workers, and the intelligentsia rather than royalty or nobility.

From my interviews with Ukrainian Canadian genealogy researchers and activists, and my explorations the field of Ukrainian Canadian genealogy in general, I estimate that Ukrainian Canadians began engaging in this new kind of family history research in the late 1970s.[40] They have done so along with other North Americans, many of whom also discovered the wonders of genealogy at roughly at the same time, inspired in part by the much-publicized television broadcast in the United States of Alex Haley's book *Roots*.[41]

Genealogical research brought many researchers out of their families and into newly created communities of genealogical research. Today, there are at least 224 such genealogical societies in Canada, according to the Library and Archives of Canada website, and a number of these regional societies have special interest groups that focus specifically on the Ukrainian genealogy research.[42] Ukrainian community organizations also support genealogical research.[43] Genealogical research is undertaken not only in the companionship of peers living in the same community but in web-based, online communities.[44] Altogether there are at least eleven specifically Ukrainian Canadian outlets that support and promote Ukrainian genealogical research in Canada, and this excludes societies housed in the United States that are conceived in broader regional terms (such as the popular Federation of East European Family History Societies). This list of genealogical regional and online communities here is not exhaustive but is designed to give the reader an understanding of how widespread and how communal Ukrainian genealogical research has become in Canada over the last three decades.

A good indication of how far genealogical research has come in the Ukrainian Canadian community would be the number of self-standing publications produced by it on the topic. Between late 1970s and early 2010s ten reference books were published in Canada, including a few reprints of previously published works, seven of which were published in the mid-1980s, coinciding with do-it-yourself genealogy seminars and workshops that various genealogical societies across Canada sponsored.[45]

While two professional academics (Himka and Swyripa) and two professional archivists (Momryk and Szalasznyj) were instrumental in the publication of the ten Ukrainian reference books, none of these publications offers critical analysis of the field of genealogical research but rather directs their intellectual energies at providing the general public with basic reference tools for genealogical research, which were much needed at the time. Three decades later, however, there has still been no scholarly analysis of Ukrainian Canadian popular genealogy.[46] Meanwhile, critical perspectives on popular genealogy began to emerge in history, anthropology, sociology, and cultural geography, along with explorations of the meaning of this cultural practice among other ethnic groups of North America.[47]

Seven of the ten Ukrainian Canadian reference books were published between 1984 and 1986, and five (!) of these came out in just one year, 1984, a circumstance that speaks to qualitative changes that had begun to take place in the vernacular domains of Ukrainian Canadian culture and especially in how Ukrainian Canadians understood themselves and their families.

While 1984 seems to have been the highlight point of genealogical publishing in the Ukrainian Canada, 1979 witnessed the appearance of the first official independent Ukrainian genealogical organization, founded in Calgary, Alberta.

In 2006, when taking a group of students to on a summer semester abroad in Ukraine, I met Walter Rusel, a retired businessman from Alberta, who signed up to take courses with our program in Lviv, Ukraine. Only later did I realize that one of the reasons Walter signed up to go to Ukraine with the university students was to do genealogical research, a long-term interest of his. A few years later we sat down for an extended life-story interview about his involvement with Ukrainian genealogy and it is then that I learned that Walter had been a long-time president of what appears to be the earliest independent Ukrainian genealogical organization in Canada, the Ukrainian Genealogical and Historical Society of Canada. It was a very moving experience for me to talk to Walter about his personal past as well as his long-term commitment to genealogical research. Walter was one of the pioneers of the preinternet Ukrainian Canadian grassroots genealogical movement. Born and raised in Manitoba, he worked on the railway as a young fellow in the 1970s before moving to Calgary, meeting his future wife, establishing his own plumbing business, and raising his family. In all respects, his life has been very typical of a Ukrainian Canadian person of Greek Catholic faith living on the prairies. Given the historical context of his youth and young adulthood years and considering his sharp and curious mind, it is not surprising that he took deep interest in the genealogical movement that was booming across North America when he was in the prime of his life.

Many scholars associate the growth of genealogical research in North America with genealogical work performed by the followers of the Church of

Jesus Christ of Latter-day Saints. The LDS Church, commonly known as the Mormon Church not only encouraged genealogical research for doctrinal reasons among its own followers but also developed resources for millions of people outside of the church.[48] Amateur and professional genealogists who are not Mormons nowadays capitalize on the widespread network of some forty-five hundred family history libraries that the LDS Church developed around the world. It happened that when Walter met his then fiancé that she was a member of LDS Church herself. When they started their family, Walter adopted the Mormon faith as his own. This change in his life opened up new possibilities and aided his own self-realization as a knowledge seeker.

Embracing his new faith, he discovered the depth and breadth of spiritual practices of documenting ancestral relationships that all LDS members need to engage in in order to perform proxy temple ordinances for those who were not yet baptized as members of the church when they died. The church also encourages its members to undertake record keeping at a more intimate and immediate level, and it is precisely this aspect of Mormon spiritual life that led Walter to become a community genealogist and establish the first independent Ukrainian genealogical organization in Canada.[49] Walter has been to the headquarters of LDS Church in Salt Lake City and its main family history library many times, and he even listened to Alex Haley's inspiring talks when the writer shared his journey into the traditional genealogy of his African and African American ancestors. Through these kinds of experiences, both educational and deeply spiritual, Walter became fully initiated into the practice of modern genealogical research.

In the preinternet times of the 1970s, genealogical research was about assembling and sharing the existing archival documentation and records that were kept on microfiches and photo plates in various public archival collections. Walter began his journey as community genealogist in the mid-1970s, identifying and assembling detailed maps depicting Western Ukrainian lands, hoping to eventually create his own gazetteer of all historical maps of Ukraine. A few years after he began his research, in 1979, he incorporated the Ukrainian Genealogical and Historical Society of Canada. Operating out of Calgary, this society served other amateur genealogists who, like him, needed to sift through many records to uncover their Ukrainian roots. Walter went on to share with me his stories of assembling microfiches that became the property in the society, organizing translation of old Cyrillic microfiches for the LDS Family History Library in Salt Lake City, buying up publications that were related to Ukrainian family history research from various local bookstores, offering workshops to Ukrainian Canadians that brought Greek Catholics and Mormons together in the same room, who otherwise led separate lives. At times the work of this society translated into fascinating journeys that Walter and his van, stuffed with re-search materials, would undertake in order to promote genealogical research across western Canada. He would go to the famous Dauphin Ukrainian Folk Festival, attend other major events on the rural prairies, offer seminars and consultations to all who were interested in genealogy. His van became both a library and family research center on wheels, especially after he moved to rural Saskatchewan, to a small community not far away from Saskatoon, to be cen-trally located, as he put it, between all the important destinations.[50]

Fast forward to the late 2000s and back to Alberta, this time to Edmonton, where in 2006, a new exciting project was initiated by the Ukrainian community of this Canadian province. With the financial support of the provincial govern-ment, the Alberta-Ukraine Genealogical Project came to life. The AUGP was the result of collaboration and cooperation among many stakeholders, ranging from such institutions as the Ukrainian Cultural Heritage Village, the Basilian Fathers Museum in Mundare, and the Provincial Archives of Alberta to genea-logical organizations such as the Alberta Genealogical Society with its Ukrain-ian arm and the Ukrainian Genealogical and Historical Society of Canada to the archival institutions and record depositories in Western Ukraine, particu-larly in the oblasts of Ivano-Frankivsk, Ternopil, Chernivtsi, and Lviv. Run from the office in Edmonton, the Alberta-Ukraine Genealogical Project was part of an international Alberta-Ukraine government-sponsored partnership, and as such the project benefited from Albertan government support, pledged to the project in the amount of $200,000.[51]

The key figure in this development was Radomir Bilash, a senior historian project manager and contributor to many fine Ukrainian Canadian research initiatives in Alberta. Radomir shared with me on several occasions many details about this project, which has an active profile and fits rather organically into a number of other family history and cultural heritage initiatives that have been launched in Alberta.[52] As its promotional pamphlet states, through this project, Albertans and others now have access to nearly thirty years of historical research conducted by the Ukrainian Village Research Programme, as well as to other resources developed by the project's various partners and stakeholders.[53] Impor-tantly, through a genealogical research agreement with Ukraine's state archives, this project also provides a formal link to archival institutions in Western Ukraine. The AUGP thus serves as a real life (rather than online) hub for a variety of genealogy-related activities, ranging from documenting rural church properties in Alberta, promoting genealogical research across Alberta and beyond, and supporting private research to offering research services to those family-history seekers who cannot pursue genealogical research on their own.[54]

The project also effectively benefits those individuals and their extended families that are interested in nominating themselves for the Alberta Centennial Program, which is significant in connection with my discussion here. The Alberta Centennial Program, or the Centenary Pioneer Recognition Program, coordinated by the Ukrainian Heritage Village near Edmonton, was established to honor pioneer families who settled in east-central Alberta prior to 1915, the cutoff year for the first immigration wave. Launched in 2003, this program provides an opportunity, as its coordinators say, to "complement celebrations" of those families who are preparing to mark the centennial of their ancestors' arrival in Canada.[55] The nominated pioneer families are recognized in a number of public ways.[56] Their ancestors (and their families) are issued a special centennial certificate that is given to them on Ukrainian Day (a popular public festivity that is held in association with Ukraine's Independence Day, celebrated annually in late August). A year later, the names of the settlers are added to a special centennial list that has been carved out on the monument prominently displayed on the museum premises. As of 2010, there were some twenty-five hundred families who had been granted the status of centennial pioneer. The program is due to wrap up in 2015. The Alberta-Ukraine Genealogical Project actively assists the seekers of the centennial status with their family history research, thus contributing to their public recognition.

All in all, the work of AUGP is the capstone of the journey that Ukrainian Canadian genealogical research as cultural practice undertook over the course of thirty years, since the late 1970s into the twenty-first century. Once a solely vernacular movement in the Ukrainian Canadian milieu, today, Ukrainian genealogical research is fully entrenched in the networks and activities of a variety of governmental, civil, national, and homeland organizations, developments that will no doubt introduce changes to Ukrainian Canadian culture, values and identity.

Back in the late 1970s, Walter and other genealogy enthusiasts were the pioneers of modern genealogical research among their peers in the Ukrainian Canadian milieu. Their participation in the widespread North American genealogical movement was grassroots, intuitive, independent, and even entrepreneurial. Walter and his peers, working in preinternet times, engaged in archival work on the ground and in real terms, handing the physical artefacts, the material traces of their ancestry that the archival world had to offer to them, and building at the same time early communities of peer genealogists. Walter's case is also illustrative of how powerful the impact of Mormonism was, with its doctrinal and spiritual emphasis on reconnecting with deceased ancestors, on the genealogical movement in North American in general, and on Ukrainian Canadian genealogy specifically.

How has the Ukrainian Canadian genealogical movement, exemplified by the work of Walter, Radomir and many other "casual" genealogists like Janet, affected Ukrainian Canadians' understanding of their own family trees, family clans, and overseas kin? Catherine Nash has suggested that genealogy, represented in the metaphor of a family tree, not only points to a specific mode of reckoning kinship through linear bilateral descent but also to the cultures of relatedness that are figured, produced, and performed in the practice of genealogy.[57] Like traditional family history writing, Ukrainian Canadian popular genealogy accounts for all relatives on both the mother's and the father's sides of the family, but instead of rooting Ukrainian Canadian family trees in Canadian soil and in the first generation of the pioneer settlers, popular genealogical research makes it possible for the Ukrainian Canadians to imagine themselves as members of far deeper kinship networks, with roots going back to the "old country. Walter's preoccupation with the maps of Ukraine and his intention to produce a gazetteer was augured this qualitative transition in Ukrainian Canadians's sense of belonging and rootedness.[58] And the undertaking of contemporary genealogical work in Ukrainian archives further confirmed the growing tendency among Ukrainian Canadians to reclaim their ancestry in Ukraine, both in personal and ethnic community contexts.

Thus, genealogical research produced qualitative changes in Ukrainian Canadians' understanding of kinship. Undertaking this modern genealogical search, Ukrainian Canadians began discovering not just the founders of their own Canadian family-clans but, importantly, their ancestors in the old country, redefining for themselves the genealogical category of ancestry and rejecting the primacy of the Canadian point zero in their genealogical accounts of their family beginnings. In other words, having embraced popular genealogy, very much like Nash claims, Ukrainian Canadians have been devising and reproducing for themselves new ideas of relatedness and relations. This replacement of Canadian ancestors with even older ones in the old country has affected the way Ukrainian Canadians see their living kinfolk overseas. These other Ukrainians, once unknown and lost in the old country, have resurfaced and are returning into the newly redefined grids of Ukrainian Canadian family trees and genealogies. Once imagined and dealt with mostly in the domain of personal family, these other Ukrainians have in the context of recent developments in the world and in the Ukrainian Canadian community become the Ukrainian diasporic other.

The search for old-country roots, ancestors, and overseas living kinfolk necessitates travel back to the country of origin, and Ukrainian Canadian genealogical research brought many people to Ukraine after the end of communist rule there in 1991. Prior to this, though, there were other journeys of homecoming that in the political context of Soviet rule acquired a unique character and led to singular homecoming experiences, distinguishing them from other well-researched and well-documented instances of homecoming among other cultural groups. Let's consider those in the next chapter.

Figure 6.1. Traditional Ukrainian bread and salt welcome, Ukrainian Canadian homecoming tour, Kyiv, 1991. Courtesy of Anne Dobry, Mundare.

6

///////////////////////////

Homecoming

$\mathcal{F}$or a long time, Ukrainian Canadians were able to connect with their ethnic homeland and places of origin only vicariously and from a distance. The primary, and many would argue, sole reason for the profound real-life disconnection that persisted throughout the twentieth century was the control that the Soviet Union exercised over its citizens, their mobility, and their relations with the outside world. The term "iron curtain" was not just a token metaphor to describe the ideological disjuncture that emerged in the world order with the establishment of communist rule in Eurasia and elsewhere but also referred to the literal impenetrability of Soviet state borders, which prevented many diaspora and homeland Ukrainians from visiting each other. As a result, Ukrainian Canadians' long-distance experiences of their homeland became firmly defined by archetypal processes of nostalgia, longing, imagining, mythologizing, narrativizing, and stereotyping, to the point that the ethnic homeland became an ethnic otherland, the land of "other" Ukrainians.

This longing for homeland was especially strongly felt by those who were separated from their immediate relatives in Ukraine, such as Stefan Wakarchuk and many other individuals whose stories have been profiled in this book. Yet the longing for homeland long ago ceased to be just a subjective desire of various individuals. Considered in the context of vernacular culture, this longing with time acquired a corporate nature, transcending individuals and his or her descendants. The corporate nature of this longing also finds expression itself in cross-generational letter writing, modern vernacular practices of family history writing, family reunions, and most recently in genealogical research, all requiring the contributions not just from the keen family researcher but from his or her other relatives as well.

Given how widespread human migration and displacement has been in modern times, I see the need and internal drive to return and reconnect with ancestral lands as a manifestation of an archetypal, foundational, and psychological need of a modern diasporic and displaced being to find and reconnect with his or her own self, a need produced by the historical circumstances of modernity. Scholars of diaspora studies have made similar arguments, asserting that homecoming is an integral dimension and feature of the diasporic consciousness.[1] Ever since the transformative 1960s, social scientists, anthropologists, psychologists and philosophers have been analyzing the social and cultural displacements that modern human beings have been subject to as an outcome of the changing world realities that mass industrialization and the development of capitalism brought about as well as the impact of these displacements. These multiple types of modern displacements, intensified by the globalization of the 1970s, also led to the fragmentation and the displacement of the modern self.[2] Many scholars argue that in order to reestablish a sense of coherence within themselves, these fragmented, displaced, destabilized modern subjects turn to narrative and the search for roots.[3]

Paul Basu, the author of an eloquent book on Scottish homecoming, advances the idea that diasporic homecoming is one of the ways by which modern selves search for their roots. As he puts it, to find the answers to the insistent questions of late modernity — "What to do? How to act? Who to be?" — a Scottish homecomer who comes in search of his or her Scottish roots turns to "the inheritance of blood and intuits there a vague memory of 'home.'"[4] I acknowledge the existence of the modern subject's need to search for his or her genealogical roots, but I also want to suggest that the return to the ancestral homeland has a vernacular origin. For those Ukrainian Canadians living out the diaspora-homeland disconnections within the genealogical networks of transatlantic kinship, the call to return and the need for homecoming are also a function of folk psychology, with its emphasis on the ideal itinerary of a diasporic journey, the mythic, cyclic journey that encompasses leaving, returning and coming back.

Because this need is rather universal, its Ukrainian case can be compared to and contextualized through the experiences of many other cultural groups, though this is not my task here. What sets Ukrainian diasporic homecomings apart from other diasporic experiences of returning home is the historical and political circumstances that made the homeland literally inaccessible to the diaspora for nearly five decades (from the late 1930s to the mid-1980s).[5] Perhaps the political circumstances in Eastern Europe that prevented the two groups of Ukrainians from visiting and directly engaging with each other, as well as the symbolic distance that grew over time between the displaced group and its homeland not only explains why Ukrainian diasporic imaginings of the homeland were so intense but also why Ukrainian homecoming experiences became so ritualized. And while diasporic visits were strictly planned, carefully regulated and zealously monitored by the Soviet authorities, they nevertheless evolved into a unique kind of vernacular practice, distinct from other well-researched homecomings, such as Irish, Scottish, Benin, British, Hadrami and others.[6]

This chapter, like others in this book, pays tribute to the cultural heritage of split and separation in modern Ukrainian culture defined globally. It concerns, once again, traveling and journeying and contributes to the scholarship on diasporic homecoming. More specifically, I focus here on visits to the ancestral lands that the Ukrainian Canadians undertook in the second half of the twentieth century as well as on the significance of such journeys for them. Following here the grassroots itineraries of modern homecoming I explore their ritual and symbolic nature, which would often culminate in pilgrimages to the ancestral villages. Exploring recollections of my informants about their "once-in-a-lifetime" journeys to ancestral villages in Ukraine and analyzing their encounters with and attitudes toward the ancestral land I argue here that these encounters became a ritual of diasporic homecoming that remains a modern rite of passage for Ukrainian Canadians. Such understanding of homecoming as ritual sets my analysis apart from the explorations of other scholars of diasporic homecoming.

These travels should also be seen as an important, and at times, concluding phase in the diasporic journey of an individual or his or her Canadian family. Homecoming in fact is not just another rite of passage for a modern displaced self but a final step in the diasporic cycle of departure, separation and absence, and reunion/return, whether we understand these experiences as manifestations of ritual (as Van Gennep and Victor Turner do) or as manifestations of a separation constraint (as Stafford does). Homecoming, however, does not automatically dissolve this separation constraint; as I have observed through my own participation in such rituals, it does not necessarily bring the two branches of the kin into real contact and can instead accentuate the symbolic distance between the two.

My efforts to highlight the principle points of homecoming should be seen in the context of my discussion of other means that Ukrainians on both sides of the binomial have relied on to sustain the connection between themselves, the letters being the most prominent one. Homecoming as a diasporic rite of passage took place while letters were being exchanged, and indeed it was oftentimes arranged through letter writing. Yet while letters offered many writers a unique opportunity to reconnect with their kin in the virtual space of letter writing, the experiences of homecoming and return offered writers and nonwriters alike an opportunity of a real-life encounter, and what happened in the space of these real encounters is the subject of this chapter.

Homecoming experiences certainly varied from individual to individual and from one historical period to another one. Many immigrants who arrived to settle in Canada as farmers during the first and second immigration waves (1891–1914, 1924–1930s) were unable to go back home for visits. The cost of traveling to Ukraine was too prohibitive for short visits, and the responsibilities in the new land were too demanding to leave new homesteads for a prolonged time. Among those early arrivers though, there was a cohort of other migrants who in today's terminology would be described as labor migrants, working as wage earners, and who indeed saw themselves as temporary, even if long-term, foreign workers.[7] There were numerous individuals in this cohort who would go back to their home villages for a prolonged visit and then return to Canada or the United States for more work. Extended homecoming was possible for those whose families were in Poland, Romania, and Czechoslovakia (home states for Eastern Galicia, the Lemko lands, parts of Bukovina, and the Transcarpathian region) before most of these territories became annexed to the USSR just before the Second World War. In the village of Hrytsevolia discussed in chapter 2, this was certainly the case for many villagers.

With the Second World War and the absorption of much of Western Ukraine into the USSR, the situation changed dramatically. Visits and home stays ceased during the war years, and with the formation of the Eastern European communist bloc, they did not resume once the war ended in Europe. After the war, with the arrival of immigrants from the displaced persons camps in Europe, the nostalgia for the now literally unreachable homeland was rekindled in Ukrainian Canadian public culture, intensified by the trauma of the war-driven exile and by the hostile takeover of Western Ukraine by the totalitarian Soviet state in 1939.

Private visits to Soviet Ukraine were hardly possible to arrange until the late 1980s. The only way diaspora Ukrainians could travel to their homeland was through organized tourism set up by the Soviet state. Only one Ukrainian travel agency in Canada was granted the privilege of conducting organized tours of Ukraine between the 1950s and 1970s, Globe Tours, operating out of Winnipeg. For many years any other Ukrainian travel agency wanting to arrange their clients' travels to Ukraine had to work through them. According to Andrij Makuch, only in the 1970s did tours to Ukraine begin to be organized by other travel agencies.[8]

Figure 6.2. Homecoming to Ukraine, first moments, Boryspil Airport, Kyiv, 1991. Courtesy of Anne Dobry, Mundare.

For the purposes of my discussion I define Ukrainian (Canadian, American, and so on) diasporic homecoming as the visits to the ancestral village. Such visits to ancestral villages in the second part of the twentieth century could be very short, just a few minutes as in the case of Lara Verny, whose story we will hear in a moment, or they could last a few days, if they were sanctioned or took place during perestroika and later. The official Soviet Intourist tours, following their prescribed itineraries, would typically bring Ukrainian Canadians first to Moscow, then to Kyiv (see figure 6.2), and then to a host of other Ukrainian historic sites and urban centers, including the cities of Lviv, Ternopil, Ivano-Frankivsk, and Chernivtsi in Western Ukraine. The tourists would stay in Intourist approved hotels and would be taken in groups to various historical sites, always chaperoned by their guides, who were also required to inform the authorities if the tourists deviated from the prescribed set of activities. To leave the tour at all was not an official option. The trips to the ancestral villages therefore had to be arranged and were carried out in a highly clandestine manner. Perestroika in the late 1980s enabled many Ukrainian Canadians to arrange their own homecoming trips, yet many continued to rely on organized tourism. Going to the USSR on the tour was seen by Ukrainian Canadians as an opportunity to return to their ancestral villages and reconnect with their homeland relatives. Was that the case, though?

Episode 1:
Sending a Child Overseas

Lara Verny shared her moving account of homecoming with one of our student researchers during an interview conducted as a part of the large-scale oral history project "Sociocultural Change on the Prairies: The Ukrainian Canadian Experience" that I coordinated with another colleague in 2002 and 2003.[9] Verny, the daughter of post–Second World War immigrants and in her late forties at the time of my interview with her, went to Ukraine at the delicate age of seventeen, to meet her ailing grandparents for the first time. Let's turn to her narrative:

> AT: Did you ever have connection with your family in Ukraïna?
>
> LV: I did. Ever since my parents left Ukraine, they had been sending *khustky* back to Ukraine, supporting them forever. They still do. See, there was always that. There were letters from T'otia [Aunt] Marusia and from [Uncle] Stepan. There was always that contact. And then, in 1970, just when I finished high school, my parents sent me on a tour to Ukraïna. So, it was before the end of communism.
>
> It was not a good experience, it was a very negative experience. I do not think I was a child at heart, but at that time I was emotionally too immature to go alone. I went with a tour, but I did not know anybody on the tour. [. . .] At that time my father was still afraid to go back, there would be problems [he thought] if he went. So, my mother, because she had the same name, was also afraid of going. They did not want to come with me. Perhaps it would have been better if she would have come, because emotionally it was a devastating trip. I just could not handle it.
>
> I grew up with the idea that I was going to be the one carrying on the Ukrainian traditions, the Ukrainian heritage. When I went for those two weeks to Ukraïna, I went there assuming that I was going as a sister. Not as a Canadian, not as a capitalist, not as a Westerner. I was going to Ukraïna, to my family. Not just to my *selo* [village] family, but to my [blood] family, to my *babtsia* [grandmother], in Ukraïna. We were brought up to think that we were all *braty* [brothers] and *sestry* [sisters].

At that time it was still required that we spend the first two days of the trip in Moscow. It was rainy all time, it was ugly. So, we went through that. And we ended up in Kyiv after that.

I was naive. I went there expecting two things. First of all, to be welcomed with open arms as a fellow Ukrainian and second, to hear Ukrainian spoken. I came to Kyiv, and nobody would speak to me in Ukrainian. Everybody would reply in Russian. I mean, now I understand that it was the capital. Even now they speak mostly in Russian. But that just blew me away! And I was not received as a sister. I was received as a capitalist pig from Western Canada. . . . from Canada.

AT: By your family?

LV: No, not by my family, in general. I was just another capitalist tourist. And I was not coming as a tourist. I was coming as a family, I was coming as a displaced Ukrainian and I was returning home. And that was so naive!

And that was one thing that was difficult. Another was my father's brother Stepan and my grandmother, who was literally half my size, a little *hrybochok* [mushroom]. They came to meet me in Kyiv. And they followed me from city to city. That was a nightmare on several levels. Again, I was what? Seventeen! Emotionally, I was not prepared for that. When I met them, or when they met me, it was obviously very emotional. I was this child of their Petro. It was nonstop emotion! One is on my one side, and the other one is on my other side. And they were constantly touching me and constantly weeping. Because this was a daughter of her son. To this day, when I am confronted with that [memory], I have to put up a wall. It was an introduction to my war.

Last year, we celebrated my parents' fiftieth anniversary. And my mother told a story that she had heard from *seliany* [farmers] from their village, which was that once my dad left the village during the war, his family there heard shortly after that he had died. And for three weeks his mother lay in the corner in the kitchen and would not eat or drink, because she was grieving for her son. He was her favorite. And he died. And they did not know until years after the war, when my parents started sending *pakunky* [packages] back, that he was alive.

So, this was what I was coming into. I did not know any of this. I could not handle it. And things like . . . my *stryi* [uncle], he was a bricklayer. Out of work. I guess he refused to join the Communist Party. So he was out of work because they would not give him work. I did not know any of this happened. So, he was poor. We stopped on the road at one point. And he took off his shoes. And his foot was just one nonstop blister. Dirty feet, holes in his socks. More holes than socks. You have to understand, I came from the upper class, I never had a hole in my sock. And his shirt, he was wearing the same shirt for four or five days. And finally I thought, I have some shirts in my bag [to give away as gifts]. And I gave him some of the shirts to wear.

I had never experienced poverty before. I had never been told that they were poor. All that stuff just hit me! I shut down. I could not . . . I was just in pain the whole time.

On my last day in Lviv they saw me off to the train. I could not even say goodbye to them. You know, when I came back to Canada, I could not write them a letter. And shortly after, within weeks, my grandfather passed away. And within several months my *baba* passed away. And I did not write them a letter. I could not handle it. In that respect, I wished my mother had come with me. So she could take some of this load off me.

Another thing, I stayed in an Intourist hotel; this is because I was a tourist. And they had to sleep on a bench at the train station, as I could not invite them into my room. This was the stuff that happened.

They had arranged for a driver. He came to pick me up in Lviv and take me to the *selo*, the village of Zubrets. It was fifty kilometers away. They had a friend who was brave enough to take me to the village. There were all kinds of things that were done in those days [to prevent the visitors from going to their home villages]. During our tour, as soon as they [the tour organizers] found out that some members of the tour had family in a particular place they would change the itinerary so that we would not to go to that place as scheduled. So, if an arrangement had been made with family members, the Canadians would not be able to meet with them.

As it happened, the timing of our going to Ternopil was also changed. So, being stupid and naive, although I do not know how I would have done it otherwise, I telegrammed them. I had their address. And I telegrammed telling them about the change of date. And, of course, everything on the tour was public knowledge. . . . I telegrammed about the changed date. One had to apply for a visa to go out to a *selo*, and I had not applied. I did not apply because I knew I would be rejected, and they would never ever honor my application. So, it was all done hush-hush. I telegrammed them, told that I was coming. The driver came up to Ternopil to pick me up. He took me to the village. We went into my grandfather's house. The reason I had to go the village was because my grandfather was ill. The story is that he had been waiting for several years, ill, to see his grandchild. If not the grandchild, then somebody from the [Canadian] family. He could not travel to Ternopil. So, that friend took me to Zubrets. The whole *selo* was there, everybody knew I was coming. He took me into the house. I had just sat down near the table, laden with food, when militia from Ternopil came in. And they took me back to Ternopil! I saw my grandpa for like two minutes [*crying*]. It was supposed to be Ukraïna I was to get back to. It was supposed to be Ukraïna I was to love. At that time I felt that Ukraïna was a total hate trip.

I came back to Ternopil. For three and a half hours they questioned me about what I was doing in the *selo*, frightening me. It did not matter that I had a dying grandfather! It did not make any sense to them! That was the end of that.

I came back home to Canada—and I totally shut down. I wrote no letters. I made no phone calls. And to this day I do not want to go back. Khrystyna went, my husband went to Sniatyn in Lviv. Several years ago. And he loved it! He wants desperately to go back. And I want my children to go. But I do not want to go back.[10]

Since no quantitative research has yet been conducted on diasporic homecoming among Ukrainian Canadians, I have no sociological evidence that would allow me to assess how widespread the phenomenon of homecoming is in Ukrainian Canadian society. I may only offer some limited observations on how common the homecoming was among the select group of individuals with whom I worked as a researcher. For example, for the oral history project, we recorded a total of 102 extended personal life stories with many rural and urban Ukrainian Canadians living in Alberta and Saskatchewan. Our respondents, in sociological terms, were a representative sample of the Ukrainian Canadian community at large, from all walks of life, different faith traditions, different generations, gender, and age groups. As the methodology of oral history allows for much flexibility in how to proceed with an interview, many respondents chose themselves what to reflect on, and a number touched on their understandings and connections to Ukraine, as well as on their own homecoming experiences. Fifty-four of the respondents discussed their lives while referring to Ukraine in general or to overseas kin. Of these fifty-four individuals, twenty-seven, or 26 percent, had traveled to Ukraine at least once. If, extrapolating from this statistic, we can assume that every fourth Ukrainian Canadian has traveled to his or her ethnic homeland at least once, then taking into the average size of a Canadian Ukrainian family, we may speculate that, on the average, each Ukrainian Canadian family has delegated a member to make a homecoming trip. Lara Verny's case is an excellent example of this kind of corporate, or family, "delegating."

Homecoming stories were typically shared by the travelers immediately upon their return home. In Soviet Ukraine the only means to share the experience and the know-how of hosting overseas kin would have been through private conversations in close circles of friends and relatives. In Canada, while no political control was exercised over the travelers, storytelling still was the dominant form in which the travelers shared their impressions. In my discussion of early immigrant folksongs and poems of departure and travel, I also mentioned how the initial separation that took place when an emigrant departed the village was subject to processes of vernacular folkloric narrativization. Narrativization is not just another dimension of folk culture but also an important sociocultural and at times political tool for formalizing collective memories of the past.[11] It differs from narration; to narrate means to tell of the experience; to narrativize the experience, by contrast, means to offer this experience in a narrative form that will always be associated with the experience and that will be used when the experience is brought up in conversations or in writing.

The stories of post–Second World War homecoming were exchanged in historically different times than the stories of departure, and their narrativization did not impose on these stories the same folkloric flare and form.[12] Yet narrativization still took place, framing the experiences of homecoming in such a way that the stories, rather than celebrating the longed-for reunion, became testimonies of an encounter with an alien world, an insurmountable distance, and an gaping chasm that grew with time between the two branches of once-separated kin. Because homecomers came from culturally similar backgrounds, because their experiences of homecoming in Soviet times were comparable, and because their stories were shared across many personal networks, the homecoming narratives also shared many features. Following a similar plot, describing similar itineraries, and accompanied by similar visuals (photographs), homecomers' narratives conveyed comparable perspectives on meeting overseas kin and on Ukraine more generally. As a result of this narrativization process, homecoming stories between the 1950s and the early 1990s taken as a whole can be seen as constituting a sort of metastory of the Ukrainian Canadian diasporic encounter with the homeland.

These stories firmly entered the plane of the Ukrainian Canadian everyday and came to occupy an important place in the vernacular domain of Ukrainian Canadian culture. During perestroika, when traveling to Ukraine eased and many Ukrainian Canadians began traveling there, homecoming stories also entered the creative spaces of Canadian art, film, and literature. Beginning with the last decade of the twentieth century, the artist Natalka Husar, the filmmaker John Paskievich, the writer Janice Kulyk Keefer and others, began using their own encounters with Ukraine to reflect on the difference, split, and incongruence between the diaspora and homeland Ukrainian cultures.[13] Narrativized and represented in public art, the distance between diaspora and homeland was further reinforced, continuing to serve as an axis of the diaspora-homeland binomial.

Ukrainian Canadian stories and testimonies of homecoming, shared in private conversations or in the context of the many research projects that I have documented over time, opened up a window into the intimate world of personal experiences of homeland and overseas kin and allowed me to develop some understanding of what these experiences meant to the travelers and their hosts. But it was not until I had an opportunity to undertake a homecoming trip myself, on behalf of a Ukrainian Canadian friend of mine, that I got the chance to experience homecoming from the inside.

Episode 2:
Playing the Overseas Relative

May 1996. A Ukrainian from Ukraine, who had already been living in Canada for several years at that point, I went to the town of Rozhniv, in Western Ukraine, to meet the Numaĭko family on behalf of the Paranchyches, my friends in Edmonton. Over the course of several years of helping Fred Paranchych and his family translate and write letters to his relatives in Ukraine we struck up a wonderful friendship that informed many of my intellectual pursuits during the time I was working on my doctorate thesis. In 1989, just two years prior to Ukraine's independence, Fred Paranchych, a second-generation Ukrainian Canadian and a retired executive from a large Alberta company, met the writer Fedir Pohrebennyk, a member of a cultural delegation from Ukraine. Fred learned from Fedir about a family called Numaĭko in the village of Rozhniv, Ivano-Frankivsk Oblast, who are descendants of the Paranchyches Fred knows to be his ancestors. Upon returning to Ukraine, the writer put the Canadian Paranchyches in touch with the Numaĭkos. Since then, the two families have been corresponding regularly with each other. After the two Paranchych branches lost contact in the early 1960s, about sixty letters were exchanged between the two families during the 1990s. Fred and his wife, Mary, neither of whom had ever been to Ukraine until then, were regularly updated with the help of letters, pictures, and, eventually, e-mail, on Numaĭko family developments, the weather in Rozhniv, crops, and household matters. As their friend and translator, on one of my own research trips to Ukraine, I volunteered

to pay a visit to the Numaĭkos on behalf of the Paranchyches, just a few years
before Fred himself went to Rozhniv.

On my trip to Rozhniv I was accompanied by Greg, a fellow Canadian and
a friend of the Paranchyches, who happened to be in Ukraine at the time and
was also interested in seeing Western Ukrainian countryside. Here are the entries
from the diary I kept during that trip:

Rozhniv, Ukraine, May 22, 1996

We arrived around 9 pm on Wednesday. That same night, despite the fact that
it is too late and everybody involved is too tired, we are served an improvised
yet elaborate dinner.

At the dinner table, Greg is put at the head of the table, the spot usually
reserved for the master of the household. I am placed on his right. I am a
female and so secondary, despite the fact that I am the one who has been intimately involved with the Paranchyches for three years not Greg, and they
already know this. To Greg's left sits the grandfather of the family, then the
grandmother, and then Petro, the husband of an older daughter of the grandparents and the male head of the household. To Greg's right and across from us
sit Petro's wife, the two other women in the household and the household's four
children.

First thing, three shots of vodka. First, "to our meeting." Second, "to both
families, here and there." Obviously by now, a mere couple of hours since our
arrival, Greg and I have been firmly placed in this family, as relatives. Third
shot, "to the reunion of both branches of one kin." Vodka takes care of the
initial awkwardness of our interaction. Yet the dinner conversation is highly
formulaic and pursues only one thread. Assigned the roles of the kin from
"over there," we are given an update on everybody in the local family, with a
clear subtext about "how hard life here is." For almost a decade this family has
been receiving financial assistance from the Paranchyches, a gesture on the
Paranchyches' part, matching perfectly local understandings of kinship responsibilities. To justify this support, one had to emphasize difficulty over joy and
hardship over success.[14]

Rozhniv, Ukraine, May 25, 1996

For two days the same scene has been repeated over and over. We have not
been allowed to walk on our own in the village, nor be left on our own. We were

escorted to the cemetery, to other relatives, to the market, to the churches, and so on (Greg told me that he felt like we were constantly on display). All our meals were large-scale ceremonies, whether it was breakfast, lunch or dinner, with the obligatory three shots of vodka and more to follow, several courses of calorie-heavy food, which was loaded onto our plates without our consent, the same seating arrangement, with Greg at the head of the table and almost the same toasts with some variations: to the meeting, to the families, to the reunion, with the difference that every time we were joined by other distant relatives of the Paranchyches, who would drop by to meet us. This script was played out again and again. What a dress rehearsal for the visit of the real kin!

By the third morning, it was obvious that everyone in the household was exhausted, especially the women, who could not take any time off from their regular sixteen- to eighteen-hour daily routines to take care of us, as the men could. While everybody insisted that we had to stay for at least a week and visit with them more ("We have not yet met you"), it was obvious to me and Greg that we should leave and allow this family to get back to their everyday world of crops, cattle, fields, and other pressing responsibilities. The ritual time of our encounter was running out.[15]

As I thought about this encounter later, I wondered why at first the Numaĭkos hadn't really known how to treat us. They had been visibly confused about whether to consider us self-invited guests (I had sent them a telegram before coming) or relations from abroad. After all, we weren't really the Paranchyches, the Canadian kin they had never met, but their chosen representatives. They knew me as a person who had been translating letters that had been sent back and forth between this village family and their Canadian kin for some years. Greg, a Canadian with no knowledge of Ukrainian, was also a friend of the Paranchyches. Greg's Canadianness, his obvious nonbelonging to Ukraine and to the local lifeworld, I believe, finally allowed the Numaĭkos to adopt a particular perspective on our presence, and to place us, by stretching their idea of the diasporic other, into a category of overseas kin. Once this was achieved, the encounter proceeded as if following one established script.

Episode 3:
Enjoying It All

I met Anne Dobry in Mundare in 2001, when I was spending the summer in the area researching the local Ukrainian museum's exhibition policy.[16] Anne was sixty-five at the time of our interview. She experienced both a privately staged and publicly organized homecoming while on a trip to Ukraine in 1991 and shared with me the following story.

Mundare, Alberta, June 5, 2001

NKF: Why did you decide to go to Ukraine to visit?

AD: Because it was always fascinating me. Dad would talk about it. He would say, boy, I wish I could go and see them again. And I talked to my children. So, they surprised us with this trip. They worked hard, they collected money, and they gave the money to Bill and me to go. And Rodney. I says, "It would be nice if Read could go with us because it is a once in a lifetime thing."[17]

NKF: When did you go to Ukraine for the first time?

AD: First, in 1991. It was the only time.

NKF: Tell me more about this trip.

AD: When [. . .] we got this money for the trip, we went to Edmonton to a travel agency. I think it is called East West here in Edmonton. And they told us that there was a trip that they'd been planning for five years, a special hundredth anniversary trip. But it was all booked. And we said, "Well, find us another trip, or if somebody cancels, let us know." [. . .][18]

After a while a war broke out in Kuwait, and I says to Bill, "I wonder . . . ," because on the news they said people weren't traveling too much, so I called East West and asked whether anybody had canceled their trip to Ukraine. And he says, "One-third of the people are not going on the trip because they are scared of the war." And I says, "Why didn't you call us and let us know? We'll go whether there is war or not!" So that's how we got booked up. We were not supposed to go on this hundredth anniversary trip, the Ukrainians from Canada celebrating Ukrainians in Ukraine. It was a special tour. [. . .]

I had suitcases full of clothing for George's family and ours. One of the ladies here in Mundare, who came from Molodiia, her mother and daughter were still in the Molodiia area, so she gave us stuff, clothes. And her suitcase was very heavy, 'cause she bought like a square twelve by twelve, it is like a foam. "They have lots of mice in Ukraine," she said. The mice eat the foam, and their stomachs swallow up and they die. So she gave me two or three. Her suitcase was small, but it was so heavy. But my husband, George, says, "You agreed to take it, you carry it." So we had to pass it on to the village where her mother and daughter are.[19]

And my brother-in-law's son and his granddaughter's son came from Minsk, White Russia. He had money for them. They traveled all night until they came to the hotel, and George gave them the money. It was two or three thousand dollars.

One of the nuns here in Mundare was working and she gave me a package. "I heard you are going to Ukraine. There is a teacher in Lviv. Phone her, and she'll come and pick up the package." And I says, "Ok." And she says, "Why don't you ask what's in the package?" I says, "I don't care. You wrapped it and told me to give to her." "It is holy water and soap. I want the teacher to give this to my parents." [. . .] We gave her the parcel and told her she was supposed to take it to the nun's parents, in the village.

NKF: Tell me more about trip to your village. Did your relatives come to meet you?

AD: They came with a van they had borrowed from the village council. It was just like a van here in Canada, but rougher looking. There were seven of them, and children. [. . .]

Then we went to the village of Berkivtsi. [. . .] We stayed for three days in the village, with the Moroshaks. But the Terletskys invited us to stay with them. They asked us to come and sleep at their place. But I thought, well, we are at the Moroshaks, just two blocks away, and they've got bedding out for three days, and our suitcases are here. And they asked us to come and sleep at their house. But we didn't. I saw them every day. We went to the graveyard, we went everywhere. I just did not want to bother, but they were offended. They weren't as friendly after because we did not stay overnight at their place. Like, I didn't think it would matter so much, but it probably did. We were the first visitors in the village for years. We have not been here for seventy years.[20]

[. . .] In our village, we had a nice supper. And they served it like in a restaurant, [with] a bowl of soup, and then they brought plates of other stuff, and I says, "That's too much." [. . .] After we finished, these two ladies were singing the songs mom and dad used to sing.[21]

Anne's homecoming story, like Lara's, illustrates once again the corporate, that is, familial, nature of homecoming. The suitcases that Anne brought over to Ukraine to distribute amongst the friend's kin also illustrate the place that friends and neighbors may occupy in the lives of Ukrainian Canadians. Anne's relations with those whose gifts she took with her to Ukraine replicate the importance of *zemliaky* networks in the expanded family-like networks of

Ukrainian villages like Hrytsevolia and reconfirm the corporate nature of
Ukrainian Canadian homecomings.

"Going Back":
Ritual Spaces of Kin Encounters

Even prior to undertaking a homecoming, the public displays of nostalgia for
homeland as well as other people's stories of "going back" that circulated
within the Ukrainian Canadian community meant that the unknown and
mythical horizons of the homeland systematically erupted into Ukrainian
Canadians' everyday lifeworlds. The English phrase "going back," having no
direct Ukrainian equivalent, worked its way into Ukrainian Canadian folk
psychology, revealing the lingering diasporic nature of a well-established
Ukrainian Canadian ethnicity. Its usual meanings swing between "returning
home after a journey" and "going to an already familiar place for another
visit." In the vernacular contexts of today's prairie Ukrainian Canadians,
"going back" evokes in the minds of many people the idea of going to the
ancestral village for a visit. Understood as such, this phrase is also used across
generations, as in the case of Mary Dorosh. Born in Canada, Mary never
traveled to her old country, but when speaking of going to her parents' village
she would habitually slip into the trope of going back. This trope itself is enough
of a commonplace, circulating also in the public domain of Ukrainian Canadian
culture, as in the case, discussed in chapter 3, of the Lastiwka Choir of Saskatoon,
whose 2002 fundraising campaign was titled "Back to the Homeland." Of
course, these references to going back do not prove that all Ukrainian Canadians
share the same understanding of this trope. Still, the widespread appeal to the
idea of going back is quite remarkable.

    How did Ukrainian Canadians experience the twentieth-century home-
comings of Soviet and early post-Soviet times? Lara Verny's highly reflective
account of homecoming offers an emotional perspective on how difficult it was
to step into the real world of the imagined homeland and how challenging it
was to enter the real networks of the overseas relatives. Did her emotional
experiences of engagement and that of others—the hugs, the tears, eating,
touring the village and, if language permitted, singing the same songs and telling
stories—result in what one would call "achieved communication" between the
two groups of Ukrainians? The three stories of homecoming presented here
point to the collision of two different sets of imaginings of what "other" Ukrainians and the homeland are about. And yet the incongruence between the two
does not suggest that communication was not achieved, and that is because what

Figure 6.3. The village gathers to meet the overseas relative after a long period of absence. The first visit of Liuba S. to her home village of Hrytsevolia, 1968 (?). Courtesy of Hanna Pyvovarchuk, Hrytsevolia.

we are dealing with here is the *ritually framed* experience of "other Ukrainianness": an experience that takes place not in the time and space of everyday, not the time and space of "here and now," that is, "real" time, but in the suspended time and space of myth and ritual that Mircea Eliade calls sacred, that Victor Turner refers to as antistructure, and that Maurice Bloch conceptualizes as transcendental.[22]

Canadian kin were long viewed by their village kinsfolk in the homeland in somewhat contradictory terms. On one hand, the Canadian relatives were regarded by the villagers as an extension of their own kin, despite the fact that these relatives were born and lived outside of their local family networks. As such, these overseas relatives were seen by the locals as ongoing relations, and as "parallel kin."[23] On the other hand, and especially if the connection to the Canadian families had been lost over time, the overseas kin were seen as inhabiting the world of elsewhere, of that beyond-the-known "otherland" of diaspora. Their presence in villagers' lives was largely mythical rather than real, punctuated rather than continuous. That is why when Canadians stepped from the mythic lands of there and then into the villagers' lived world of here and now, they were met with as much ceremonial hospitality as possible, for these were truly dignitaries in the villagers' eyes, most honored guests from the unreachable outer world, who were also members of one's family (see figure 6.3).

Materialization of a relative from Canada in one's village was such an out of ordinary development that it provoked much interest among the villagers (as was the case with Liuba S. visiting the village of Hrytsevolia in 1976, the community discussed in chapter 2; see figure 6.3) and so much angst (as was the case with Lara Verny's visit to her village as described in the episode here).

At the same time, Canadian Ukrainians stepping onto the terrain of their ancestral homeland for the first time brought with them not just bags with Western goods as gifts but all the baggage of ideology and their personal imaginings of the homeland and the overseas kin. In lieu of these varied imaginings, in the second part of the twentieth century the distance between Ukrainian Canadian families and their kin in Ukraine may have been constructed in a number of ways. Yet in each instance such distance only asserted the incongruence between the two branches of a family.

This incongruence was experienced differently by the immigrants of different immigration waves, as well as by their children and grandchildren. As we have seen, Ukrainian Canadians who compiled family histories on the occasion of their centennials in Canada saw Ukraine as the land of their ancestors rather than the land of living *rodyna* (a Ukrainian word for family). Amateur genealogists, seeking deeper personal roots for themselves in the ethnic homeland, subsequently incorporated the overseas kin into their family trees. Yet during their first homecoming trips, all homecomers, no matter their background, age, and political views, experienced distance and cultural incongruence between the two worlds and two family networks.

Thus, when coming into contact, in order to reach the other Ukrainians through the layers of their own imaginings of who these diasporic others are and in order to enter the nearly mythical landscapes of the old country, the two groups have to first resort to *ritual* interaction. My visit to Rozhniv on behalf of Fred and his Canadian family—which I thought would be just a casual get-together—turned out to be a fully staged ceremonial hosting of the overseas kin. Assigning Greg and myself the status of the overseas relatives helped our hosts to gain better control over an otherwise unclear, socially muddy, and culturally unruly situation. They thus gave us a highly ceremonial reception, which local ideas about overseas kin and hospitality dictated was the best (and only) way to welcome overseas relations. The framework of the ritual, which assigned particular ceremonial roles to all participants, provided both sides with a template for relating to each other in a face-to-face interaction and thus enabled initial communication between the two branches of what used to be a single family. As a result, while experiencing this overwhelming hospitality (which is universally cited in interviews and private conversations among the Ukrainian Canadians), first-time visitors do not normally interact with their hosts within the time-space of their mundane everyday life. The everyday world of routine chores and joys is abandoned for the world of the ritual. Both groups' interaction is also "diagnostic" in the sense that their interaction speaks to and of the ongoing un(der)realized diaspora-homeland genealogical connectedness, which likewise is not experienced at the level of the mundane. Rather, ritual is summoned up to mediate the two different planes of people's lives, that of mundane daily existence of the here and now, on the one hand, and that of the unresolved longing for kin and homeland that have been lost in space and time, on the other. Lara Verny's homecoming failed in part because both she and her homeland relatives were denied an opportunity to enact this ritual where it had to be enacted, in the village, among the kin, by a table laden with food. Had she been given this opportunity, Lara may have come back with different memories, perhaps, more along the lines of Anne Dobry's, whose homecoming followed the script.

It is not by chance that the visits to the villages last only a few days, for like any ritual, the ritual of homecoming has its own prescribed time frame. Mary Ellen P., a third-generation Ukrainian American in her forties, cut her two-week stay to a three-day visit in 1998.[24] Vera A., a first-generation Ukrainian American in her fifties, shortened her seven-day preplanned visit to a two-day stay in the early 1990s.[25] Three days seem to be the limit; after that, both sides begin to exhaust the resources that allow them to relate to each other in ritual time and space and are ready to shift back to their usual, "normal," that is, long-distance, way of relating, through letter writing, sending money and parcels to the village, sharing stories about the old country, and falling back into familiar patterns of expressing private nostalgia and public longings for the homeland. What appears to be the "real" time and "real" space of a diaspora-homeland family encounter turns out to be constructed in the symbolic and ritual terms of homecoming. Real homecomings for many took place upon their return to Canada.

Did the diaspora and homeland Ukrainians find a path toward each other through the thickness of ritual acting? Did such ritual engagements indicate an "achieved communication" between the two groups? When I asked Anne whether she had had a chance, while on her tour of Ukraine, to communicate, meet, and talk with Ukrainians other than her kin, her immediate response was, "Oh yeah, I had pins and candies and stuff. Everybody got something. I distributed them to the little kids and the bigger kids too."[26] In Anne's case, communicating, dealing with the locals, perhaps meant distributing tokens of the Canadian world rather than engaging with real people here. Acting out of a culturally prescribed understanding of kindness and partially out of a diaspora-cultivated image of Ukrainians as "poorer brothers and sisters," Anne was offended when confronted by a local man who challenged her way of seeing the locals as needy. She told me that she quickly collected herself: "I felt upset, I felt, I was giving you things for free, like toothbrushes and other things, why are you so rude? [. . .] And then I thought, they are poor, why should I get upset?"[27] The story of Lara Verny speaks for itself and serves as a striking example of communication failure on many levels. Lara is a highly reflective individual, and she herself provided some answers to the question of why the encounter was such a failure when it came down to such primary tasks as re-establishing contact with her grandparents. Her village relatives were outside their home terrain and therefore were constrained in how they could relate to Lara, and Lara herself was triply displaced, young and fully inexperienced in transatlantic kinship relations.

True communication—with real human beings reaching out to each other, seeking each other's identities, and understanding each other's views of the world and themselves—was very hard to achieve during initial homecoming visits because it is difficult to access real individuals behind the prescribed ritual roles of "local hosts" and "foreign visitors from the unknown world." Not all participants were even trying to accomplish this. In Rozhniv as a replica relative, I found it hard to go beyond the busyness of the ritual; there was already so much to be done, all the actors were busy performing the prescribed roles and tasks, partaking in elaborate meals, talking about families and family business, meeting numerous relatives and partaking in dinners organized by them, looking over the photos, going to the graveyards, and so on. I just remained a fictive relative, since I also felt I had a duty to report about this visit back in Canada. Prescribed by the ritual structure, all these activities and corresponding behaviors exerted a strong hold on the other participants. The communication was between actors rather than between individuals.

Paradoxically, many Ukrainian Canadians felt that communication during the first homecoming was achieved because the local relatives first of all represent a genealogical link to their shared ancestors, and oftentimes this is the most important connection that a diasporic pilgrim seeks to make. For many Ukrainian Canadians, their overseas village kin were abstract and distant figures in their genealogies in the first place—great-aunt, third cousin, great-grandfather, second niece—whose real personalities did not surface in letters. First visits to the village usually confirmed their established view of their relatives as merely relations while also providing an opportunity to meet the "others" face to face, albeit in the framework of ritual. It could be that during subsequent visits to home villages and towns the grip of ritual would give way to the interaction of real individuals within the "real" time and space of "here and now." Angie, a former student of mine, a third-generation Ukrainian Canadian from Saskatoon in her mid-twenties, told me after spending a year in Ukraine and visiting her ancestral village on many occasions, "I just loved it there. Loved them all. They were so, so great. I've got to *know* them. I could go there anytime."

Episode 4:
From Private to Public Homecomings, the View from Ukraine

Along with the personal homecomings that took place in the postwar period, on several occasions the organized diaspora, namely its socialist camp, which was on friendly terms with the Soviet governments in Kyiv and Moscow, organized a few official homecoming visits to Ukraine for select dignitaries from the socialist wing of the Ukrainian Canadian community. Unlike private village homecomings, these official diaspora-homeland encounters on the homeland's territory were publicized in the Soviet Ukrainian media and in socialist Ukrainian Canadian public discourse.[28]

During the summer of 2002 I spent four days in the village of Nebyliw, Ivano-Frankivsk Oblast, to record local stories about various government-sponsored homecoming tours from Canada that were brought into this village by officials from Kyiv. Nebyliw is firmly engraved in the Ukrainian Canadian mythic landscape as the home of the first officially recognized immigrants from Ukraine to Canada. In public discourse it is often assumed to be the community where "it all began." Therefore, the name of the village is known to many Ukrainian Canadians who are active participants in Ukrainian Canadian public life. After the Second World War, several delegations from the prosocialist camp of the Ukrainian Canadian community visited the community. Olha Velychko, the great-granddaughter of one of the first "official" immigrants to Canada and at one time head of the village council, was chosen on several such occasions to be a "poster girl," appointed, in 1966, for example, to ceremonially greet and accompany an esteemed overseas guest (figure 6.4). In an interview, she described to me her experiences with these homecomings.

Figure 6.4. Olha Velychko, an appointed representative of the village, welcomes Vasyl' Pylypiw, a descendant of the "first" immigrant to Canada in 1891 from Nebyliw, 1966. Courtesy of Olha Velychko, Nebyliw.

NKF: When did the Ukrainians from Canada and the U.S. start coming to visit?

OV: No one could come and visit us here. We were a closed zone. Completely. No one could come. When Hanna Tatarchuk came once to Lviv, it was some time in 1975 or 1976, and we had to take her *kradky* [clandestinely], so no one would see that we were taking her to the village, putting her on the bus, risking our own skin, as the saying goes, bringing her to the village so she could see it for herself. She was born here, in 1907, and when she left for Canada she was a sixteen-year-old girl. Of course she wanted to come.

When that Vasyl' came from Canada to Nebyliw, our collective farm organized a large-scale *hostyna* [reception] for him.[29] The head of the collective farm and the local head of the Communist Party were there. So it was quite a representative *hostyna* for Vasyl'. That old man came, the village met him with salt and bread, as it is supposed to be, you know. The whole village came out to meet Vasyl'. I was to walk along with the old man through the streets, and I felt so important, you know how it is! It was the best *hostyna* ever. They put so much on the tables, the way Ukrainians do.

You know how it is. You have to put so much on the table, no matter where all this (uneaten) food will be going afterward.

NKF: That's how you received him in 1966, right?

OV: That old man lived at my place. For three days! And those other misters went to the mountains to rest. They gave me a car so I could take the old man around, wherever he needed to go. Who had cars at that time? Nobody! So I had to drive the old man around, from one relative to another. And what about those relatives? When they learned that the old man had no gifts to distribute, they lost interest in hosting him. Why wouldn't they?[30]

NKF: So that was the first time someone from Canada came to the village, right?

OV: Yes, the first time, and then no one came for a long time. Only when those official delegations came with Krawchuk, for example. But other than that, no one could travel.[31]

NKF: So the villagers would go to (Ivano-)Frankivsk to pick up their Canadian relatives to bring them to the village, clandestinely, right?

OV: Rather to Lviv. I went three or four times to meet people there, when Anna Tatarchuk came, for example. Others went to meet their family in hotels as well.[32]

As this exchange suggests, official Ukrainian Canadian homecomings to Soviet Ukraine borrowed extensively from the set of practices developed within the framework of private rituals of homecoming. There is a trip to the village, there is a table laden with food, there are gifts delivered, there are "brothers" and "sisters" from both sides of the Atlantic present, there is walking around the village with many gawkers on the street. But such a public homecoming ritual is imposed on the locals rather than staged by them on their own initiative. That is why the distant relatives of Vasyl' were unexcited to host him, as it was not their celebration but those of the officials. In public discursive terms, not just select left-wing Ukrainian Canadian officials but the entire diaspora paid a visit to the village that gave the diaspora its first members. As in private rituals of homecoming, in the context of public rituals, the two parties, not being directly related, ended up being even further distanced from each other. Olha Velychko's skeptical tone while describing the visitors highlights this distance quite powerfully.

In July 1991, right before the Soviet Union collapsed, the same leftist political leaders from the Ukrainian Canadian community (from Tovarystvo Obiednanykh Ukraïntsiv Kanady [TOUK], under the leadership of Petro Krawchuk), together with the Soviet authorities, staged a large-scale ritual of homecoming to celebrate the one-hundredth anniversary of Ukrainian immigration to Canada.[33] The event, planned while Ukraine was still a part of the Soviet Union, took place just weeks before Ukraine's parliament proclaimed its independence from the USSR. Organized by the Association of the United Ukrainian Canadians together with the Ukraine Society, the 159 participants on this tour, one of whom was Anne Dobry, who were from all parts of Canada and of all ages, traveled for four weeks from one community to another. As one of the reports written upon the completion of the tour describes it,

> It was a historic journey of Ukrainian Canadians, to pay tribute to the land of their ancestry, Ukraine, and to visit the Precarpathian village of Nebyliw, whose first two Ukrainian émigrés opened the door for further Ukrainian immigration to Canada. The tour participants were offered three itineraries. Two groups chose to visit the western regions of Ukraine, which included Lviv, Ternopil, Ivano Frankivsk, and Chernivtsi. The third, the "Peace Group," visited Moscow, Leningrad, and the Baltic Republics.
>
> After these tours, made by bus, the tour participants gathered in Kyiv where they boarded a ship to travel down the Dnieper River to Odessa and return. This eleven-day trip included stops and excursions to the main cities and historic centers along the route, with meetings and ceremonies with the local population. In Kaniv, the tour participants visited the grave of Taras Shevchenko on Chernechev [sic] Hill, a beautiful spot above the Dnieper, where they placed wreaths and flowers at the monument of the great poet. Throughout the whole tour, the passengers were entertained with a cultural program offered by professional artists who traveled along with them as well as by local choral and orchestral groups, who boarded the ship during stopovers.
>
> A memorable highlight for the two groups touring Western Ukraine was the visit to the village of Nebyliw, from where Ivan Pylypiw and Vasyl' Eleniak began the mass emigration of Ukrainians to Canada [see figure 6.5]. A fine monument to their memory has been erected in the village, and it was around this monument in the village center that the ceremonial visit of the Canadian tour groups and the villagers was held. Flowers were placed at the foot of the monument, as the visiting groups offered greetings and the local populace gave them a welcome. The ceremonies ended with a concert program provided by local talent.[34]

The centennial homecoming as organized by the Soviet authorities and TOUK was designed to serve the same purpose as other official, past government-sponsored homecomings, namely, to assert century-old brotherhood between

Figure 6.5. Petro Krawchuk, the leader of prosocialist Ukrainian Canadians, is welcomed to Nebyliw during the official homecoming tour, 1991. Courtesy of Anne Dobry, Mundare.

the diaspora and Soviet Ukrainians, who otherwise, in the context of their everyday lives, hardly knew each other. The ritual drama of homecoming, at times grotesque, was played out in every community the participants visited, accompanied by the obligatory Ukrainian ritual of welcoming with bread and salt, staged speeches, and concerts. The tour participants, who were not necessarily political like the organizers of the homecoming tour, whose roots were in Ukraine's west and whose beliefs in a free Ukraine aligned with pronationalist aspirations, also visited central and southern Ukrainian communities while cruising the Dnieper on a ship, ironically, named after Lenin (see figure 6.6). In terms of engaging with each other, this was once again a ritual of "passing the 'other Ukrainians' by," for the encounters between the diasporans and the locals were staged at every moment of the tour. In fact, in his memoir, Krawchuk repeatedly states that local regional authorities ruined the plan to just celebrate the centennial of emigration to Canada and not engage into any discussions of imminent political changes in Ukraine by criticizing Soviet rule in Ukraine.[35]

In their attempts to bring diaspora and homeland together, to reunite the two branches of the family into one transnational Ukrainian family, the tour organizers arranged for two small boxes of soil, taken from the graves of the

Figure 6.6. Traditional bread and salt welcome, Kyiv, 1991. Notice the name of the cruise ship *Lenin* that housed and transported the visiting Ukrainians along the Dnieper River. Courtesy of Anne Dobry, Mundare.

two official "first" immigrants buried in Alberta, to be brought back to Nebyliw. One of these boxes was presented by Petro Krawchuk. On July 7, Krawchuk passed on to the villagers the earth from the grave of Ivan Pylypiw. A few days later, another group of touring Canadian homecomers would arrive in the village, and another leader, Nick Hrynchyshyn, would present the village with earth from the grave of Vasyl' Eleniak.[36]

Twelve years later, the boxes with the soil were still sitting behind the class door of one of the classroom cabinets in Nebyliw secondary school, in the classroom transformed into a mini museum created to commemorate the diaspora Ukrainians who left Nebyliw for work and life overseas (figure 6.7). Bringing the soil from the graves of beloved ones who are buried outside of home back to their home community is a common practice among Ukrainians. Another common practice is spreading the soil around in the field one worked, by the river one grew up on, in the graveyard one's family is buried in, in the yard of the church one attended, and so on. In any case, the soil from the grave elsewhere is to be returned to nature, to be put back in the earth from whence it came, in some ways replicating the established practice of the burial itself and concluding the cycle of life. What comes from the earth goes to the earth, and what leaves home returns home.

Figure 6.7. Boxes containing soil from the Canadian graves of Vasyl' Eleniak and Ivan Pylypiw, the "first" Ukrainian immigrants. Nebyliw Public School, Nebyliw, 2003. Photo by author.

This brings me back to the act of initial diasporic departure, so well documented and monumentalized in the early immigrant songs and so well forgotten in Ukrainian Canadian official discourse. Within the framework of folk psychology, acts of departing, leaving, emigrating, and exiling are expected to be matched by some kind of returning. The bringing of the soil from the graves of the first immigrants back to their home village in fact is a symbolic attempt at diasporic return, an attempt undertaken by the officials representing the diaspora at large. Has this metaphorical homecoming been accomplished? Is the ideal diasporic itinerary completed with the act of return? Represented by the containers of soil from the Canadian graves, did the diaspora and its eternal wanderers, as the early immigrants were represented in the early emigrant folklore, return home? Has the separation constraint been overcome in the context of the diaspora-homeland hundred years of disconnection?

The grave soil that has been brought home would ideally be returned to the earth, not placed on a shelf behind the glass door of a museum cabinet. My own encounter with these two boxes back in 2002, eleven years since they had been put behind that glass door, was unsettling, reminiscent of my trip at the age of twelve to Lenin's mausoleum, where the embalmed and deteriorating body of the Soviet leader who died in 1924 was publicly displayed for mass consumption. The nonreturn of the grave soil, that physical evidence of the Ukrainian diasporic other in Canada like a nonreturn of a body to the ground, violates the space and time of its own ritual as well as the folk psychology that insists on bringing that ritual to completion.

The boxes with soil from the Canadian graves of the first Ukrainian immigrants from Nebyliw, themselves the arrivees from the "world beyond the known," the Ukrainian otherland of the diaspora, and their entrapment in the time and space of a real journey they were on speaks poignantly of incompletability of the diasporic return and of the importance of ritual when it comes to homecoming. Together with stories of homecoming, the fate of the grave soil conveys the challenges of real-time communication with the diasporic other and confirms that no diasporic homecoming will ever complete the eternal emigrant journey. Ordinary Ukrainians with lost and found kin overseas will continue facing, and dealing with, the separation constraint that has characterized their relationship with their own other Ukrainians over the last hundred years.

That most diaspora-homeland encounters have been unfolding within the mythical domain of ritual space and time, where little real communication takes place, only extends the diasporic dimension of today's Ukrainian ethnicity. With the Soviet regime in Ukraine, though, the diasporic dimension of Ukrainian Canadian ethnicity had certainly been subjected to a new test. By and large, the collapse of the USSR opened up new avenues for the mutual rediscovery of the century-old Ukrainian diasporic other. So did the invention of the internet, email, Skype, and other wonders of communication technology. Profound geopolitical change and the accelerated technological revolution of the last two decades might have been expected to shorten the distance between the old diaspora and the homeland and to shatter old conceptions of the other. And ultimately, these changes offered an opportunity for many people on both sides of the binomial to do this. The twist is that with the collapse of the USSR and Ukraine entering the uncertain and untested road of postsocialist transition, its citizens began leaving the country again en masse, as legal and illegal migrants, in search of work, cash, and a better life. With millions of Ukrainians living and working outside of Ukraine first as migrants and then as emigrants, the separation constraint has reemerged in Ukrainian culture, and the diaspora-homeland binomial has once again come into the spotlight. Let's turn to these new diasporic contexts to see what means are being utilized by the new diasporas to sustain their connection with the homeland.

Figure 7.1. Ukrainian poet Oksana Sikora-Hayda getting ready for a public dance performance, Lisbon, 2012. Photo by Viktor Hnatiuk. Courtesy of Oksana Sikora-Hayda.

7

///////////////////////////////////

Into the Twenty-First Century

Son

S'ohodni mama u miĭ son pryĭshla
Tykhen'ko sila na kraiu posteli.
Dyvuius': v Portuhaliï znaĭshla,
U desheven'kim nomeri hoteliu.
—A ty dytyno, na kraiu zemli,
Chohos' shukaiesh u dvori chuzhomu?
—A nenandovho mamo, po zymi
Planuiu povernutysia dodomu
[. . .]
—Ne zhal' meni, shcho ty zreklas' ideĭ
Lyshyla vsikh, koho ty liubysh, znaiesh.
Ta zhal', shcho tam, sered chuzhykh liudeĭ,
Pisen' svoïkh ty zovsim ne spivaiesh.

—Meni tut, spravdi, ne do spivanok
Nema koly: robota i robota.
—Sered tvoïkh zhyttievykh storinok
Tsia—mala buty. Shchob piznaty,
Khto ty.

Dream

Today my mother came into my dream
And quietly sat on my bed's edge.
I am surprised: how did she ever find me
In Portugal, in a cheap hotel room.
—My child, at the edge of the world,
What are you searching for in someone else's yard?
—Mother, I am not here for long.
When winter comes, I will be heading home.
[. . .]

185

—It doesn't worry me that you betrayed your dreams
And left all those who you loved and cared for behind.
What worries me that there, among the strangers,
You never sing your own songs anymore.

—Indeed, the songs have left me, as
I have not time to sing: I work and work.
—Among your various life paths,
This one had to happen, so you could learn yourself
Who you really are.[1]

June 17, 2006. Ternopil–Halych Road. My friend Bohdan Struk and I are traveling in his car to the town of Halych, where I am about to interview an acquaintance of his who recently returned from Italy after working there as an illegal migrant for a few years. Since 2003, as director of the study abroad semester in Ukraine that my college runs, I have spent three months a year in Western Ukraine, first in Lviv, and as of 2005, in Ternopil where our program is now based. My prolonged trips to the region and my teaching have brought me to a variety of locations in Western Ukraine where my students and I pursue our studies, meet and work with local people, and experience the country and its people in a most intimate way. By spending three months a year in the Ternopil region, the most Ukrainian part of Ukraine, as the locals like to say, and sharing the life of my local colleagues who have become close friends, I got the chance to personally experience the depth and strength of the diasporic dimension of local Ukrainian culture—and recently, its new meanings.

Bohdan and I just crossed the city boundary, having gone through one area of Ternopil known locally as Kanada. I am reminded of many chats I eavesdropped on while waiting for the bus, shopping at the market, or sharing a meal in the university cafeteria with my colleagues, along the lines of "'Where did you disappear to last night?' 'I was in Kanada, went there to visit my aunt,'" or, "'Where does this bus go?' 'To the market first, and then to Kanada.'" If New Yorkers live in Harlem, the East Village, or the Upper West Side, Ternopolians live in BAM, Alaska, and Kanada, the names of these neighborhoods attesting to the great sense of humor and global citizenship the Ternopolians share.[2]

Young locals may not even know why one of their city districts, built in Soviet times, is nicknamed Kanada. Indistinguishable in many ways from other Soviet urban *mikroraĭons*, it is just another typical midrise neighborhood, with five-story and nine-story apartment buildings dotting the terrain. But as old-timers tell, the area acquired its name because in the 1970s when the neighborhood was being developed, Soviet authorities, to ease the well-known Soviet housing shortage, began to let citizens put their personal savings toward the construction of new cooperative apartments. Personal savings for many in this region came from the parcels that were sent to the local relatives from Canada. And so it went, Kanada got built on the remittances that the Canadian overseas kin had been sending to many locals, with *khustky*/headscarves being the main cash voucher among other items in the parcels.[3]

I smile to myself as we pass Kanada, reminded of another incident in Hrytsevolia when in 1998 on my first day in the village, walking the sandy village road, I stumbled on a lonely pink price tag in English, a foreign vessel casually floating in the sandy waves of the village road, which I immediately recognized as coming from Value Village, a popular chain of secondhand stores in Canada.[4] The pink piece of paper, having been taken off an item of clothing that must have recently arrived in a parcel from Canada to a local family, was a powerful reminder of how the diasporic world erupts into the local everyday and of how, like the letters and parcels, regular and well-punctuated these eruptions have been, arriving regularly, even back in Soviet times, in Western Ukraine, once or twice a year, just in time for Easter or Christmas. The diasporic dimension is so entrenched in the local culture of many villages here that at times what used to be of diasporic origin, has become a local cultural feature. As is the case with *kanada*, a dance performed to the *kolomyika* song "Heĭ Hop Kanada" ("Numo khloptsi ne sydimo, ta ĭ Kanadu zavodimo / Heĭ Hop Kanada / starykh bab ne nado / molodykh davajte / a vy khloptsi hraĭte") a traditional local dance, very popular at local weddings, despite the reference to the country of Canada.[5]

We left the city. Bohdan turns the CD player on and the sounds of *kolomyika* immediately take over our conversation, filling up the car with their cheerful beat:

> Vsia rodyna za kordonom hroshi zaroblieie.
> Tsiotka kohos' dohliadaie, vuĭko vikna myie.
> A dva brata akrobata to zhe se spravuiut'
> Des' u Rymi, v Italiï kolizeĭ buduiut'.

> Za kordon, za kordon, pisen'ka khaĭ lyne.
> Za kordon, za kordon, z ridnoiï Vkraïny.
> Nashi sestry ta ĭ braty, vy tam ne skuchaĭte.
> Neĭ na svieta velykodni dodomu vertaĭte!

> [...]
> Z Portuhaliy ĭdut', z Chekhiv, ta azh do Londonu,

Vsiudy chuty u nediliu ukraïns'ku movu,
Bo na ts'omu bilim sviti ie nashoho brata,
Pryïzhdzhaïte het' domiv, vas chekaie khata.[6]

All the family's abroad, all are making money.
Auntie's looking after someone, uncle washes windows.
And two brothers, the two jokers, they are always plotting,
Building the Coliseum in Italy, somewhere in Rome.

Go abroad, go abroad, let my song fly there.
Go abroad, go abroad, from our native Ukraine.
Our brothers and our sisters, don't feel very lonely.
Come back home for a visit during Easter holidays.

[...]
They arrive from Portugal, the Czech Republic, and even from London.
One can hear the Ukrainian language everywhere.
In this world, as it happens, there are so many of our people.
Hey you all, do come home, your old house is waiting for you.

The upbeat rhythms of *kolomyika* are recognizable immediately; after all, *kolomyika* constitutes one of the most impressive achievements of the Ukrainian folk music culture here in Western Ukraine. Its popularity never ebbed even in Soviet times, attesting to the vitality of this folk tradition in this part of Ukraine. It is also one of the most lively genres of Ukrainian folklore, as its music and beat lend themselves wonderfully to dancing and singing, and many local *kolomyika* songs are still composed and sung at village weddings, family gatherings, and other get-togethers. They are especially known for their humorous and satirical qualities, and the *kolomyika* we are listening to right now in the car is no exception:

Mis'ko ïkhav za hranytsiu—vizy pidlyvaly
Shtyry dni, shtyry nochi ïoho provodzhaly.
Zakololy patsiuka ta shche dva telieta
Dovho bude Mis'ko nash to vse vidrobliety

A Marusia na paneli tiezhko kypyruie
A dodomu pyshe vsim zhe vona shchos' buduie.
A Petro ie rakod'orom, khto ïoho ne znaie.
Khloptsi hroshi zarobliaiut' a vin zabyraie.

Mike was going abroad—marking the occasion,
People were feasting for four days and four nights.

A boar and two calves were slaughtered—
It would take Mike a while to pay them back for the feast.

And Marusia on the streets is working very hard,
Writing home that she is doing some construction work.
Our Petro is a racketeer, everybody knows that.
The boys are making money, and he is robbing them later.

This song mocking the experiences of "ours abroad" had been following me around before on this trip, loudly broadcasted at the city market, played in music kiosks around the city, in public transit or in people's cars and homes. I am thrilled to find out that Bohdan owns a CD that has it and to learn that Vasyl' Mel'nykovych, the songwriter and singer, like many other local singers and writers, has written other *kolomyikas* whose subject is the most far-reaching current social development in post-Soviet Ukraine, mass labor migration abroad.

The collapse of the USSR brought about major changes in the lives of people once populating Soviet Ukraine, soon resulting in the emigration of many Ukrainians, who began leaving their home en masse in search of work, very much like their predecessors had hundred years before. These changes, which affected individuals in their immediate lifeworlds, stemmed from the collapse of the central economy and central government, leaving many citizens economically disoriented, without work, income, or prospects for a stable future. Whatever the uneasy transition from socialism to postsocialism that generated so much debate in social sciences in the 1990s came to mean in various contexts, in practical terms it led to many departures in the lives of many individuals and families.[7] Ordinary Ukrainians once again have found themselves split into distinct social entities, those at home and those who have recently gone abroad. Despite living in a very different technological environment from their ancestors, one with the potential to minimize separation, shorten distances between people, and compress time and space, they have nevertheless been called on to draw on their cultural reserves, folk psychology, and vernacular creativity to deal with the newly imposed separation constraint in their families and communities.

Though many Ukrainians were given an opportunity to travel abroad even in the late 1980s, before the official dissolution of the USSR, the large-scale migration of Ukrainians heading west in search for labor began to take shape in the mid-1990s, against the background of the deteriorating economy, food shortages, fast-growing inflation, and the decollectivization of agricultural collectives in the villages. Labor migrants' destinations ranged from near- to far-abroad, from former socialist countries to the European Union, the Middle East, North America, and beyond. In the early 2010s, for example, there were about 1.3 million Ukrainian nationals working in Russia, about 168,000 in Poland, some 191,000 in Italy, around 51,000 in Portugal, about 77,000 in Spain, some 20,000 in Turkey, and 20,000 in the United States.[8]

And it so happened that at the turn of the twenty-first century, popular culture in Western Ukraine, like the songs of Vasyl' Mel'nykovych, once again turned to the theme of emigration, very much like the folk culture of the early twentieth century had, when Ukrainian people were emigrating en masse over the ocean first to South America and then to North America. Once again songs, poetry, storytelling, anecdotes, all these vernacular means of self-maintenance and communication, helped people share their experiences of living and working abroad as legal and oftentimes illegal labor migrants.

Tamara Moroshan's beautifully crafted poem that opens up this chapter effectively gives voice to the primacy of song (of native song and the poetic word) in the lives of many Ukrainians, insisting through the words of the deceased mother of a labor migrant that a person shall never abandon the song even if one has to leave behind the loved ones and home. This chapter highlights exactly this relationship between the time of rupture and vernacular creativity, between the trauma of separation and the self-expression that draws on traditional practices. More specifically, I focus here on the role and place that the "native" or vernacular song, and specifically its companion, vernacular poetry, play in the lives of those Ukrainians who have found themselves working illegally abroad and thus subject to the diaspora-homeland separation and split.

My discussion here begins with the general overview of the phenomenon of vernacular reflectivity on Ukrainian labor migration as it emerged first in Ukraine at the turn of the twenty-first century. I proceed to outline the general parameters of this vernacular creativity as it has evolved into a powerful stream in the domain of Ukrainian popular culture. Given the prominence of poetic representations of labor migration within this stream of vernacular creativity, I turn here to an exploration of migrant poetry writing. Following the poems, the poets, and their stories in Portugal and Italy, I describe the nature of Ukrainian migrant poetry writing at the turn of the twenty-first century and analyze the relationship between the poetic and the diasporic, the vernacular and the modern, asserting that poetry is more than just rhymed words, that poetry and poetry writing is about action and agency. I also return to the question of how this poetry creates a new divide between the two groups of Ukrainians, the homelanders and those in the diaspora, and how ultimately this poetry revives and serves the diasporic binomial in the Ukrainian culture.

Vernacular Reflections on Labor Migration

Scholarly and political accounts of contemporary migration from Ukraine began to appear in Ukraine at the very beginning of the twenty-first century, lagging some five to ten years behind the phenomenon of labor migration itself.[9] In the early 2000s, in their efforts to document the phenomenon, scholars wrote about migrants' absence from the Ukrainian society, the loss of an electorate, the loss of a labor force, the absentee parents.[10] As migration continued, a steady public discourse on labor migration and its political, cultural and economic outcomes for Ukrainian society emerged. These extensive academic and political debates on labor migration were preceded and informed by earlier reflections on the migration, shared in the regions within smaller social networks as conversations, stories, anecdotes, litanies, and so on.

With labor migration gaining momentum in the mid-1990s, family stories about being separated from kin, the problems and dilemmas of the migrants, and the pros and cons of laboring abroad began circulating widely within communities and family networks in Western Ukraine. By the late 1990s, these personal stories, initially limited to networks of family and friends, began reaching larger audiences when out-migration reached exponential levels. Local media fully committed itself to exploring the life of "ours abroad." The publications concerning labor migrants in Europe and elsewhere appeared in numerous media as warning tales about the dangers of working abroad, personal diaries, letters written to the family, ordeal tales, recommendations how to succeed abroad, and philosophical reflections on the experiences of migrants abroad.[11] Re-created at the intersection of both traditional and modern conceptions of the world, this new lore has been quietly, and for a while without much critical evaluation, imposing on people qualitatively new ideas about diasporic split and separation.

It took nearly a decade for labor migration creative writing to emerge as a new strong current in Ukrainian popular culture. In the early 2000s, when I decided to explore the vernacular creative culture of the new diasporas in Europe, I knew that I was seeing the early trickles of what would soon become a strong pulsating current in the domain of the Ukrainian popular culture.[12] Locating early examples of migrant's creative writing was no easy task, though, as most texts were self-published or printed by small publishing houses in small quantities without ISBN numbers, creating a challenge for the collector. Throughout the 2000s, during six summers that I was based in Ukraine, I traveled widely throughout the country, especially its west, gathering popular writing and interviewing villagers, town folks, writers, poets, and theater directors on the topic of contemporary labor migration. I traveled to Italy once with the migrants, some legal and some illegal, on the minibus from Ternopil to Rome. In Italy and later in Portugal, I continued my search for Ukrainian migrants' creative writing, interviewing poets, clergy, and newspaper publishers and editors, participating in local Ukrainian Italian or Ukrainian Portuguese events, and overall sharing the experience of being in a new diaspora. Recently, locating such texts has become easier, as bibliographical information for book-length publications have begun to appear on the internet.

Drawing on my research, recently I produced an annotated bibliography of this literature and offered a critical and statistical analysis of it. This work, to my knowledge, is the first of its kind, as creative writing about labor migration has not triggered much interest among cultural studies specialists, anthropologists, sociologists, and the like. My own work in this direction, I hope, will open up new avenues of research into this new cultural phenomenon.[13] Let me now consider briefly the overall parameters of this phenomenon and then move on to discuss the place of poetry within it.

Labor Migration Creative Writing:
The Scope of the Phenomenon

Interested in overall representations of labor migration in contemporary popular culture of Ukraine, I began collecting literary works with the focus on labor migration in 2003.[14] Because creative writing on labor migration can be found in a variety of media, I focused in my search on identifying full-length published or self-published books, whether single author or edited. Furthermore, I looked at the books that were either solely focused on the phenomenon of labor migration or that profiled this phenomenon as a constitutive and integral dimension of the book's narrative. In the bibliography I compiled, I include works authored by established writers, by newly emerging writers, by labor migrants themselves, and by those who never directly experienced the world of *zarobitchanstvo*.[15] In the course of my research, I discovered subcategories, such as books that explore the theme of "ours abroad" whose protagonists are not labor migrants in the strict sense of the word but who also face difficulties in adjusting to their new countries of residence. I exclude these books from the labor migration bibliography proper, though I list them under a separate category. While trying to sort through the literature, I relied on the category of topic as a principal characteristic according to which the books were either included or excluded from the final list.

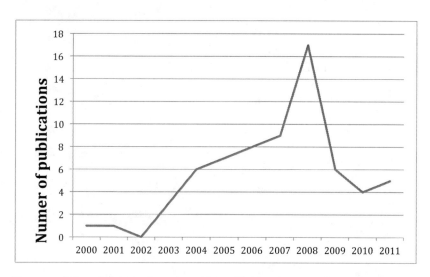

Figure 7.2. Labor migration and creative writing publications by year. Eight publications in the bibliography are listed without the year of publication and are not included in this figure.

The bibliography consists of eighty-two entries written in a variety of literary genres (seventy-six of which focus on labor migration strictly defined; see figure 7.2).[16] The earliest publications date to 2000, and the peak was 2008, when eighteen books were published. The overwhelming majority of the authors are women (eighty-six out of ninety-six authors total).[17]

Another point I would like to raise here concerns the geographic focus of literary reflections on labor migration. A somewhat expected outcome of the statistical analysis is distribution by region in Ukraine. Fifty percent of all books in the bibliography were published in Lviv, Ternopil, and Ivano-Frankivsk (see figure 7.3).

As far as migrants' destinations are concerned, the books I found focus exclusively on labor migration in Europe and North America. I have failed to find thus far texts that look at *zarobitchanstvo* outside of these two large geographic domains. Interestingly, even acknowledging that the current bibliography misses perhaps another 15–25 percent of what has been published (sources that I could not identify or access), the life of labor migrants in Italy receives the most attention among the books I looked at.

Ukrainian labor migration literature recently ceased to be a monolingual phenomenon. Since 2006, a small number of publications have appeared in Russian and Italian, in addition to Ukrainian. As the number of such publications is

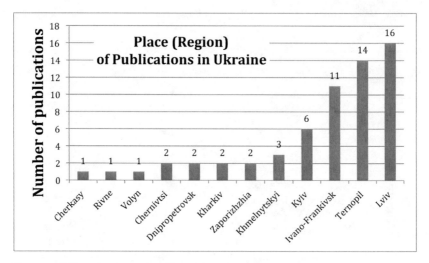

Figure 7.3. Labor migration and creative writing publications by region within Ukraine.

quite small to date, however, we can conclude at this point that labor migration, as well as the creative writing about it, remains a "very Ukrainian" phenomena.

All in all, vernacular creative writing on labor migration from Ukraine has been expanding as cultural phenomenon. It would be nearly impossible to assess the scope of this phenomenon, as it unfolds in many media. And while it is logical to assume that such vernacular reflectivity, having first appeared in various local media, predates the full-length books I have identified, focusing on these full-length book publications offers the researcher an opportunity to statistically profile the phenomenon of labor migration creative writing. Focusing on book-length publications allows one to appreciate the depth of this phenomenon and how widespread it is as well as to grasp the chronological parameters of creative writing now circulating in print.

While working on this project, I also continued on with my field research among the communities and people who were the purveyors and producers of these vernacular representations of the experiences of labor migration, following them much along the lines of George Markus's suggestion.[18] This research informed my focus on poetic expression for my follow-up analysis of the vernacular creativity of the labor migrants. Ultimately, it is my working with the people in the first place as well as their stories and their poems that led me to see how important poetry has been to many who ended up abroad as illegal migrants in postsocialist times in Europe. When in the field, it was clear to me that poetry writing had become a common personal and communal means of dealing with

trauma of separation, split, and distance between those abroad and their intimate universes of family, home, and friends. As folklorist, I also understood
that poetry was a highly productive genre of this new body of creative writing
that I was assembling into a bibliography back at my desk in Canada. Working
on this bibliography at the same time, I was pleased with the statistical confirmations of what I intuitively understood to be the case, as nearly 40 percent of
all books containing creative writing about labor migration included poetry.
This statistic demonstrates the high popularity of poetry among the labor
migrants.

Vernacular Poetry: From Texts to Agency

Let me begin with the following story:

> It is a warm and long evening and I am still immersed in the wonders of this
> immense spiritual site to which I was welcomed by community leaders, who
> invited me to attend this evening's ceremony and made me feel welcome.
> Together with other spiritual leaders, undistracted by the bright evening sun,
> the headman led the evening ceremony, which was well attended and well
> received by all who gathered tonight in this place. In my spot, I have a good
> view of this ceremonial site. It is expansive and accommodating. In the glow of
> the evening sun, I recognize some familiar faces from my earlier encounters
> during this field trip to this remote, as far as I am concerned, place. The cere-
> mony, with its extended singing, is now over; people begin to disperse from the
> site but linger under the nearby trees, all enjoying the shade and an opportunity
> to visit. I remain in my seat, still embracing the atmosphere, thankful to the
> local people for letting me be part of their lives here.
>
> One of the women I have become friends with over the course of my last
> year's visit to this community comes over and warns me that she just called
> another couple of women to join us for a chat. I am very happy to see my friend
> and equally happy to meet her two friends.
>
> Once the three of them exchanged greetings I immediately find myself yet
> again transported to a different universe. Not a minute into our exchange, the
> first woman begins reciting a long verse, as the others silently follow the rhythm
> of her voice and the rhymes of her verses. She ends by reciting what appears to
> be a ballade of love and betrayal, and we all descend back onto the plane of our
> conversation. The other woman promptly takes over, responding to the first

woman in verses again, rhyming her words on the spot, expressing her admiration for her and thanking her for sharing her beautiful story. Then my friend joins in. The exchange lasts for good ten minutes, and all three of my acquaintances take turns stepping in and speaking in rhyme, either reciting verses they knew before our get-together or rhyming their words spontaneously.

Mesmerized, I felt transported to an unknown world, where conversing meant exchanging rhythmic verses, where listening meant looking directly into the stranger's eyes without blinking, where social skills meant the ability to produce, on the spot, rhymed lines, and where poetry talk was just a normal course of conversation. The women looked pleased with themselves, evidently satisfied with their interaction and performance in front of each other and life in general. Once all had a chance to flash their skills at poetry, the ritual time of this spontaneous spiritually flavored poetic engagement ran out, and we all left the site. We spent that evening together, drinking coffee, talking, sharing our experiences of being far away from home, reminiscing about the meaning of life, and feeling like newly found kin reconnected after a long period of separation.[19]

The place in this story, which is extracted from my field diary, is Lisbon, and the spiritual site is the Roman Catholic Church that the Ukrainian Greek Catholic Parish was using for its services. The time is December 2012, and my interlocutors are twenty-first century Ukrainian women, Nadia, Nelia, and Halyna, who are in their early forties and who have been living and working in Portugal for quite some years as domestic workers, first illegally, than legally, with their families still in Ukraine. I have deliberately left out the ethnographic details from the story to illustrate the power of orality, and of poetry specifically, in the lives of today's Ukrainian migrants in southern Europe and to show how comparable Ukrainian culture is in its predisposition toward the poetic word and poetic conversations to other cultures. Both orality and poetic expression (poetry being the most common tool of orally transmitted texts) is alive and well among the modern Ukrainians, especially those from smaller urban centers and villages.

Having been exposed on many occasions to these kinds of experiences and having met many migrant poets, I wanted to understand how contemporary migrant poetry "works," what motivates people to write poetry and why it is in such demand these days in various diasporic settings. In part, my interest in trying to figure out why poetry is so popular in the new diasporas is driven by the fact that when I was exploring early immigrant songs, I could not enter the social worlds of the early migrants who left Ukraine to go across the Atlantic.

In many ways, the vernacular poetic reflectivity of today's migrants is highly reminiscent of poetic production at the turn of the twentieth century, which has also been characterized by Ukrainian Canadian scholars as permeated by folklore.[20] The only way to access the minds of those early immigrants for me was to enter the printed poetic word itself and to explore the inner workings of the immigrant songs' narratives.

Now, the situation is different. I do have an opportunity to engage with the poets themselves and to observe poetry "in action." Perhaps that is why I am less interested in the examination of literary or folk qualities of these vernacular texts, something that has been attempted by others, albeit not in any sustained or extended fashion.[21] Instead, my interest in migrant poetry writing pertains to its status as a cultural practice of late modernity informed by and directed at overcoming the separation constraint that has continued to accompany Ukrainians in their postsocialist diasporic journeys over the last twenty years. Recognizing that the poetic word primarily serves the individual migrants in their personal efforts to deal with their own displacement, I also understand that the poetry they produce quickly acquires social value, serving also the communal needs of the new diasporas. Nadia, Nelia, and Halyna all needed affirmation from each other that poetry was a valid way of negotiating the migrant's life. They also intuitively knew that the ability to craft poems gave them an edge in their social networks, and all three embraced the opportunity to lend their poetic talents to social activities.

In sum, as an anthropologist interested in the processes of cultural recreation, I see labor migrant poetry as a unique symbolic commodity that is being produced, distributed and consumed within the new diasporic settings of Ukrainians. The production, distribution, and consumption of migrant poetry are three interrelated processes in the symbolic maintenance of emerging diasporic cultures and are similar to the production, distribution, and consumption of economic goods that constitute the three facets of local economic systems. This poetic economy is a unique dimension of diasporic community life, and as a commodity, poetry can also bring value, status, and prestige to those who produce, distribute, and consume it. Born in times of profound sociocultural change, Ukrainian migrant poetry writing has become an important communal practice directed at sustaining and expanding the sense of the community for those who partake in any of its three phases.

While growing production (and consumption) of poetry in newly created Ukrainian communities in southern Europe may serve as an indication of qualitative changes that communities of migrants experience on their way to becoming new diasporas, poetry writing is also a manifestation of growing sense of agency that many migrants find and nurture within themselves while transitioning from being members of a community of migrants to members of diaspora and adapting to their lives abroad as transnationals.

Poetic Creativity of Labor Migrants: The Dimensions of the Phenomenon

Poetic renderings of labor migration came hand in hand with the unfolding of mass migration. While working in Ternopil from 2004 to 2007, I examined several local newspapers in depth, focusing on *Ternopilska Hazeta*, which, I found, had begun publishing migrant poetry as early as 1995. This was roughly the same time that the citizens of Ternopil Oblast started leaving their homes as mostly illegal migrants and heading west.[22] *Ternopilska Hazeta* certainly is not unique. Like many other newspapers I consulted, it represents rather well the surge of poetic reflectivity that accompanied the phenomenon of migration itself.[23] The earliest Ukrainian periodicals abroad (*Do Svitla* in Italy and *Pysanka* in Portugal) continued this trend, publishing poetic reflections on the experiences of Ukrainian labor migrants abroad. For example, between 2002 (the year of its inception) and 2007 *Do Svitla* received nearly three thousand letters from recent Ukrainian migrants to Italy, each containing a piece of creative writing, most commonly a poem and less frequently a humorous story.[24]

Although quantifying the extent of poetry writing is hard, as it is not easy to estimate the parameters of creative writing associated with labor migration in general, of which poetry is an integral part, my bibliography allows us to offer additional statistical observations on migrants' poetic productivity. Out of the eighty-two books that comprise this bibliography, twenty-four of them contain poetry and another eight books are a mix of both prose and poetry.

Poetry writing is not only a widespread phenomenon but one truly "owned" by labor migrants and their families, who are both the writers and primary consumers of the poetic word, in both the personal and public domains. While not all the prose works I list in my bibliography are authored by migrants, all the poems about labor migration are either written by migrants or by their children left in Ukraine.[25] This makes the poetic expressive culture of the migrants truly a folk or vernacular phenomenon.

"Folk" in this context does not mean "folkloric" in the traditional sense of the word.[26] Produced at the beginning of the twenty-first century, Ukrainian migrant poetry is best understood as the poetry of modern folk, who are the inheritors of more than one intellectual tradition. Thus, the content, the form, and moral message of many poetic narratives, as well as the very predisposition toward such creativity, have been dictated by long established cultural, ideological, and literary conventions of the society the migrants come from. The roots of migrant poetry writing go back to traditional Ukrainian culture, which itself is rooted in the so-called deep history of *longue durée* responsible for the most lasting elements of human culture that comprise the backbone of folk psychology. Ukrainian migrant poetry writing is also directly informed by Soviet culture, itself a product of the medium-range historical time (social time) that can only sustain cultural values we associate with temporal ideologies. These diverse roots fundamentally define the vernacular character of Ukrainian migrant poetry that unfolds nowadays in a truly transnational fashion, that is, both in the homeland, as a part of homeland vernacular literary processes, and in the diaspora, as ethnic creative writing. It is true that singing Ukrainian folk songs is a widespread cultural practice among Ukrainians, even those who may have been heavily Russified. The persistent love of singing among Ukrainians can be seen as continuation of traditional culture, but at the same time, love for the poetic word has its roots in the culture of the Soviet intelligentsia, which saw familiarity with literature and poetry as important aspect of its identity. Nadia, Nelia, and Halyna represent the Ukrainian intelligentsia as well, as all three had a university or college degree and all three had worked in a white-collar sector of Soviet Ukrainian society before becoming domestic workers in Portugal.

To better understand the processes of production and consumption of poetry in the new Ukrainian diasporas and to appreciate the poetry itself, it is important to understand who produces it. This vernacular literature has a distinctly female face. Out of 201 poets whose work is included in book-length poetry collections, 193 authors are women and 20 are men. This means that 96 percent of the poets in the book-length poetry collections are women. Women poets do not typically write about contemporary political affairs, though during the 2004 Orange revolution, patriotic themes emerged in female as well as male migrant poetry.[27] Female migrant poetry is usually informed by the authors' experiences of working abroad, being away from family and children, being assigned a lower social status in the country of employment than back home, and so on.

Overall, poetic reflections on the fate of the (female) labor migrant in southern Europe tend to project a particular identity of a female migrant. What is this identity? Who is the lyrical heroine constructed in labor migration poetry? Is there a relationship between the author and her lyrical heroine? I turn to these questions now.

Authors and Lyrical Heroines

Lisbon, Portugal. Saturday, December 2011. I am seated in one of the class-rooms in a Portuguese public school rented out by the local Ukrainian cultural organization Dyvosvit to run a Ukrainian Saturday school (figure 7.4). Across from me is Nadia Baranovs'ka, on Saturdays a teacher in the Ukrainian school and from Monday to Friday a housekeeper slash nanny for one of the well-to-do families of Portugal's capital. Enveloped in the loud and cheerful sounds of school recess, we are oblivious to the external noises, fully focused on our conversation. The conversation concerns Nadia's life as a poet, and it fully consumes us both as the morning in the school progresses. I learn about how poetry "came" to Nadia, still back in Ternopil Oblast, where she is from; I learn how, after having moved to Lisbon, the poetic word once again "found" Nadia and how scenes from Portuguese life inspired many of her poems. I am deeply moved by Nadia's emotional recitations of her poetry, all by heart, all becoming an integral part of my interviewing her for the project on labor migrant creative writing.

Nadia was the first poet that I interviewed for this project in Portugal, and it is thanks to our exchange that I decided to focus specifically on the intersections of poetry and female agency, that is, on the role poetry by women plays in the formation of Ukrainian communities in southern Europe.[28] It is not just Nadia's poetry that inspired me to look deeper into this question but also the way in which her engagement with poetry acquired a distinctively new quality when she found herself abroad. Like many other migrant poets' writing, Nadia's poetry has a distinctive Ukrainian folkloric flare. Her verses are highly melodic and her poetry is nostalgic, lyrical, and strongly feminine. Her well-crafted verses are not just rewarding and pleasant to read but also reminiscent of much other contemporary migrant poetry writing I encountered in my research on vernacular migrant creativity.

Of importance to me was to find out to what degree the lyrical heroine and the author coincide and where they depart. I spent a lot of time with Nadia, observing her in action, in her professional environment (school), in her dealing with her peers (other women migrants in Lisbon), in the church, and during public events hosted by the Ukrainian Association in Portugal. I read a lot of Nadia's poetry as well and I would like to think that we became relatively close. Our relationship, which is now sustained by advanced modern communication, allowed me see that Nadia's lyrical heroine was endowed with the same personal features as Nadia herself. In other words, Nadia and her lyrical heroine, whose voice is heard in the poetic word and whose identity is projected through the text, come across as truly the same person.

Figure 7.4. Ukrainian poet Nadia Baranovs'ka (*left*) and the author discussing migrant poetry production in Lisbon, November 2011. Photo by Yuriy Unhurian.

Nadia's work and the work of many other Ukrainian female poets living abroad raises questions about the projections scholars make about women migrants as victims of socioeconomic change.[29] The lyrical heroine of Nadia's poetry is highly feminine in her thoughts, actions, and stated values; her identity is informed by her roles in her own family as wife, mother, daughter and by the economic necessity of her leaving the social nest of her relations. In other words, her sense of self is projected through these family-informed and family-oriented identities, redirecting attention from self to the self's relationship to others in the woman's circle of intimate relations. The protagonist in woman's poetry has been "left" and "exiled," verbs that convey the sense that things are happening to the heroine rather than that the heroine is taking charge of circumstances. Ironically, Nadia also speaks of her poetic gift in passive language. Poetry "returned" to her when she began her career as an illegal migrant in Portugal, and themes and topics that she reflects on in her poems "descend" on her or she "stumbles" on them while living her daily life. Downplaying her own personal agency seems to be a must for Nadia.

But should and can projected authors' identities, like the one in Nadia's poems, be regarded as "true" representations of Ukrainian migrant women abroad?

Rome, November 3, 2011

After I had worked all day in the office of *Ukrainska Gazeta*, Marianna Soronevych, the chief editor, invited me to join "The Ukrainian Days in Rome," a series of events organized in conjunction with the city-wide initiative "The Worlds of Rome 2011." The symposium on Ukraine and the accompanying art exhibits are set up in the Museum of Roman Civilization, in the part of Rome known as EUR, or "Mussolini's quarters." The event is primarily focused on Ukraine and its own old civilization and by extension it also profiles the Ukrainian community of Rome. Amid replicas of ancient Roman statues and reliefs, there are a couple of art shows from Ukraine. A conference hall hosts a mini-conference on Ukraine, and another hall profiles the art of local Ukrainian artists, in this case, the artwork of Ukrainian migrant women.

There, my eyes turned to another wall, and I found myself lost in the greenery of very many paintings displayed across it. The paintings all appeared to be done by a self-taught artist, or so I thought, and before I even finished the thought, I noticed a table with the two books of migrant poetry by Pani Viktoria that I had studied in the office of the *Ukrainska Gazeta* just that morning.[30] These volumes had impressed me the most among the various volumes I had perused in the office of *Ukrainska Gazeta* as strong examples of vernacular female migrant poetry, containing many poems that project the image of a hardworking, humble, but persevering lyrical heroine whose life has been defined by suffering and determination to overcome it. I started browsing the audience and a second later found Pani Viktoria herself.

"Pani Viktoria, is that you? I am thrilled to meet you, I loved your books. I am a professor from Canada, researching Italian Ukrainian poetry. Can I buy your books, I see you have a few?"

That was the beginning of distinctly different encounter with a female migrant poet from other encounters I had had. Pani Viktoria promptly took me under her powerful wing. "Are you from Canada? Writing about me? I have a cousin in Canada. I tell you what, we should publish my books there. Just don't run away from me tonight, I see in you a soul mate. I read people, I read people's minds and see you are my person." She started speaking to me using *ty*, two sentences into her greeting. "Call me Viktoria. 'Pani Viktoria' is my pen name," she says.

"I will tell you so you will understand," she continues, grabbing my arm. "Yes, I am a writer, and I am a painter, I work twenty-four hours a day, I look after an eighty-seven-year-old man. I paint in the evening, write poetry at night, and in the morning I am back to work. When he dies I will get his house. How long are you in Rome for?" She walks me into the conference hall, where presentations about how ancient and beautiful Ukraine is are being delivered. "You should come and stay in my house, it is on the sea. You will like it. I will tell you so you will understand, I have an Italian husband, he is not here tonight. You will come to the banquet with me. With me, they will let you in of course. You will be my guest. I will tell you so you will understand, I have had a difficult life, my husband in Ukraine was a monster, [. . .] I have two sons. My eldest is in Ternopil, doing *aspirantura*. I bought him an apartment there. My youngest is seventeen, and he is here with me."[31]

Over the course of three hours of presentations Pani Viktoria literally held me by my sleeve. She told me many elaborate and highly self-centered stories while managing to hold several exchanges with many more people in the audience at the same time. At a certain point, she even decided to switch to English (that was done in the presence of a handsome Italian male politician attending the event) further proving to me, and to him of course, the diversity of her talents.

All in all, that quiet, pious-looking and soft-featured woman that had looked up at me from the back cover of the book I had studied that morning with excitement turned out in reality to be a confident, driven, and motivated self-advocate. And yet of all the poetic collections I have consulted, Pani Viktoria's work is perhaps the most strongly folkloric, and her poetic voice stands out among those of her peers. Her lyrical heroine is also highly feminine, suffering at the hands of history and local circumstance. Her poetry is like her paintings—prolific, repetitive, yet fluid, not without some appealing folkloric qualities that ultimately make it exemplary of contemporary migrant folk poetry. Still, the image of a lyrical heroine, projected by the author as tender, sensitive, and passive, strongly contrasts with the author's own personality.

The Social Life of Poetry

Julie Cruickshank has written beautifully about how personal stories that may come across as being relevant to individuals only can in fact serve important social purposes when regularly exchanged. They thread together, enhance and sustain the social fabric of community in which they circulate.[32] In Portugal, I witnessed on many occasions, including the one I described above in which Nadia, Nelia, and Halyna spoke to each other in rhyme, how personal poetry that is orally circulated in small and large settings can promptly become valuable communal property.

Back in Lisbon on another occasion, in the same Ukrainian Saturday school, after my first encounter with Nadia Baranovs'ka, I learned that the school runs a poetry club. "Would you like to meet our poets?" the school director asked me. "We have very many fine poets among the students," added the assistant director, and before I could say anything or consider ethical implications of talking to young poets without first obtaining the parental consent, the teachers summoned a cohort of young students to the office, all of whom wrote poetry and were members of the poetry club. One by one the girls introduced themselves and recited their poems, without consulting any written sources. Their poems spoke about their nostalgia for Ukraine and family, about the long-distance relationships they endured before rejoining their mothers in Lisbon, and about many other things that were of importance to them. It was a most memorable experience to listen to the seven students reciting, at length and by heart, their own poetry. The youngest poet was eight years old and the oldest was sixteen. How did this club come into existence? What motivates students to sign up for it? What motivates the children to engage in the pastime of poetry writing?

It took me another year and another research trip to Lisbon to come to understand what kind of relationship exists between the poets, their poetry, and their immediate community, in this case the school. Observing the students and teachers in December 2012, I saw what a vibrant and truly remarkable cultural institution the Saturday school was. Operating as a Ukrainian secondary school under the guidance of the Ministry of Education of Ukraine that coordinates an extended network of Ukrainian schools in the new diaspora, the school attempts to teach the regular school curriculum during the only day a week it is open. Preparations for Christmas at the school were underway and in the midst of these preparations the director approached me and Nadia Baranovs'ka, who was the head of the poetry club, asking her for "the new texts." I first did not understand what he meant, but soon it became clear. Every month, the school commemorates a certain theme or event, be it the Ukrainian language, Ukrainian history, the anniversary of the Ukrainian independence, or Christmas. To mark the occasion the school organizes a concert or a series of presentations and prepares thematic wall posters (*stin-hazetas*). The poetry club apparently is regularly tasked with producing poems appropriate for the occasion, which are recited during the event, reproduced on the posters, and even broadcast on the local Ukrainian radio station. The poets thus are assigned the very practical role of sustaining the social life of the school, and they are quite celebrated by Lisbon's Ukrainian community as purveyors of cultural stuff.

About a quarter of the twenty-five teachers at Dyvosvit School happen to write poetry. They get gently "recruited" (by Nadia Baranovs'ka and the school administration) to contribute their poetry to the wide variety of school and community events. Svitlana, a kindergarten teacher, tells us in the teacher's room during another recess that she "used to be inspired" and wrote poems often. "Now," she says, "I write only when I feel nostalgic for home back in Ukraine." "In that case," Nadia Baranovs'ka responds, smiling at me and Svitlana, "you should start feeling nostalgic very soon. We have to prepare for the radio show. Please call your muse back."

My follow-up interviews with other Ukrainian migrant poets in Lisbon revealed a similar pattern at work in the community at large. The Ukrainian poets of Lisbon write their poetry with full awareness of the imminent public consumption of their work, either in Lisbon or back in their home communities in Ukraine. In Lisbon, for example, when various anniversaries are celebrated and cultural festivals are organized, the organizers scout for the poets, counting on them to write and recite poems for the occasion (see figure 7.5). Radio show hosts are in need of content and frequently invite the poets to share their poetic word with the listeners. Cultural organizations like Dyvosvit engage their members, in this case both students and teachers, to write poetry for concerts and other school projects. Newspapers also publish readers' poetic submissions. Poets are in high demand in the community, and they have come to recognize their important role. When poets get together for tea or coffee, they also enjoy the opportunity to engage in an impromptu recital contest, showing off their skills to each other and demonstrating once again the social capital their poetic gift earns them. And when local writers achieve the reputation of established poets, they soon begin considering producing collections of their own work, as with Tamara Moroshan, whose poem opens up this chapter.

This cycle of vernacular poetry production, distribution and consumption has become an important communal phenomenon and a significant dimension of Ukrainian life in the new diasporas of Portugal and Italy. And despite the fact that poetry writing begins as a private undertaking, it long became a tool of community development. The turn to the production of poetry collections also corresponds to the transition from fluid migrant communities to settled diasporic ones that has begun to take place in Italy and Portugal (and in other European countries where Ukrainians have been working as labor migrants). I am reminded of the words of Mr. Yuriy Unhurian, the director of Dyvosvit, who spoke of a qualitative transition that has taken place among Ukrainians in Portugal. "In 2002–3, there were two hundred thousand Ukrainians in Portugal," Mr. Unhurian told me, "and those were the labor migrants. Now, we have only

Figure 7.5. Ukrainian poet Iryna Yamborak at a community event, Lisbon, 2011. Courtesy of Iryna Yamborak.

about sixty-five thousand, and these are the members of the diaspora." Poetry not only helps these Ukrainians who chose to remain in Portugal to realize themselves but it produces social networks and contributes to the formation of new cultural institutions, and as such it plays a direct role in the formation of new diasporas. With this transition taking place, we now see the emergence of new communal cycles of poetry production and consumption.[33]

Unlike at the turn of the twentieth century, when Ukrainian poetry was written and published in Canada predominantly by men, at the turn of the twenty-first century, engaging in poetry writing appears to be a woman's undertaking. Women seem to benefit the most from the art of rhyming. Poetry writing has become a "cool" thing to do; it is a fashionable and respectful undertaking that attracts many women. Some women, like Pani Viktoria, see the social value of poetry and use it openly as a means for self-advancement. Pani Viktoria, no doubt skillful at poetic wording, embraced poetry writing as an opportunity to advance herself in her Ukrainian milieu, and she effectively uses her identity as a poet and an artist to promote herself in Italian mainstream communities. Others rely on it to become socially engaged, to access social networks, to build friendships and relationships.

All in all, poetry writing in these diasporic settings has become a unique cultural and, importantly, gendered practice that not only helps migrant women make sense of their experiences as migrants in a host country but also provides them with the opportunity to rise above the mainstream, to assert themselves, to reach new social heights, and to build their own new communities. In such new diasporic communities, poetry writing emerges as both personal and communal practice, driven by both an individual and communal sense of agency. Despite being a seemingly private undertaking, it oftentimes exemplifies social or ethnic grassroots activism characteristic of diaspora communities. Importantly for my discussion in this book, poetry writing serves as strong manifestation of the vitality of folk psychology and the vernacular cultural tradition of Ukrainians.

Constructing New *Other* Ukrainians?

Among contemporary Ukrainian migrants, vernacular poetry has become the cultural domain where the new kinds of distance between the proverbial us and them and the emerging differences between the new diasporas and homeland are actively registered, pronounced, and re-created in a poetic form. Poetry has also become a cultural plane on which the conceptualizations of the "diasporic other" are being implicitly yet effectively produced. While contemporary labor out-migration has provoked much discussion of what the labor migrants mean to Ukraine and what kind of ambivalent present/absent members of Ukraine they have become, the specifically diasporic perspective on those left in the homeland has just began to emerge in southern European contexts.[34] At the turn of the twenty-first century, given new historic circumstances in which electronic communication is assumed to effectively compensate for separation, distance, and longing and the fact that new diasporas have established themselves on the same continent as the homeland, the new round of negotiating the diaspora-homeland binomial could be rightly expected to follow an altogether different pattern of development compared to how it evolved a century ago. Yet what unites these two different historical times and geographic contexts is the fact that in both settings poetic expression promptly came to a foreground.

Relying on traditional poetic means, new migrant poetry, very much like the emigrant folklore of the early twentieth century, effectively constructs the difference between the so-called us, or the Ukrainian same, and them, or the Ukrainian "diasporic others." Back in Portugal, when I was discussing the Ukrainian Portuguese minority with George Mahleiros, Portugal's leading specialist on the country's cultural minorities, on the campus of the University of Lisbon, he asked me whether Ukrainian migrant poetry in Portugal focuses on Portugal and the Portuguese. I promised to explore this matter, but I immediately thought of the fact that the Ukrainian migrant lyrical poetry that I encountered in Portugal—and for that matter in other diasporic contexts over the last ten years—in the overwhelming majority of cases focuses on homeland and the experiences of separation, distance, and longing. In Portugal, I heard only two poems composed by women poets that focused, in gratitude it seemed, on Portugal as a new home, one of which was a poem written in Ukrainian and the other in Portuguese. Most lyrical poems explore the tension between migrant's displacement and his or her nostalgia for the homeland and loved ones, effectively projecting his or her ideas about the growing distance between us and them and underscoring his or her views of those left behind.

One way this tension has been explored is by way of a particular folk metaphor known to every one socialized in the Ukrainian culture. Chapter 2 of this book opens with a poem written by a young girl in Ukraine, Kalyna Berlad, that explores the fate of a white stork (*leleka*) who left the home nest and had to build a new one in faraway countries. Though her poem proceeds to assert the kinship connection between the two branches of kin here and there, the young poet implicitly and conventionally employs the time-tested cultural metaphor of a stork to effectively differentiate these two branches of the kin and the resulting two groups of Ukrainians, the homelanders and those elsewhere.

The figure of *leleka* occupies an important position in traditional and contemporary vernacular Ukrainian culture. The storks commonly build their nests in the villages on high posts with platforms erected to attract them, and the households they select have always been considered to have better luck. Like in other European folklore, in traditional Ukrainian culture the stork was believed to bring children to couples, and some young children in Ukraine are still being told so. Migratory birds, storks are thought to be intelligent, homebound, and wise. They appear in many folklore tales and folk songs, and in today's context, the connection between singing and these birds is further asserted by the fact that the words "leleka" and its synonym "zhuravel" are oftentimes found in the names of local choirs.

With the onset of modernity in Ukrainian lands at the end of the nineteenth century and all its rapid economic changes and calamities such as the First World War, accompanied by mass migration overseas, the old meanings of "leleka" gave way to new cultural interpretations. In the twentieth century, storks began to symbolize the split of Ukrainians into the two distinct and separate contingents, those in the diaspora and those in homeland. This shift in meaning is expressed, in a representative way, in the fate of a widely known poem by the renowned Ukrainian poet, writer, scholar, and national activist Bohdan Lepky (1872–1941) who spent much of his life in exile abroad. Published in 1910 in one of Lviv's literary magazines and put to music by Lepky's brother, the poem-song soon become very popular among the Ukrainians, especially those outside of their homeland and those fighting in First World War. As a song of departure, the poem in a most concise form possible ("Do you hear, my brother, my friend, how the storks are leaving for better lands, calling 'croo, croo, I will die in the alien land, flying over the ocean, and wearing out my wings, croo, croo'") describes the same experiences of separation, distance, and split as other early twentieth-century immigrant folklore discussed in the chapter 1.[35] Perhaps that is why it remains popular. The song was subjected to true folkloric fine-tuning when its lyrics were changed and it became known by the title "The Storks Song" rather than by the original title assigned to the poem by Lepky himself.[36]

While the literary heritage of Bohdan Lepky was little known in the former Soviet Ukraine that suppressed dissemination of information about nationalist cultural elite in exile, the trope of the stork as an itinerant emigrant remained in circulation. In the 1980s, as perestroika loosened the USSR's ideological control over the relationship between the diaspora and Ukraine, the attention to the Lepkys' song revived in Ukraine, triggering poetic tributes and new musical productions and leading to its inclusion into the school curriculum.[37] Since the mid-1990s, it has been a sort of beacon to all those who have been affected by mass labor out-migration from Ukraine.

Nadia Baranovs'ka and many other poets in new diasporas followed the established practice of associating migrants, emigrants, and overseas kin with these powerful migratory birds:

> You know, when I came to Portugal, I remembered Lepky. The storks, labor migrants, emigration. And when I encountered our labor migrants' children, I thought Lepky's poem is about our school in Lisbon. I just had a poem in my mind, also about the storks. My poem is also about how the storks leave their homes every year, how they fly away to the alien lands. But they are returning to their own nests. As if it is a parallel world. Like our own. Parents leave home, children leave home, but then return. If only there would be no separation. This is what my stork poem is about.[38]

As attested by its history, throughout the twentieth century, the stork metaphor served as effective means for popular culture to communicate the "presence" of a split and the dominance of separation in the lives of many contemporary Ukrainians. The metaphor, having had its meaning adjusted to better suit new sociocultural contexts, firmly positioned Ukrainians, the storks, who left their homeland, on the fringes of familiar networks of local families and communities. In times of accelerated social change, the breakdown of structures of the familiar lifeworld creates a need for many to come to terms with their disappearing world. The growing distance between people's lives in the present and the former familiar lifeworld with its conventional unquestioned meanings, transforms them into viewers of their own life. The risk of losing sight of this disappearing life incites people to reflect on it, to renarrate it, and to write about it. Among many Ukrainian migrants, whose lives were unfolding in the midst of the profound social change of the late twentieth century and now outside of their homelands, vernacular poetry appears to be the most powerful tool of modern social reflectivity to deal with such a breakdown of established familiar social worlds. Relying on established stock of common metaphors, clichés, and other folkloric expressive forms, poetry has proved to be highly appealing in the communities of Ukrainians in Europe. As a means of dealing with the changing realities of their lives, poets turned to contemplate a different fate for themselves and those they left back home.

Undoubtedly, outside of the vernacular poetic domain, new Ukrainian communities in Europe and elsewhere utilize many other means to formulate and express their opinions of Ukraine and their compatriots there (amateur journalism and participation in social media being the most pronounced such means). These means, though, serve the most immediate needs of the new diasporic communities, allowing these communities to promptly react to various ongoing political situations and developments back in homeland. Migrants' vernacular lyrical poetry, on the other end, tends to focus on the inner dimensions of emigration; it does not address the here and now of Ukrainian politics, which continues to negatively affect those in homeland and those in the new diasporas, but the universal experiences of the diaspora-homeland separation, split, and longing for unity.

Pursuing these experiences and focusing on the familiar and the familial, this vernacular poetry effectively revives and further sustains the diaspora-homeland binomial in the Ukrainian culture that these days should indeed be defined in global rather than national terms. Importantly, public production, consumption, and redistribution (through publishing) of such vernacular migrant poetry effectively signals the qualitative changes that migrant communities have been undergoing recently, gradually transforming themselves from temporary communities of migrants into new diasporas, fully rooted in new homelands. With this transformation, sustained by folk psychology, the diaspora-homeland binomial in Ukrainian culture cuts even deeper into the body of the Ukrainian culture.

Figure 8.1. Nesting storks in the garden of labor emigrants, village of Lanivtsi, Ternopil Oblast, Ukraine, 2002. Photo by author.

Epilogue

The Folk Connection

*I*n May of 2005, I spent a few memorable days in the village of Bili Oslavy, a community that throughout its entire history knew too well long-distance separation, seasonal labor elsewhere, emigration, and the terminal splitting of kin. Located in the heart of the Carpathians, spread across the steep hills of the valley, for generations the village would see its residents travel to other regions in Europe or beyond in an effort to sustain their local lives. The most recent destinations for the Oslavians wanting to make an earning include southern Europe and the United States, especially Chicago, where, as the villagers shared with me, there is a community of Oslavians who work there to support their families and households back home. Any Oslavian born and raised in the village, as a result, has more than one relative abroad, some distant and some close. I visited Oslavy with my friend Bohdan Struk, who had insisted that I would have to get to know the village and the villagers if I wanted to write about the diasporic connections of Ukrainians. I accepted Bohdan's advice, and he took me there for a three-day stay with his family. In the village I met many people who talked at length with me about their experiences working abroad as labor migrants and exploring their long-term connections with the old diasporas.

There I also met Vasyl' Leb'iuk, an employee in a local state forestry company, whose video recording hobby over the last twenty years had become a part-time job serving the entire community. Vasyl''s passion for video recording had by the time of our encounter taken on a whole new meaning in light of the recent growth in travel between Oslavy and the Oslavian migrant communities elsewhere in the world, sustaining the video connection between local families and their members elsewhere. Video recording in 2005 in Oslavy meant relying on bulky VHS tapes, and hundreds of these tapes occupied a lot of space in Vasyl''s otherwise compact home, taking over the half of the main room and turning this half into what looked like a makeshift video production studio, filled up with various electronics, two old TV sets, a computer, several VHS players, plenty of cords, wire, and videotapes. The family socialized and met guests in this same room, and some guests slept in an area just above the large old-fashioned *piec*, or oven. I spent two evenings with Vasyl', chatting with him about his filming and watching his recordings of local weddings as well as video letters filmed in Chicago and New York that were sent back to families in Oslavy.

My encounter with Vasyl' had a certain surreal quality to it. Vasyl''s home, built in the local vernacular architectural style soon after the Second World War, was a typical Ukrainian wooden *khata*, exterior walls whitewashed with a touch of blue, three interconnected rooms, main room containing old wood-heated *piec*, with a sleeping area on top of it, and amenities outside. Surrounded by other homes of the same style and age, Vasyl''s *khata* evoked tradition, tranquility, and rootedness in local history and vernacular culture. Yet inside of his home stuffed with electronics, the two of us were fully consumed by endlessly moving images of Chicago's streetscape, Manhattan's skyscrapers, suburban immigrant families' gatherings, the realities existing elsewhere across the ocean, all simultaneously projected for us on the two old TV screens (figure 8.2). Vasyl''s wife was in the same room, sitting high above us in the *piec* sleeping area, embroidering a piece of cloth in the local tradition of crisscross stitching, epitomizing some imagined idyllic Ukrainianness many people associate with rural Ukraine.

Over the course of many years Vasyl''s very local life became infused with sounds and images of faraway lands, flickering on an old computer or a TV screen, filling up this house, as he transferred newly arrived tapes into the European format. I could not stop thinking about how much Vasyl''s personal life had been affected by recent global developments and the cultural flows of people, capital, ideas and images that accompanied them, the flows well described by Arjun Appadurai and briefly discussed in the introduction.[1] Vasyl', it appeared, was deeply immersed in these cultural flows that connected the two Ukrainian worlds, one in diaspora and one in homeland, forming the peculiar zone of "in-between," filled with diasporic longing and nostalgia for "other Ukrainians" whose life was unfolding on the opposite end of the diaspora/homeland binomial. In his case, these flows of imagery, ideas, and people effectively connected his own local lifeworld with the Oslavians living in the United States as well as with their old diasporic kin who had emigrated earlier from Bili Oslavy, placing him in the epicenter of their intersections.

For Vasyl', immersion in this diasporic space offers a range of experiences with "other Ukrainians," and these experiences are a regular occurrence in his

Figure 8.2. Watching a video letter from family members who emigrated to New York State in the early 2000s in the home of Vasyl' Leb'iuk, village of Bili Oslavy, Ivano-Frankivsk Oblast, Ukraine, 2005. Photo by author.

otherwise quite local life. Because of this, I felt a great sense of affinity with Vasyl', recognizing in him a fellow documentalist who has been deeply immersed in the world of "other Ukrainians," not unlike myself. For both of us, this simultaneous immersion in the world of here and there has been a common occurrence. While Vasyl' got exposed to the world of "other Ukrainians" through circumstance, in my case I have been deliberately seeking these experiences out in my work. Such constant exposure to and involvement in both worlds of homeland and diaspora beyond one's own immediate networks is perhaps comparatively unique and rare. The majority of people with real or imagined connections to the opposite side of the diaspora-homeland binomial do not constantly think of "other Ukrainians" over there in highly reflective manner, especially of those "other Ukrainians" who are not related to them.

Vasyl''s and my sustained involvement with the cultural flows of diasporic kin are rooted in the historical circumstances of the end of the twentieth century and the beginning of the twenty-first century as well as in our personal circumstances. We both happened to live in the times of intensified diasporic traffic and accelerated diasporic exchanges between various localities in the world where Ukrainians live nowadays, and I have moved between the continents myself, having come to study in Canada in the 1990s and having been based in my new home country ever since while regularly going back to Ukraine. We both witnessed how the twentieth century ended, bringing about a new round in the negotiations between the diaspora and the homeland. Curious to explore earlier manifestations of the diaspora-homeland binomial, in this book I set out to dig up the roots of the diasporic dimension of Ukrainian culture. I proceeded to show how both the diaspora and the homeland were imagined throughout the twentieth century. Now, facing the task of writing this concluding chapter, I am presented with a challenge of offering an epilogue to the discussion of a cultural phenomenon that still unfolds in time and space.

The very idea of exploring twentieth-century noninstitutional (dis)engagements between those in the diaspora and the homeland and their ideas about each other stemmed from two developments. First, no one has ever attempted to examine Ukrainian grassroots practices of diaspora/homeland (dis)engagement in the twentieth century in a sustained and focused way, practices that largely developed in the days before the internet, jet travel, and mobile phones. Secondly, the twentieth century is over, offering the researcher an opportunity to revisit it from a different vantage point.

For Ukrainians, the twentieth century was a historic period, a time when they faced the emergence of a new modern condition that began quietly determining, for the rest of the century, many local peoples' lives and many local communities' affairs. This condition, that I have labeled the diasporic dimension of Ukrainian culture, was brought about by profound global transformations that the world experienced in the last quarter of the nineteenth and the first two decades of the twentieth century, including mass migration from Europe to the Americas, the development of capitalism in Ukraine, the First World War, and the eventual redrafting of the political map of Europe that rendered, for the rest of the century, Ukrainians and their lands subordinate within the new nation-states that emerged in Europe.

Mass displacement, voluntary and otherwise, of Ukrainians at the end of the nineteenth century and in the early twentieth century was an outcome of these transformations, and subsequent political conditions in Ukraine prevented those who were separated from their families in the whirlpool of these global changes from ever reconnecting in real time and real space. This displacement was accompanied by the profound experiences of separation and split from and longing for other family members who ended up on opposite sides of the Atlantic or on opposite sides of the political divide between the USSR and

Western Europe that was further reinforced after the Second World War. The words "exile," "diaspora," and "emigration" began to be widely used to refer to those who ended up living outside Ukraine, and remained common currency throughout the entire twentieth century and beyond. And while many separations and departures were endured by the Ukrainian people during the twentieth century, in my research I focused specifically on separation and departure that stemmed from emigration understood in its most traditional terms as economic or political emigration, which in the case of Ukraine encompasses at least four immigration waves over the course of the twentieth century.

The diasporic dimension of Ukrainian ethnicity (which I see here as a social category) supported by the diasporic consciousness of individuals of Ukrainian heritage gave rise to the specifically diasporic conceptions and local practices that I have discussed in the preceding chapters. This diasporic dimension of Ukrainian culture is revealed in the lives of Ukrainians in both the diaspora and the homeland and, as I argue in this book, is here to stay, given the new round of mass displacement of Ukrainians from Ukraine that began taking place at the turn of the twenty-first century. It has become a new cultural principle, a structure, a binomial one, with its roots in a particular historical period (twentieth century), and I envision that from now on, this cultural condition will continue to define many aspects of Ukrainian culture. This diasporic dimension is firmly planted in Ukrainian culture, and it will eventually give rise to a new and permanent feature of Ukrainian folk psychology, very much in Bruner's terms as discussed in the introduction to this book.

While I have advanced here such an understanding of the interdependence between the Ukrainian diaspora and the Ukrainian homeland, I have not focused on its institutional, organizational, and political aspects but on the actions, thoughts, undertakings of individuals who pursue their lives in the way they understand they should and who may have nothing to do with the organized communities, their institutions and political tensions. It is in this vernacular domain that the diasporic dimension of ethnicity is experienced most intimately and most meaningfully and therefore sustained more lastingly. It is in this domain that diasporic practices, as discussed in previous chapters, pursue *personal* engagement with Ukrainians on the other side of the binomial. It is in this vernacular domain that ideas about "other Ukrainians" are shaped, and this is in this domain that individuals' diasporic consciousness plays itself out to the fullest.

The diasporic consciousness in most people's lives is not in the foreground all the time but rather operates on the periphery. All the informants I consulted for this book were living lives as engineers, farmers, pharmacists, teachers, and nurses and also as parents, daughters, sons, husbands, and wives, and attending to their responsibilities in these capacities was always primary, pushing diasporic concerns into the background, until circumstances were such as to make it necessary to address them. Nevertheless, in both worlds, there were parallel (though not identical) processes and practices of diasporic longing and imagining, which formed that precarious space of in-between, the space belonging to both cultures, that of the homeland and that of the diaspora.

This space that is not fully occupied in either of them but lingers as a backdrop, a background against which the lives of people unfold. In some ways, in exploring how split, absence, distance, separation is felt and lived out by both groups on both sides of the homeland/diaspora binomial, I have been exploring this space in between. This space can perhaps be said to constitute the very axle that holds the two sides of the binomial together. Like any other structure that stands the test of time, this binominal is adaptive, shedding certain features and adding new ones over time. But the axle, the space in between, is here to stay, at least for now, while the world order and world culture still depends on the separation of space and time.

This brings me to the next point, namely, that the only way to access this zone and its circuits of diasporic vernacular subjectivity, which I understand to be a part of folk psychology, is through the examination of various vernacular practices and representations that may not always openly concern "other Ukrainians." And this is what I have attempted to do. I have turned to traditional folklore to describe how "other Ukrainians" and Ukrainian "otherlands" have been conceived by Ukrainians on both ends of the binominal. Presenting the reader with this rich mesh of vernacular diasporic practices and representations, themselves all interrelated, I hoped to have demonstrated the vitality of Ukrainian folk psychology and its utility when it comes to diaspora-homeland conceptions of each other. The growing distance between the cultures of diaspora and homeland and the changes in the way this distance was experienced in the twentieth century were managed not only by traditional folklore practices but also by new forms of folk practices that emerged throughout the century.

Even in the wake of the modern technological revolution of the last quarter of the twentieth century, which changed how people experienced space, time and communication, vernacular practices continued to define the ways in which the diasporic dimension of Ukrainian ethnicity was sustained. With renewed mass migration from Ukraine in the 1990s, vernacular approaches to the diasporic condition of Ukrainian culture were revived with new force. New means of communication served as a springboard for such approaches and effectively supplemented the traditional oral circuits of communication, letter writing, and other traditional local media. New technologies of communication also make new vernacular representations of the diasporic dimension of Ukrainian culture far more easily accessible.

Because I see the diasporic dimension of ethnicity as being informed by conditions of modernity, novel yet permanent, at least for the foreseeable future, my research here should be treated as a prologue to future explorations of the diasporic condition of Ukrainian culture. Given the emergence of new Ukrainian diasporas in Europe and the revival of the interaction between diaspora and homeland in the late twentieth century in the context of old diasporas, I am confident we will be seeing these kinds of studies very soon.

Notes

Introduction

1. George and Janet Zenkiw are pseudonyms.

2. Cited in Paul Basu, *Highland Homecomings: Genealogy and Heritage Tourism in the Scottish Diaspora* (New York: Routledge, 2007), xi.

3. James Clifford, *Routes: Travel and Translation in the Late Twentieth Century* (Cambridge, MA: Harvard University Press, 1997), 255.

4. Oksana Pakhl'ovs'ka, "Binom "Ukraïna—Diaspora" S'ohodni: Kryza i Perspektyva" [Ukraine-Diaspora Binomial Today: The Crisis and the Potential Future], *Visnyk Ukraïns'koï Vsesvitn'oï Koordynatsiïnoï Rady* 6–7 (2002): 9–12.

5. Robin Cohen, one of the trailblazers of diaspora studies, states that diasporic consciousness is rooted in the myth of common origin that is shared by both those in the diaspora and those in the homeland (*Global Diasporas: An Introduction* [Seattle: University of Washington Press 1997], 184). However, Cohen does not elaborate on the meaning of diasporic consciousness. Recently, scholars have revisited it in a more focused way. For example, Paul Basu devotes an entire monograph to the question of Scottish diasporic consciousness (*Highland Homecomings*, 24). Stephen C. Lubkemann describes diasporicity as a persistent social condition of Liberians ("Diasporas and Their Discontents: Return without Homecoming in the Forging of Liberian and African-American Identity," *Diaspora: A Journal of Transnational Studies* 13, no. 1 [2004]: 127).

6. Matthew Frye Josephson, *Special Sorrows: The Diasporic Imagination of Irish, Polish, and Jewish Immigrants in the United States* (Cambridge, MA: Harvard University Press, 1995).

7. Arjun Appadurai, "Global Ethnoscapes: Notes and Queries for a Transnational Anthropology," in *Recapturing Anthropology: Working in the Present*, ed. Richard G. Fox (Santa Fe, NM: School of American Research Press, 1991), 191–216.

8. Olena Malynovska, *International Migration in Contemporary Ukraine: Trends and Policy* (Geneva: Global Commission on International Migration, 2004); Olena Malynovska, "International Labour Migration from the Ukraine: The Last Ten Years," in *New*

Waves: Migration from Eastern to Southern Europe, ed. Maria Ioannis Baganha and Richard Maria Lucinda Fonseca (Lisbon: Luso-American Foundation, 2004), 11–22.

9. Father Iosafat, interview by Natalia Khanenko-Friesen, Krekhiv, Ukraine, June 2003.

10. See, for example, Irina Pribytkova, "Trudovye Migranty v Sotsial'noï Iierarkhii Ukrains'kogo Obschestva (okonchanie)" [Labor Migrants in the Social Hierarchy of the Ukrainian Society (part 2)], *Sotsiolohiia: Teoriia, Metody, Marketyng* 1 (2003): 109–24; Irina Pribytkova, "Trudovye Migranty v Sotsial'noï Iierarkhii Ukrains'kogo Obschestva (nachalo)" [Labor Migrants in the Social Hierarchy of the Ukrainian Society (part 1)], *Sotsiolohia: Teoriia, Metody, Marketyng* 4 (2002): 156–67; and Viktor Susak, "Ukraïnski Host'ovi Robitnyky ta Immihranty v Portuhaliï (1997–2002 rr.)" [Ukrainian Guest Workers and Immigrants in Portugal (1997–2002)], in *Ukraïna v Suchasnomu Sviti: Konferentsiia Ukraïns'kykh Vypusknykiv Prohram Naukovoho Stazhuvannia u SShA, Ilta, 12–15 Veresnia 2002 r.* (Kyiv: Stylos, 2003), 194–207.

11. David Harvey, *The Conditions of Postmodernity: An Enquiry into the Origins of Cultural Change* (Oxford; Cambridge, MA: Blackwell, 1989); William Safran, "Comparing Diasporas: A Review Essay," *Diaspora: A Journal of Transnational Studies* 8, no. 3 (1999): 255.

12. Arjun Appadurai, "Disjuncture and Difference in the Global Cultural Economy," *Theory, Culture and Society* 7, nos. 2–3 (1990): 296–310; Ulf Hannerz, *Transnational Connections: Culture, People, Places* (London: Routledge, 1996); Anthony D. Smith, *National Identity* (Reno: University of Nevada Press, 1991), 157.

13. Natalia Shostak, "On Local Readings of Overseas Kin: Visions from Ukraine," in *Reverberations: Representations of Modernity, Tradition, and Cultural Value In-between Central Europe and North America*, ed. by Susan Ingram and Cornelia Szabo-Knotik (Frankfurt am Main: Peter Lang, 2002), 201–22.

14. Jerome S. Bruner, *Acts of Meaning* (Cambridge, MA: Harvard University Press, 1990), 35.

15. See Fernand Braudel, *The Mediterranean and the Mediterranean World in the Age of Philip II*, 2 vols. (Berkeley: University of California Press, 1996). Braudel develops the notion of at least three time horizons of history in this seminal work that was first published in France in 1949.

16. William H Mott, *Globalization: People, Perspectives, and Progress* (Westport, CT: Praeger, 2004), 71.

17. Ibid.

18. Bruner, *Acts of Meaning*, 42.

19. Similar observations have been made in relation to autobiographical narratives within the framework of anthropology (Vieda Skultans, *The Testimony of Lives: Narrative and Memory in Post-Soviet Latvia* [London and New York: Routledge, 1998], 25–26), psychology (Bruner, *Acts of Meaning*, 11), and ethnic studies (Stephen Cornell, "That's the Story of Our Life," in *We Are a People: Narrative and Multiplicity in Constructing Ethnic Identity*, ed. Paul Spickard and W. J. Burroughs [Philadelphia: Temple University Press, 2000], 44–45).

20. The timeframe of our investigation here is limited to the so-called short twentieth century, bracketed by the First World War and the collapse of socialist system and the dissolution of the USSR in 1991, which opened the new era in the relationship between newly independent Ukraine and its diasporas.

Chapter 1. Separation

1. Maria Genek is a pseudonym.

2. Maria Genek, interview by Natalia Khanenko-Friesen, Mundare, Alberta, January 31, 2001.

3. Shtefka Hurnia to Maria Genek, April 2000, tape donated to the author by Maria Genek.

4. This melody is known in various regions of Ukraine and associated with many songs.

5. The adjective *ridnyĭ*, translated here as native, stems from the noun *rid*, or kin.

6. Even more separation and displacement ensued from the USSR's annexation of Western Ukraine in 1939 and subsequent political purges, the Second World War, and postwar collectivization in Western Ukraine.

7. Sofiia Hrytsa, "Ukraïns'ki Narodni Pisni pro Emihratsiiu" [Ukrainian Folk Songs about Emigration], *Ukraïns'ka Diaspora* 1 (1992): 111. See also her introduction in *Bud' Zdrava, Zemlytse: Ukraïns'ki Narodni Pisni pro Emihratsiiu* [Stay Well, My Land: Ukrainian Folk Songs about Emigration], ed. Sofiia Hrytsa (Kyiv: Muzychna Ukraïna, 1991), 9–10.

8. Hrytsa, *Bud' Zdrava, Zemlytse*, 13.

9. The song was recorded by Mykhaĭlo Pavlyk and published in Ivan Franko, ed., *Etnohrafichnyĭ Zbirnyk*, vol. 5 (Lviv: Naukove Tovarystvo Imeni Shevchenka, 1898), 73–75, cited in Sofiia Hrytsa, introduction to *Naĭmyts'ki ta Zarobitchans'ki Pisni*, ed. Sofiia Hrytsa, Oleskiĭ I. Deĭ, and M. H. Marchenko (Kyiv: Naukova Dumka, 1975), 28. Volodymyr Hnatiuk documents the history of the song as well, stating it was sent by the emigrant deacon to his son as his last words: "As we will meet only in the other world, pay respect to your church, your priest and all the kind people, and kiss our sacred land. Then you will be respected as well" ("Pisenni Novotvory v Ukraïns'ko-Rus'kiĭ Narodniĭ Slovesnosti" [Novel Folk Songs in Ukrainian-Rus Folk Literature], *Zapysky Naukovoho Tovarystva Imeni Tarasa Shevchenka* 50, no. 11 [1902–3]: 44–45).

10. Such was the case with the song "At, Bozhe Miĭ, Iak v Tiĭ Amerytsi," as pointed out by Sofiia Hrytsa in the introduction to *Naĭmyts'ki ta Zarobitchans'ki Pisni*, 28. For additional information in English on emigrant songs published in various early twentieth-century periodicals, see Yarema Kowalchuk, "The Emigrant Verses of Hryhorij Olijnyk: An Analysis" (MA thesis, University of Alberta, 1981).

11. Volodymyr Hnatiuk, "Pisenni Novotvory v Ukraïns'ko-Rus'kiĭ Narodniĭ Slovesnosti" [Novel Folk Songs in Ukrainian-Rus Folk Literature], *Zapysky Naukovoho Tovarystva Imeni Tarasa Shevchenka* 50, no. 6 (1902–3): 1–18.

12. Ibid., 1–37; Volodymyr Hnatiuk, "Pisenni Novotvory v Ukraïns'ko-Rus'kiĭ Narodniĭ Slovesnosti" [Novel Folk Songs in Ukrainian-Rus Folk Literature], *Zapysky Naukovoho Tovarystva Imeni Tarasa Shevchenka* 50, no. 2 (1902–3): 38–67; Filaret Kolessa, "Ukraïns'ka Narodna Pisnia u Naĭnovishiĭ Fazi Svoho Rozvytku" [The Ukrainian Folk Song in the Newest Phase of Its Development], in Filaret Kolessa, *Fol'klorystychi Pratsi* [Studies in Folkloristics] (Kyiv: Vyshcha Shkola, 1970).

13. See Maria G. Bochko, "Emihrants'ka Pisennist' v Osvitlenni Dozhovtnevoï i Radianskoï Fol'klorystyky" [Emigrant Songs in Pre-October and Soviet Folklore Studies Accounts], *Narodna Tvorchist' ta Etnohrafiia* 4 (128) (1974): 74–79; Maria G. Bochko, "Nove i Tradytsiĭne v Emihrants'kiĭ Pisennosti" [New and Traditional in Emigrant Songs], *Narodna Tvorchist' i Etnohrafiia* 4 (132) (1975): 49–53; and Maria G. Bochko "Spil'ni Rysy Emihrants'kykh Pisen' Ukraïntsiv i Slovakiv" [Common Features of Emigrant Songs of Ukrainians and Slovaks], *Narodna Tvorchist' i Etnohrafiia* 6 (130) (1974): 72–77. The reader may also wish to consult Robert Klymasz's *A Bibliography of Ukrainian Folklore in Canada, 1902–64* (Ottawa: Queen's Printer, 1969) for further references.

14. The earliest academic studies of the emigrant song cycle in Canada that were undertaken in an extended and sustained manner using fieldwork date to the early 1950s and were produced by Jars Rudnyckyj, who also trained a new cohort of young folklorists, including Robert B. Klymasz. See the four volumes of Jars Rudnyckyj's *Materialy do Ukraïns'ko-Kanadiĭs'koï Fol'klorystyky i Dialektolohiï* [Ukrainian-Canadian Folklore and Dialectological Texts] (Winnipeg: Ukrainian Free Academy of Sciences, 1956–63). Klymasz is to be credited for his extensive field research into the topic of Ukrainian Canadian folklore and immigrant songs specifically, which he launched in the 1960s and has continued to engage to this day. See his *Introduction to the Ukrainian Canadian Immigrant Folksong Cycle* (Ottawa: National Museum of Canada, 1970), 16, which provides a listing of various sources on Ukrainian immigrant songs.

15. Anthony Smith, "Ethnic Myths and Ethnic Revivals," *European Journal of Sociology* 25, no. 2 (1984): 283–305.

16. Of course, in the public domain of Ukrainian Canadian popular writing, there are origin stories that focus to a great degree on the old country and on the departure and the journey across the Atlantics and the Canadian interior. Such stories were typically passed down to children and other curious people by the original immigrants themselves, as for example, the story of coming to Canada of the "first" official Ukrainian immigrants, Eleniak and Pylypiw. Recorded in 1932, the oral narrative soon became the official story of the first official immigrants' arrival to Canada in 1891 (see Natalia Khanenko-Friesen, "From Family Lore to a People's History: The Role of Oral Culture in Ukrainian Claims to the Canadian Prairies," in *Orality and Literacy: Reflections across Disciplines*, ed. Keith Carlson, Kristina Fagan, and Natalia Khanenko-Friesen [Toronto: University of Toronto Press, 2011], 177–96). The theme of departure and traveling overseas has also been explored in Ukrainian Canadian art, for example, in William Kurelek's paintings.

17. Charles Stafford, *Separation and Reunion in Modern China* (Cambridge: Cambridge University Press, 2000), 7.

18. Ibid., 5.

19. Ibid., 4-28.

20. Bohdan Medwidsky, "Songs from the New World," in *Ukrainian Folksongs from the Prairies*, ed. Robert Klymasz (Edmonton: Canadian Institute of Ukrainian Studies Press, 1992), 84.

21. Bochko, "Emihrants'ka Pisennist'," 75-78; Hrytsa, introduction to *Naĭmyts'ki ta Zarobitchans'ki Pisni*, 18-19.

22. Hrytsa, introduction to *Naĭmyts'ki ta Zarobitchans'ki Pisni*, 19.

23. Viktor Beliaev, ed., *Sobranie Narodnykh Russkikh Pesen s Ikh Golosami: Na Muzyku Polozhil Ivan Prach* [Collection of Folk Russian Songs with Voices: Put to Music by Ivan Prach] (Moscow: Gosudarstvennoe Myzykal'noe Izdatel'stvo, 1955), 297-98, cited in Hrytsa, introduction to *Naĭmyts'ki ta Zarobitchans'ki Pisni*, 19.

24. Arnold Van Gennep, *Rites of Passage* (1909; repr. London: Routledge, 2004); Terence Turner, "Transformation, Hierarchy and Transcendence: A Reformulation of Van Gennep's Model of the Structure of *Rites de Passage*," in *Secular Rituals*, ed. Sally Falk Moore and Barbara G. Myerhoff (Amsterdam: Van Gorcum, 1977), 53-70; Victor Turner, *Ritual Process: Structure and Anti-Structure* (Ithaca, NY: Cornell University Press, 1969); Maurice Bloch, *Prey into Hunter: The Politics of Religious Experience* (Cambridge: Cambridge University Press, 1992); Valeriia Eremina, *Ritual and Fol'klor* [Ritual and Folklore] (Leningrad: Nauka, 1991); Al'bert Baĭburin, *Ritual v Traditsionnoĭ Kul'ture: Strukturno-Semanticheskiĭ Analiz Vostochnoslavianskikh Obriadov* [Ritual in Traditional Culture: The Structural and Semantic Analysis of East Slavic Rites] (Saint Petersburg: Nauka, 1993).

25. Kathy Kulmacz, "Rites of Passage at the Mohyla Institute," course paper, University of Saskatchewan, 2002.

26. Hrytsa, introduction to *Naĭmyts'ki ta Zarobitchans'ki Pisni*, 18-19.

27. Medwidsky, "Songs from the New World," 84.

28. "Potoĭbichnyĭ svit" is a common Ukrainian phrase describing the world of the dead. It derives from the phrase "po toĭ bik," or "on/over on the other side." As in English, the phrase hints at "the other side" of something but does not specify what this something is. Semantically, this is very interesting, as it is not clear what is between (is constituted by) this side and the other side—a river, an ocean, a chasm, etc.?

29. Translated from Volodymyr Hnatiuk, "Pisnia pro Brazyliiu" [Song about Brazil], in *Etnohrafichnyĭ Zbirnyk*, vol. 5 (Lviv: Naukove Tovarystvo Imeni Shevchenka, 1898), 73-75.

30. The Valley of Josaphat (Joel 3:2 and 3:12) is understood in vernacular Ukrainian culture to be a place where the dead gather for final judgment.

31. In linguistic terms, a sentence, for instance, is a syntagm of words; the paragraphs and chapters are the syntagms of sentences. Syntagmatic relations are the various

ways in which elements within the same text relate to each other and to the whole text.
See Daniel Chandler "Semiotics for Beginners," Aberystwyth University, www.aber
.ac.uk/media/Documents/S4B/sem03.html. In immigration songs, the various motifs
are presented in a particular and predictable order, which is to say, they are organized
syntagmatically.

32. Hnatiuk, "Pisenni Novotvory," 13.

33. Osyp Oles'kiv, *Pro Vil'ni Zemli* [About Free Lands] (Winnipeg: Ukraïns'ka
Vil'na Akademia Nauk, 1975), 18.

34. *Naïmyts'ki ta Zarobitchans'ki Pisni*, 417.

35. Hrytsa, *Bud' Zdrava, Zemlytse*, 53.

36. Ibid., 52.

37. Vladimir Propp, *Morphology of the Folktale*, 2nd rev. ed. (Austin: University of
Texas Press, 1968), 21. First published in Russian in 1928.

38. Liminality derives from the Latin word "limen" that means "threshold." The
term refers to a variety of threshold states a person can experience, psychological,
neurological, and metaphysical subjective, conscious and unconscious, and so on. In
anthropology the term has received much attention in works by Victor Turner; see his
"Betwixt and Between: The Liminal Period in *Rites de Passage*," in *The Forest of Symbols*
(Ithaca, NY: Cornell University Press, 1967), 93–111, and his *The Ritual Process*.

39. Bohdan Medwidsky makes similar observation about the motive of the itinerant
traveler in his article "Songs from the New World."

Chapter 2. Mediating Absence in Homeland

1. Kalyna Berlad to Christine Pawluk, February 29, 2000.

2. I am grateful to Christine Pawluk for allowing me to read and analyze the
Berlad-Pawluk letters.

3. I had a chance to read this correspondence, and every letter I read vividly
communicated the impact that the Canadians' homecoming had had on the Ukrainian
family back in Khutir-Budyliv.

4. In Hrytsevolia, I stayed with the Bakus'kos, while the head of the household was
on *zarobitky* (an "earning stay") in Canada. While in the village, I attended local public
and private events (church services, local weddings, graduation concerts in local school,
and so on), conducted interviews, recorded oral histories, and studied personal correspondence of Hrytsevolians with their overseas relatives. I also wrote and translated
letters addressed to relatives in North America that I was to mail on my return to
Canada. All these experiences contributed to my understanding of the long-distance
imagination of overseas Ukrainians in rural areas of Ukraine. See Natalia Khanenko-
Friesen, *Inshyǐ Svit abo Etnichnist' u Diï: Kanads'ka Ukraïns'kist' Kïntsia Dvadtsiatoho Stolittia*
[The Other World; or, Ethnicity in Action: Canadian Ukrainianness at the End of the
Twentieth Century] (Kyiv: Smoloskyp, 2011).

5. The village dates to the early thirteenth century. Local stories tell the history of the village in various ways. See the local history book about Hrytsevolia produced by the local school: "Istoriia Sela Hrytsevolia" [History of the Village of Hrystevolia], scrapbook, Hrytsevolia Public School (Hrytsevolia, n. d.).

6. "Zvit po Naselenniu na 01.01.99 Berezivs'koï Sil's'koï Rady" [Population Report, Berezivka Rural Council, January 1, 1999], Berezivka Rural Council Archives, Berezivka, Lviv Oblast.

7. "Istoriia Sela Hrytsevolia."

8. Ibid.

9. Local persecutions were a part of long-term Soviet operations (1944–51) against the Ukrainian Insurgent Army, an underground military unit of Ukrainian nationalists that actively fought the annexation of Western Ukraine to the USSR after the Second World War ended.

10. The Soviet authorities imposed their government system onto Hrytsevolia in 1944 while the war was still being fought. During the same time, the newly established village council started gathering various statistical reports on villagers and their households and recording the gathered data in special annual books. I counted 130 households while working through several volumes of these books ("Khoziaĭstvennaia Kniga Osnovnykh Proizvodstvennykh Pokazateleĭ Khoziaistv v Sel'skikh Sovetakh, Hrytsevolia: Tom za 1945–1948" [The Book of Main Indicators of Productivity in Rural Councils, Hrytsevolia: Volume for 1945–1948], fond 1–1185, description no. 1, item no. 1, Berezivka Rural Council Archives, Berezivka, Lviv Oblast).

11. "Pohospodars'ka Knyha Berezivs'koï Sil'skoï Rady Narodnykh Deputativ na 1996, 1997, 1998, 1999, 2000 roky" [Household Statistics Book of Berezivka Rural Council of People's Deputies, 1996–2000], Berezivka Rural Council Archives, Berezivka, Lviv Oblast.

12. Volodymyr Diiesperov, "Selo Stalo Kartoiu Politychnnoï Hry" [A Village as a Card in Political Games], *Viche* 4, no. 73 (1998): 67–78; Ihor Zhovtaniuk, "Ahrarne Pidpryiemnytstvo: Buty chy Ne Buty" [Agrarian Entrepreneurship: To Be or Not to Be], *Viche* 4, no. 73 (1998): 62–67.

13. I learned this from my discussions with the Bakus'kos, my host family in the village. The size of the household garden land had grown in size from an average of 0.26 hectares per household prior to 1992 to 0.9 hectares in 1999. The increase is nearly four times and the work in these large gardens has been traditionally done manually. From "Pohospodars'ka Knyha," vol. 6, Berezivka Rural Council Archives.

14. According to Genka Mandz'o, during a conversation with me on May 7, 1998, members of four Hrytsevolian households emigrated to Brazil.

15. "Istoriia Sela Hrytsevolia."

16. One should not forget that throughout the second part of the twentieth century, rural communities in Soviet and later post-Soviet Ukraine were technologically disadvantaged in comparison to urban centers. Only a few rural households had a private

phone line by the late 1980s. To make a phone call, one would have to go to the post office or to the neighbors who had a phone line. Cell phones became available only in the late 1990s, and the internet still was unavailable in the early 2000s.

17. *Gemeinschaft* here refers to community defined against the broader social organization of the *Gesellschaft* type, that is society. See Ferdinand Tönnies, *Community and Society*, trans. Charles P. Loomis (East Lansing: Michigan State University Press, 1957).

18. Nadia Trach, private conversation with author, May 10, 1999. Nadia was fifty-four years old at the time.

19. Author's field notes, Hrytsevolia, May 1999.

20. Author's field notes, Hrytsevolia, May 1998.

21. Author's field notes, Hrytsevolia, May 1999.

22. Ibid.

23. Author's field notes, Hrytsevolia, May–June 1998.

24. Ibid.

25. Maria Smal', interview by Natalia Khanenko-Friesen, Hrytsevolia, May 21, 1999.

26. Author's field notes, Hrytsevolia, May 1999.

27. Author's field notes, Hrytsevolia, May–June 1998.

28. Author's field notes, Hrytsevolia, May 1999.

29. Ibid. Note the use of "their," *po-ïkhn'omu*, rather than the proper adjective "German," a linguistic choice that underscores the boundary between "them" and "us."

30. Ibid. Vanchuk is a pseudonym.

31. Ibid.

32. Ibid.

33. In-laws are all assigned special terminology in Ukrainian, there being no collective term like "in-law," a fact that confirms that each relationship has its own significance. The cumulative English "in-laws" that lumps different relationships and people's special in-law identities together into one category suggests the minimal importance of the new relatives to an individual.

34. Al'bert Baïburin, *Ritual v Traditsionnoï Kul'ture: Strukturno-Semanticheskiï Analiz Vostochnoslavianskikh Obriadov* [Ritual in Traditional Culture: The Structural and Semantic Analysis of East Slavic Rites] (Saint Petersburg: Nauka, 1993), 52–53.

35. See, for example, Petro Rohatynskyj, "Zarobitchanska i Politychna Emihratsiia z Butchachchyyny" [Labor and Political Emigration from Buchach Region], in *The City of Butchach and Its Region: A Historical and Memoiristical Collection*, Ukrainian Archives, vol. 27 (New York: Shevchenko Scientific Society, 1972), 683–96.

36. Maria Smal', interview by Natalia Khanenko-Friesen, Hrytsevolia, May 21, 1999.

37. For further discussion of similarities between laments for the deceased and the laments for the conscripts, see Valeriia Eremina, *Ritual i Fol'klor* [Ritual and Folklore] (Leningrad: Nauka, 1991), 25–28.

38. Peter Svarich, *Memoirs, 1877–1904* (Edmonton: Ukrainian Pioneers' Association of Alberta, 1999), 75–80; Volodymyr Hantiuk, "Pisenni Novotvory v Ukraïns'ko-Rus'kiĭ Narodniĭ Slovesnosti" [Novel Folk Songs in Ukrainian-Rus Folk Literature], in *Zapysky Naukovoho Tovarystva Imeni Tarasa Shevchenka* 50, no. 6 (1902–3): 1–18; Vasyl' Stefanyk, *Kaminnyĭ Khrest* [Stone Cross] (n. p.: Vidkryta Knyha, 2011), originally published in 1899; the cycle of poems "Letters from Brazil," cited in Ivan Franko, "Lysty z Brazyliï: 1897–1898" [Letters from Brazil: 1897–1898], in *Davnie i Nove: Druhe pobil'shene vydanie zbirky "Miĭ Izmarahd," Poeziï Ivana Franka* [The Old and the New: Second Enlarged Edition of the Collection "My Izmarahd," Poems by Ivan Franko] (Lviv: Ukraïns'ko-Rus'ka Vydavnycha Spilka, 1911), 153–61. Svarich's book is one of the earliest Ukrainian Canadian memoirs.

39. The singular personal pronoun "ty," or "you," is reserved in Ukrainian for those with whom interlocutor is on familiar terms. In the village culture, "ty" is not used when addressing the elder member of one's kin. The plural personal pronoun "vy" is used instead.

40. [. . .] indicates omitted text.

41. Nadia Trach, private conversation, May 10, 1999.

42. Dressing the deceased maiden as a bride was mentioned to me on several occasions in my extensive fieldwork in rural Central Ukraine between 1989 and 1992 as a part of my work for the Museum of Folklife and Architecture in Kyiv. See also Eremina, *Ritual i Fol'klor*, 166–92, for a discussion of merged wedding and funeral rituals in Slavic and world folklore.

43. Scholars of Slavic folklore have discussed at length the workings of this structuring principle in the folk culture of the Slavic people. Among others, see Al'bert Baĭburin, *Zhylischhe v Obriadakh i Predstavleniiakh Vostochnykh Slavian* [Residence in the Rites and Beliefs of Eastern Slavs] (Leningrad: Nauka, 1983), and Tat'iana Tsyv'ian, "Dom v Fol'klornoĭ Modeli Mira (na Materialakh Balkanskikh Zagadok)" [House in the Folkloric Model of the World (Based on the Materials of Balkan Riddles)], *Trudy po Znakovym Sistemam* 10 (1978): 65. Although one should not underestimate Hrystevolians' worldliness or their entrepreneurial skills and readiness to explore the world, in conversations, during the interviews, in those slow times of pontificating about life, the traditional views came to the surface as conversational tools to keep the conversation going and to explain the world and the happenings in the village community in a meaningful way.

44. Author's field notes, Hrytsevolia, May 1999.

45. Maria Smal', interview by Natalia Khanenko-Friesen, Hrytsevolia, May 21, 1999.

46. That she later told me that her mother was sixteen years younger than her husband, had married him at sixteen, and probably did not learn to love him as he was overseas all the time does not erase the importance of her public statement of fearing the water that Maryntsiunia mentioned during the interview.

47. A common slippage in local discussions where the emigrants who left for Canada are discussed as living in America.

48. Maria Smal', interview by Natalia Khanenko-Friesen, Hrytsevolia, May 17, 1998.

49. Ibid.

50. Ibid. I heard another variation of this story a year later (Maria Smal', interview by Natalia Khanenko-Friesen, Hrytsevolia, May 21, 1999).

Chapter 3. Constructing Longing in Diaspora

1. Mary Dorosh is a pseudonym.

2. John is the stepfather of Mary's children.

3. Notice the usage of the expression "going back," which implies the return to the place of origin. I return to this trope in the chapter on homecoming.

4. Mary Dorosh, interview by Natalia Khanenko-Friesen, Mundare, Canada, October 17, 1997. Mary was born in 1926. [. . .] indicates omitted text.

5. Scholars of diaspora studies seem to agree that those in the diaspora are endowed with unique qualities informed by multifocal and multilocal identities and preferences rather than just by local ones. See, for example, Vijay Agnew's introduction to *Diaspora, Memory, Identity: A Search for Home*, ed. Vijay Agnew (Toronto: University of Toronto Press, 2005), 3–17.

6. See among many others, William Safran, "Diasporas in Modern Societies: Myths of Homeland and Return," *Diaspora* 1, no. 1 (1991): 83–99; James Clifford, *Routes: Travel and Translation in the Late Twentieth Century* (Cambridge, MA: Harvard University Press, 1997), 247, 267; and Dominique Schnapper, "From the Nation-State to the Transnational World: On the Meaning and Usefulness of Diaspora as a Concept," *Diaspora* 8, no. 3 (1999): 225–54.

7. Longing for homeland is an archetypical feature of human life, and it acquired a whole range of meanings in the social context of diasporic communities. For most recent discussion of various imaginings of homeland across various cultures, see Ewa Morawska, "'Diaspora' Diasporas' Representations of Their Homelands: Exploring the Polymorphs," *Ethnic and Racial Studies* 34, no. 6 (2011): 1029–48.

8. Yaroslav Federkewicz, personal communication with the author and interview, Edmonton, Alberta, January 24, 1998.

9. Natalka Husar, personal e-mail correspondence with the author, May–December 2011.

10. The interpretive tools adopted by me at the beginning of this journey across diaspora-homeland imaginings are informed by my training in folklore and anthropology. If one adopted other disciplinary lenses or chose different tools for one's analysis, the outcome would be different from mine. I therefore do not advance here the claim that what I offer as a discussion will hold true for everyone. In addition to the diversity in methods one can use in studying the understandings of homeland, there is also much diversity in the Ukrainian Canadian community informed by class-based, East/West, rural/urban, generational, denominational, gendered, political, and other divides. This

complexity will muddy up and complicate any efforts to produce neat representations of what Ukraine as a homeland means to Ukrainian Canadians.

11. According to the 2011 National Household Survey in Canada, 1,251,170 Canadians claim a Ukrainian background, and among them 276,055 people claim their origin to be wholly Ukrainian (Statistics Canada, "2011 National Household Survey," www12.statcan.gc.ca/nhs-enm/2011/dp-pd/dt-td/index-eng.cfm).

12. Frances Swyripa, "From Sheepskin Coat to Blue Jeans: A Brief History of Ukrainians in Canada," in *Art and Ethnicity: The Ukrainian Tradition in Canada*, ed. Robert B. Klymasz (Hull, Quebec: Canadian Museum of Civilization, 1991), 21.

13. According to statistical sources of 1909, most migrants were peasants (51.4 percent), while others were hired workers (13.7 percent). Their dependents (women and children) comprised 20.5 percent of the emigration profile. Only 1.1 percent of all migrants were qualified specialists in one or another area. The percentage of illiterate migrants reached 50 percent and possibly more. See Arnol'd Shlepakov, *Ukraïns'ka Trudova Emihratsiia v SShA i Kanada (kinets' 19-pochatok 20 st.)* [Ukrainian Labor Emigration in the USA and Canada (Late Nineteenth to Early Twentieth Centuries)] (Kyiv: Vydavnytstvo Akademiï Nauk of the Ukrainian Soviet Socialist Republic, 1960), 18. At the time of first migration wave (between 1870 and 1914), Galicia, Bukovina, and Transcarpathia were under the rule of the Austro-Hungarian empire, and Eastern Ukraine was part of Russian empire.

14. Orest Martynowych, *Ukrainians in Canada: The Formative Period, 1891-1924* (Edmonton: Canadian Institute of Ukrainian Studies Press, 1991), 170-71.

15. Swyripa, "From Sheepskin Coat to Blue Jeans," 22.

16. Rose T. Harasym, "Ukrainians in Canadian Political Life," in *A Heritage in Transition: Essays in the History of Ukrainians in Canada*, ed. Manoly R. Lupul (Toronto: Canadian Publishers, 1982), 112.

17. Swyripa, "From Sheepskin Coat to Blue Jeans," 22.

18. Such readings clubs and societies began to appear in 1903-4 (Shlepakov, *Ukraïns'ka Trudova Emihratsiia*, 135).

19. Martynowych, *Ukrainians in Canada*, 289.

20. Maurice Bloch, Christel Lane, and various others have analyzed the ideological role of ritual. See Maurice Bloch, *From Blessing to Violence: History and Ideology in the Circumcision Ritual of the Merina of Madagascar* (Cambridge: Cambridge University Press, 1986); Christel Lane, *The Rites of Rulers: Ritual in Industrial Society, the Soviet Case* (Cambridge: Cambridge University Press, 1981); and Joseph R. Gusfield and Jerzy Michalowicz, "Secular Symbolism: Studies of Ritual, Ceremony and Symbolic Order in Modern Life," *Annual Review of Sociology* 10 (1984): 417-35.

21. "Sviato Derzhavnosty i Sobornosty Ukraïny" [Day of the Statehood and Sovereignty of Ukraine], *Ukraïns'kyĭ Holos*, February 24, 1971, p. 4.

22. Martynowych, *Ukrainians in Canada*, 289. According to Arnol'd Shlepakov and his colleagues, the first Shevchenko day was held on May 1, 1904, in the hall of the first Shevchenko Reading Club founded by Kyrylo Genyk (*Ukraïns'ki Kanadtsi v Istorychnykh*

Zviazkakh iz Zemleiu Bat'kiv [Ukrainian Canadians and Their Historic Connections with the Land of Their Ancestors] [Kyiv: Dnipro, 1990], 38).

23. Translation provided by Orest Martynowych (*Ukrainians in Canada*, 290).

24. "Celebration of 100 Anniversary of Shevchenko's Birth in Winnipeg, 1914," in *Propamiatna Knyha Ukraïns'koho Domu u Vinipehu* [Memorial Book of the Ukrainian National House in Winnipeg] (Winnipeg: Trident Press, 1949), 155.

25. *Ukraïns'kyĭ Holos*, May 20, 1914. p. 2.

26. Based on my reading of the reports on the celebrations of Shevchenko related events published in *Ukraïns'kyĭ Holos* between 1910 and 1986. Although the majority of reports in *Ukraïns'kyĭ Holos* were about the celebrations held in March, in some communities these celebrations were held on other days. For example, in 1933, in Toronto, Shevchenko Day was held on January 19 (*Ukraïns'kyĭ Holos* 5, 1933).

27. See "Shevchenkivs'kyĭkontsert v Edmontoni" [Shevchenko Concert in Edmonton], *Ukraïns'kyĭ Holos*, April 19, 1972, p. 8.

28. "Sviato Derzhavnosty i Sobornosty Ukraïny." *Ukraïns'kyĭ Holos*, 1971, p. 4.

29. Maurice Bloch, *Ritual, History, and Power: Selected Papers in Anthropology* (London and Atlantic Highlands: Athlone Press, 1989), 19–45.

30. "Celebration of 100 Anniversary of Shevchenko's Birth in Winnipeg," 155.

31. The word "Ukraïna" is a feminine noun in the Ukrainian language.

32. Historians will observe that this reimagining took place in the context of the formation of a new Ukrainian republic, albeit within the walls of the Soviet Union. Orest Subtelny for example, rightly points out that the creation of the Soviet Ukraine and its further expansion in 1939, when lands in Western Ukraine lands were incorporated into the UkrSSR, provided the first historical referent for national unity among Ukrainians and for Ukrainian statehood (*Ukraine: A History* [Toronto: University of Toronto Press, 2009], 456–57).

33. Natalia Khanenko-Friesen, *Inshyĭ Svit abo Etnichnist' u Diï: Kanads'ka Ukraïns'kist' Kintsia Dvadtsiatoho Stolittia* [The Other World; or, Ethnicity in Action: Canadian Ukrainianness at the End of the Twentieth Century] (Kyiv: Smoloskyp, 2011).

34. The image first appeared in the hall as a photograph of the artwork, published in one of the popular Ukrainian wall calendars. As a print, it briefly decorated the National Hall in the mid-1920s, just before the building burned in a fire. In 2000, it was selected for the inclusion in the mural. The painting depicts three prominent male figures in Ukraine's history, Taras Shevchenko (1814–61), Mykhailo Drahomanov (1841–95), and Ivan Franko (1856–1916). All three have been symbols of Ukrainian national culture shared worldwide, but only Shevchenko and Franko were the poets. As symbols, they have been appropriated and reappropriated by various Ukrainian ideologies at different historical conjunctures many times. Known for their efforts in building the Ukrainian nation, culture, or economy, all three figures were especially celebrated in Ukrainian communities (including Ukrainians in Canada) at that time.

35. Mundare, an urban center of the Canadian West, was put on the map with the construction of the Lloydminster-Edmonton line of the Canadian Northern Railway in

1905–6. The Lloydminster-Edmonton area eventually constituted the southern boundary of the Ukrainian bloc in East Central Alberta. See Joanna E. Krotki, *Local Histories of Alberta: An Annotated Bibliography* (Edmonton: Division of East European Studies, University of Alberta, 1980), 275.

36. The monastery's quarters were not originally located in Mundare, where they are now, but "on the farms" at Beaver Lake, "the northwest quarter of section 10 of range 16" (Nykon N. Svirs'kyi, *Tudy lynut' Nashi Sertsia: Istoriia Monders'koho Manastyria* [Our Hearts Go There: History of Mundare Monastery] [Monder: Vydavnytstvo Ottsiv Vasyliian, 1963], 6).

37. A detailed account of the Basilian fathers' activities in Ukraine and Canada may be found in Martynowych, *Ukrainians in Canada*, in the chapter "The Catholic Clergy," 182–213. On the Basilians in North America, see Meletiĭ Voĭnar, *Vasyliiany v Ukraïns'kim Narodi* [Basilians in the History of Ukrainian People] (New York: Vydavnytstvo O. O. Vasyliian, 1950); Bohdan Kazymyra, *Pershyĭ Vasyliüanyn u Kanadi* [The First Basilian in Canada] (Toronto: Dobra knyzhka, 1961); *Propamiatna Knyha Ottsiv Vasyliian u Kanadi: 50 Lit na Sluzhbi Bohovi i Narodovi (1902–1952)* [Memorial Book of the Basilian Fathers in Canada: 50 Years of Serving God and People] (Toronto: Basilian Fathers Press, 1953).

38. Detailed discussion of this event may be found in Jason Golinowski, "Gold, Silver, Bronze: Reflections on a Ukrainian Dance Competition" (MA thesis, University of Alberta, 1999), 39–64.

39. With the arrival in 1952 of Ivan Semeniuk, a post–Second World War immigrant from Ukraine and an educated musician and choir conductor, a choir was set up that has been active in the community for decades (Mundare Historical Society, *Memories of Mundare: A History of Mundare and Districts* [Edmonton: Friesen Printers, 1980], 71).

40. Marsha Woloschuk, personal communication with the author, October 10, 2000.

41. Mundare certainly witnessed Ukrainian commemorative events prior to the seventies, events that likewise reflected local concern for preservation of its Ukrainian heritage. Reference to those may be found in Ukrainian Pioneers' Association of Alberta, *Ukrainians in Alberta, 1891–1900*, vol. 2 (Edmonton: Ukrainian Pioneers' Association, 1981); *Memories of Mundare*; and Peter Svarich, *Memoirs, 1877–1904* (Edmonton: Ukrainian Pioneers' Association of Alberta, 1999).

42. Ed Bilyk, "Paul D. Bilyk—Family," in *Memories of Mundare*, 201–3; Gertrude Bilyk, "Bilyk, John A. and Katherine," in *Memories of Mundare*, 200–201.

43. "Lysyk William and Elizabeth," in *Memories of Mundare*, 356.

44. "The Roman Warawa Family 1900–1980," in *Memories of Mundare*, 523.

45. The notion of the lifeworld is Edmund Husserl's, developed in the 1920s; see his *The Crisis of European Sciences and Transcendental Phenomenology* (Evanston, IL: Northwestern University Press, 1954).

46. Alfred Schutz, *The Phenomenology of the Social World*, trans. George Walsh and Frederick Lehnert (Evantson, IL: Northwestern University Press, 1967); Alfred Schutz and Thomas Luckmann, *The Structures of the Life World*, trans. Richard M. Zaner and H. Tristram Engelhardt (Evanston, IL: Northwestern University Press, 1989).

47. Schutz, *Phenomenology of the Social World*, 139–214.

48. Ibid., 142.

49. Ibid., 142–43.

50. Narrative presentations of the local lifeworld are also realized through metaphors of kinship and generations. In addition, the lived time of individual families is marked in narrative by references to the major events in the life cycle (such as births, deaths, and weddings of individual family members), by listings of all the "firsts" (the first house the family built, the first farm machinery they acquired, the first car they bought, and so on), and by major events in the family history (farm accidents, fires).

51. No other old country is brought into this narrative, either as a textual reference or a map, only Ukraine, even though a sizable number of non-Ukrainians have always lived in this community. In 1996 the Canadian Census listed thirteen other ethnic origins in Mundare (Natalia Khanenko-Friesen [Shostak], "Local Ukrainianness in Transnational Context: An Ethnographic Study of a Canadian Prairie Community" [PhD thesis, University of Alberta, 2001], 204–5).

52. Benedict Anderson, *Imagined Communities: Reflections on the Origin and Spread of Nationalism* (London: Verso, 1991), 187.

53. Anna Wlasenko-Bojcun, *Ukraïns'ki Nazvy u ZSA ta Inshi Pratsi* [Ukrainian Place Names in the USA and Other Selected Articles], ed. Iwan Owechko (Bismarck, ND: Sixtieth Anniversary of the Author Committee, 1977), 7–55. See also Peter Krawchuk, "Ukrainian Place Names in Canada," *Ukrainian Canadian*, September 1980.

54. Other Ukrainian geographic names of Lamont country include Ukraina, Stanislawow, and Podola. Canadian geographer John Lehr discusses similar topographic practices of Ukrainian settlers in Manitoba. See his "The Rural Settlement Behavior of Ukrainian Pioneers in Western Canada 1891–1914," in *Western Canadian Research in Geography: The Lethbridge Papers*, ed. Brenton M. Barr (Vancouver: Tantalus Research, 1975), 51–66, and "Kinship and Society in the Ukrainian Pioneer Settlement of the Canadian West," *The Canadian Geographer* 29, no. 3 (1985): 207–19. Peter Krawchuk discusses Ukrainian place names in "Ukrainian Place Names in Canada," *Ukrainian Canadian*, September 1980, www.virtualmuseum.ca/sgc-cms/histoires_de_chez_nous-community_memories /pm_v2.php?id=story_line&lg=English&fl=0&ex=00000464&sl=5522&pos=1 (accessed September 14, 2011). See also Wlasenko-Bojcun, *Ukraïns'ki Nazvy u ZSA ta Inshi Pratsi*.

55. Vieda Skultans, *The Testimony of Lives: Narrative and Memory in Post-Soviet Latvia* (London: Routledge, 1998), 31–32.

56. James W. Pennebaker and Becky L. Banasik, "On the Creation and Maintenance of Collective Memories: History as Social Psychology," in *Collective Memory of Political Events: Social Psychological Perspectives*, ed. James. W. Pennebaker, Dario Paez, and Berhard Rimé (Mahwah, NJ: Lawrence Erlbaum, 1997), 3–19.

57. "Dream with Me of Days Gone By," preface to *Memories of Mundare*, iv.

58. Gwen Polomark, "Natural History," in *Memories of Mundare*, 1.

59. Ibid., 3.
60. "P. Bahry," in *Memories of Mundare*, 180.
61. Ibid.

Chapter 4. Enveloping Distance

1. Personal memoirs as a unique modern phenomenon of ethnic reflectivity have not been thoroughly researched in the Ukrainian Canadian scholarship. At the Prairie Centre for the Study of Ukrainian Heritage, I continue to collect and document personal memoirs. The bibliography now accounts for seventy memoirs whose publication dates from early twentieth century to the present.

2. *Labuza* is a wild tall grass used for animal feed.

3. Stefan Wakarchuk, Davydivtsi, Ukraine, to Wasyl Wakarchuk, Werigin, Saskatchewan, March 15, 1964, Wakarchuk Letters, binder 4 (1924–72), Personal Sources Archive, Prairie Centre for the Study of Ukrainian Heritage, St. Thomas More College, University of Saskatchewan. Paraskitsa is Wasyl's sister. According to Hrinchenko's dictionary of the Ukrainian language, *badika* was used by Bukovinians in reference to older men including older brothers (http://hrinchenko.com/slovar/znachenie-slova/584-badika.html). Presumably, *lylika* is the feminine counterpart of *badika*.

4. Author's field notes, Edmonton, October 7, 1992.

5. Author's field notes, Hrytsevolia, May 10, 1999. My guess is that this incident with the audiotape took place in late 1970s.

6. Author's field notes, Mundare, October 4, 2011. Christine most likely refers here to the incident that took place in the late 1950s or early 1960s.

7. *Vybyty* literally means "to beat out."

8. Author's field notes, Ternopil, October 26, 2011.

9. The *khustka* was the most common item sent in parcels to Ukraine. In Soviet Ukraine, especially in the countryside, the plain, smaller kerchiefs from overseas were exchanged for up to thirty Soviet rubles on the black market, and the large and decorative ones could fetch eighty to ninety rubles (Stefan Wakarchuk to Wasyl Wakarchuk, March 15, 1964, binder 4 [1924–72], Personal Sources Archive, Prairie Centre for the Study of Ukrainian Heritage). It is not surprising that the *khustka* assumed the role of currency in local village economies. Both the purchasing and symbolic power of the *khustkas* was high.

10. Robert B. Klymasz, "The Letter in Canadian Ukrainian Folklore," *Journal of the Folklore Institute* 6, no. 1 (1969): 39–49.

11. Shtif Tabachniuk [Yakiv Maidanyk], *Kaliendar Sh. Tabachniuka* [Calendar of Sh. Tabachniuk] (Winnipeg: n.p., 1918), 142–45.

12. See, for example, Teodor Fedyk, ed., *Pisni Imigrantiv pro Staryi Krai i Novyi Krai (Pisni pro Kanadu i Avstriiu)* [Immigrants' Songs about the Old World (Songs about Canada and Austria)] (Winnipeg: Ukrainian Booksellers and Publishers, 1927).

13. Andrei Sheptytskyi, "Lysty do Zarobitchan: 1901–1943" [Letters to the Labor Migrants (1901–1943)], Ukraïns'kyĭ Tsentr, http://www.ukrcenter.com/Література /Андрей-Шептицький/25348/Листи-до-заробітчан (accessed January 10, 2012).

14. I chose to refer to such correspondence as immigrant letters, though other researchers may discuss them as emigrant letters.

15. Klymasz, "Letter in Canadian Ukrainian Folklore," 39–49.

16. Oleksandr Sych, comp., *Z Novoho Kraiu: Lysty Ukraïns'kykh Emihrantiv z Kanady* [From the "New Land": Letters of Ukrainian Emigrants from Canada], Research Report No. 45 (Edmonton: Canadian Institute for Ukrainian Studies Press, 1991); Oleksandr Sych, *Z Novoho Kraiu: Lysty Ukraïns'kykh Emihrantiv z Kanady* [From the "New World": Letters of Ukrainian Labor Migrants from Canada] (Chernivtsi: Editorial Department of Oblpolitgrafvydav, 1991).

17. Volodymyr Marchuk, "Lysty Emihrantiv iak Dzherelo do Vyvchennia Hospodarstva i Pobutu Ukraïntsiv v Parahvaï v Druhiĭ Polovyni 30-kh Rokiv 20 st." [Emigrants' Letters as a Source of Studying the Household Activities and the Daily Life of the Ukrainians in Paraguay in Late 1930s], in *Naukovi Zapysky Instytutu Ukraïns'koï Arkheohrafiï ta Dzhereloznavstva im. M. Hrushevs'koho*, vol. 20 (Kyiv: Instytut Ukraïns'koï Arkheohrafiï ta Dzhereloznavstva im. M. Hrushevs'koho, 2010), 366–73.

18. Halyna Myroniuk et al., "The Migration Letter: Archiving Intimacy in Postal Era," paper delivered at "Introducing the IHRC Digital Pilot Project: Letter Writing as Emotional Connection among Finnish, Ukrainian, Italian, and Latvian Immigrants," Immigration History Research Center, University of Minnesota, May 17–18, 2010.

19. Marchuk, "Lysty Emihrantiv Ukraïntsiv v Parahvaï," 2010; Jeffrey Picknicki Morski, *Under the Southern Cross: A Collection of Accounts and Reminiscences about the Ukrainian Immigration in Brazil, 1895–1914* (Winnipeg: Watson and Dwyer Publishing, 2000).

20. William I. Thomas and Florian Znaniecki, *The Polish Peasant in Europe and America*, 2nd ed. (New York: Dover, 1958); William I. Thomas and Florian Znaniecki, *The Polish Peasant in Europe and America*, ed. Eli Zaretsky (Urbana: University of Illinois Press, 1984). This work was first published between 1918 and 1920.

21. Theodore C. Blegen, ed., *The Land of Their Choice: Immigrants Write Home* (Minneapolis: University of Minnesota Press, 1955); Arnold H. Barton, *Letters from the Promised Land: Swedes in America, 1840–1914* (Minneapolis: University of Minnesota Press, 1975); Leo Schelbert and Hedwig Rapport, eds., *Alles Ist Ganz Anders Hier: Auswandererschicksale in Briefen aus Zwei Jahrhunderten* (Olten, Switzerland: Walter, 1977); Witold Kula, Nina Assorodobraj-Kula, and Marcin Kula, *Writing Home: Immigrants in Brazil and the United States, 1890–1891*, ed. and trans. Josephine Wtulich (New York: Columbia University Press, 1986); Adolf E. Schroede and Carla Schulz-Geisberg, eds., *Hold Dear, As Always: Jette, a German Immigrant Life in Letters*, trans. Adolf E. Schroede (Columbia: University of Missouri Press, 1988); Walter D. Kamphoephner, Wolfgang Helbich, and Ulrike Sommer, eds., *News from the Land of Freedom: German Immigrants Write Home* (Ithaca, NY: Cornell University Press, 1991); Herman Ganzevoort, *The Last Illusion: Letters from Dutch Immigrants in the "Land of Opportunity"* (Calgary: University of Calgary Press, 1999).

22. Charlotte Erickson, *Invisible Immigrants: The Adaptation of English and Scottish Immigrants in Nineteenth-Century America* (London: Weidenfeld and Nicolson, 1972).

23. Johan Stellingwerff and Robert P. Swierenga, *Iowa Letters: Dutch Immigrants on the American Frontier* (Grand Rapids, MI: Eerdmans, 2004), originally published as *Amsterdamse Emigranten: Onbekende Brieven uit de Prairie van Iowa, 1846–1873* (Amsterdam: Buijten and Schipperheijn, 1975); Herbert J. Brinks, *Dutch American Voices: Letters from the United States, 1850–1930* (Ithaca, NY: Cornell University Press, 1995); Kamphoephner et al., *News from the Land of Freedom*; Sonia Cancian, *Families, Lovers, and Their Letters: Italian Post-War Migration to Canada* (Winnipeg: University of Manitoba Press, 2010); David Fitzpatrick, *Oceans of Consolation: Personal Accounts of Irish Migration to Australia* (Ithaca, NY: Cornell University Press, 1994); Solveig Zempel, ed., *In Their Own Words: Letters from Norwegian Immigrants* (Minneapolis: University of Minnesota Press, 1991); Eero Kuparinen, *Maitten ja Merten Takaa: Vuosisata Suomalaisia Siirtolaiskirjeite* [Beyond the Seas: Hundred Years of Immigrant Letters] (Ekenas: Turum Historiallinen Arkisto, 1985).

24. Natalia Khanenko-Friesen, "Letters from the 'Old Country': Exploring and Defining Ukrainian Canadian Vernacular Letter Writing," *Canadian Ethnic Studies Journal* (forthcoming).

25. The Personal Sources Archives, initiated in 2009, grew out of my long-term research projects, "Ukrainian Canadian Personal Memoirs" and "Letters to/from the 'Old Country.'" The goal of this program is to build a collection and create an inventory of vernacular documentation that is of importance to the study of the Ukrainian cultural experience in Saskatchewan, Canada, and around the world. As a research program, our mandate is to actively seek, collect, and preserve such personal documents as letters written to and from Ukraine, diaries, family histories, personal memoirs, photos, and other relevant documentation. Both projects are the outcome of a larger research program, "Diaspora, Homeland and the Ukrainian Other in the Twentieth Century," supported by Canada's Social Sciences and Humanities Research Council (2007–11) through the council's standard research grant. Over the course of last five years, more than eleven hundred personal letters belonging to twenty-one different series have been identified and archived in our archival holdings.

26. See Jennifer Attebery, *Up in the Rocky Mountains: Writing the Swedish Immigrant Experience* (Minneapolis: University of Minnesota Press, 2007), 1–20, for further discussion of scholarship focusing on vernacular nature of immigrant correspondence.

27. Jerome Bruner, *Acts of Meaning* (Cambridge, MA: Harvard University Press, 1990).

28. Sonia Cancian, for example, considers the place of correspondence in the maintenance of kinship, but she only focuses on how the writers exercised their kinship roles in writing (how parents tried to parent their children in Canada, for example); see *Families, Lovers, and Their Letters*, 41–69. And in his seminal work *Authors of Their Lives: The Personal Correspondence of British Immigrants to North America in the Nineteenth Century* (New York: New York University Press, 2006), David. A. Gerber, an authority on immigrant letters, focuses on familial relations that frame personal correspondence, but in his

analysis of immigrant letters he emphasizes synchronic familial relations that enmesh the writer in his/her time. In his earlier work, Gerber asserts that "personal correspondence . . . is composed by individuals and intended for the attention of the individuals closest to them in emotional terms" ("'You see I speak wery well English': Literacy and the Transformed Self as Reflected in Immigrant Personal Correspondence," *Journal of American Ethnic History* 2, no. 2 [1993]: 56–62).

29. Khanenko-Friesen, "Letters from the 'Old Country.'"

30. See also Natalia Khanenko-Friesen, *Inshyĭ Svit abo Etnichnist' u Diï: Kanads'ka Ukraïns'kist' Kintsia Dvadtsiatoho Stolittia* [The Other World; or, Ethnicity in Action: Canadian Ukrainianness at the End of the Twentieth Century] (Kyiv: Smoloskyp, 2011), 19.

31. It is important to note here that despite the assumed correlation between the phases in the transatlantic letter writing and the phases of the growth of the Ukrainian Canadian community, the changes in letter writing first and above all correlate with the timeline of a particular family history in Canada (and with the immigration of the original migrants). In other words, each letter is as much governed by the circumstances of individual writers and their families as it is subject to the workings of larger history of community development in Canada or Ukraine. Still, given that the immigration took place in massive waves, family letter writing in general follows a shared chronology in its development.

32. Other collections of letters from Ukraine that we have gathered so far display the opposite tendency; in these, the writing is sustained predominantly by female members of extended families.

33. The couple farmed together until 1965, when they retired and built themselves a new home in Yorkton. There they led active lives as members of various Ukrainian organizations and the Ukrainian Orthodox community. Wasyl died in 1985, leaving behind four children, Alexander, Mary, Pauline, and Sylvia (Pauline Semenuik, interview by Natalia Khanenko-Friesen, Yorkton, Saskatchewan, November 12, 2010). The family history of the Wakarchuks can also be found in the unpublished family history that Wasyl's son wrote in the late 2000s (Alexander Wakarchuk, "Wakarchuk Family History," unpublished, n.d.).

34. There is a vast body of literature on the political repression of Western Ukrainians by the Soviet authorities. See, for example, B. O. Iarosh, *Totalitarnyĭ Rezhym na Zakhidnoukraïns'kykh Zemliakh u 30–50-i roky 20 Stolittia: Istoryko-politolohichnyĭ aspect* [Totalitarianism in Western Ukraine, 1930–50: Historical and Political Aspects] (Luts'k: Nadstyria, 1995); Mykhaĭlo V. Sen'kiv, *Zakhidno-ukraïns'ke Selo: Nasyl'nyts'ka Kolektyvizatsiia 40-kh poch. 50-kh rokiv 20 st.* [Western Ukrainian Village: Forced Collectivization, 1940–50] (Lviv: Instytut Ukraïnoznavstva NANU, 2002).

35. Founded in 1929, Intourist was the state-owned and operated Soviet company, solely responsible for handling foreign tourism in the USSR. Only organized foreign tourism was allowed in the USSR. The Intourist offices were thought to be staffed by KGB agents.

36. For the discussions on the prescriptive and regulatory powers of letter writing as a genre, see, for example, Gerber, *Authors of Their Lives*, 162–200. See also Attebery, *Up in the Rocky Mountains*, "Thanks for the Letter: The Shape of Genre," 21–43.

37. Attebery, *Up in the Rocky Mountains*, 1–20; Orm Øverland, *The Western Home: A Literary History of Norwegian America* (Northfield, MT: Norwegian American Historical Association, 1996); Linda Dégh, "Two Letters from Home," *Journal of American Folklore* 91, no. 361 (1978): 808.

38. If *badika* is the term used by the younger siblings in reference to the oldest brother in the family, similarly, *lylika* is the term reserved for the oldest sister. In the context of this correspondence, Stefan refers to Wasyl's wife as *lylika* out of respect for his old brother and, perhaps, to symbolically shorten the insurmountable distance between all the participants in this transatlantic kinship.

39. On Good Friday, one fasts for the entire day.

40. Stefan Vakarchuk to Wasyl Wakarchuk, September 15, 1963, Wakarchuk Letters, binder 4 (1924–72), Personal Sources Archive, Prairie Centre for the Study of Ukrainian Heritage.

41. Pauline Semenuik, interview by Natalia Khanenko-Friesen, Yorkton, Saskatchewan, November 12, 2010; see also Alexander Wakarchuk, "Wakarchuk Family History."

42. Wasyl's interest in his own family genealogy is very much in line with that of many other members of other families who have searched for their overseas roots and relatives, a trend that has accelerated since the 1980s. The 1980s were the years in which some Canadian provinces were celebrating their seventy-fifth anniversaries (Alberta, Saskatchewan), and these were also the years in which many families of the original settlers were actively exploring their own family roots in anticipation of centennial family reunions to mark both their families' personal immigration anniversaries in Canada and the centennial of Ukrainian settlement (which was widely celebrated in Canada in 1991).

43. Pauline Semenuik and her brother engaged in correspondence with several of their father's relatives in Davydivtsi throughout the 1990s (Pauline Semenuik, interview by Natalia Khanenko-Friesen, Yorkton, Saskatchewan, November 12, 2010).

44. Stefan Wakarchuk to Wasyl Wakarchuk, December 1984, Wakarchuk Letters, binder 4 (1924–72), Personal Sources Archive, Prairie Centre for the Study of Ukrainian Heritage.

45. Arnold van Gennep, *The Rites of Passage* (London: Routledge and Kegan Paul, 1960); Victor Turner, "Variations on a Theme of Liminality," in *Secular Ritual*, ed. Sally F. Moore and Barbara G. Myerhoff (Amsterdam: Van Gorcum, 1977), 48–65; Hein Viljoen and Chris van der Merwe, eds., *Beyond the Threshold: Explorations of Liminality in Literature* (New York: Peter Lang, 2006).

46. Mikhail Bakhtin, "Forms of Time and of the Chronotope in the Novel: Notes toward a Historical Poetics," in *The Dialogic Imagination: Four Essays*, trans. Caryl Emerson and Michael Holquist, ed. Michael Holquist (Austin: University of Texas Press, 1981),

259–422; Mikhail Bakhtin, *Rablais and His World* (Bloomington: Indiana University Press, 1984). I would like to thank Peter Larson for our productive dialogue back in 2008 on the nature and interpretation of space and specifically *liminal* space in the contexts of myth and literature.

Chapter 5. Imagining Kinship in Diaspora

1. Jerome Bruner, *Acts of Meaning* (Cambridge, MA: Harvard University Press, 1990), 42.

2. Zenon Pohorecky, "Kinship and Courtship Patterns," in *Continuity and Change: The Cultural Life of Alberta's First Ukrainians*, ed. Manoly R. Lupul (Edmonton: Canadian Institute of Ukrainian Studies Press, 1988).

3. Michael G. Peletz, "Kinship Studies in Late Twentieth-Century Anthropology," *Annual Review of Anthropology* 24 (1995): 360–62.

4. Sarah Franklin and Susan McKinnon, introduction to *Relative Values: Reconfiguring Kinship Studies*, ed. Susan Franklin and Susan McKinnon (Durham, NC: Duke University Press, 2001), 1–28; Janet Carsten, introduction to *Cultures of Relatedness: New Approaches to the Study of Kinship*, ed. Janet Carsten (Cambridge: Cambridge University Press. 2000), 1–36; Peter Schweitzer, introduction to *Dividends of Kinship: Meanings and Uses of Social Relatedness*, ed. Peter Schweitzer (London; New York: Routledge, 2000), 1–32; Catherine Nash, "'They're family!': Cultural Geographies of Relatedness in Popular Genealogy," in *Uprootings/Regroupings: Questions of Home and Migration*, ed. Sara Ahmed, Claudia Castaneda, Anne-Marie Forties, and Mimi Sheller (Oxford, New York: Berg, 2003), 180.

5. Natalia Khanenko-Friesen, *Inshyĭ Svit abo Etnichnist' u Dĭi: Kanads'ka Ukraïns'kist' Kintsia Dvadtsiatoho Stolittia* [The Other World or Ethnicity in Action: Canadian Ukrainianness at the End of the Twentieth Century] (Kyiv: Smoloskyp, 2011).

6. Manoly Lupul, ed., *Visible Symbols: Cultural Expression among Canada's Ukrainians* (Edmonton: Canadian Institute of Ukrainian Studies Press, 1984).

7. Author's field notes, Mundare, Alberta, October 13, 1997.

8. Edward Shils, *Tradition* (London: Faber, 1981), 2, cited in Anthony Giddens, *Modernity and Self-Identity: Self and Society in the Late Modern Age* (Stanford, CA: Stanford University Press, 1991), 146.

9. Martin A. Conway, "The Inventory of the Experience: Memory and Identity," in *Collective Memory of Political Events: Social Psychological Perspectives*, ed. James. W. Pennebaker, Dario Paez, and Berhard Rimé (Mahwah, NJ: Lawrence Erlbaum, 1997), 43.

10. See Giddens, *Modernity and Self-Identity*, 146, 160.

11. Anthony D. Smith, "Ethnic Myths and Ethnic Revivals," *European Journal of Sociology* 25, no. 2 (1984): 283–305; Anthony D. Smith, "The Myth of the 'Modern Nation' and the Myths of Nations," *Ethnic and Racial Studies* 11, no. 1 (1988): 1–25; Anthony D. Smith, "Chosen Peoples: Why Ethnic Groups Survive," *Ethnic and Racial Studies* 15, no. 3 (1992): 437–40.

12. Detailed information on Ivan Pylypiw (1859–1936) and Wasyl Eleniak (1859–1956), as well as on commemorative Ukrainian Canadian projects related to these two men, can be found in Marschal Nay's thoroughly researched book *Trailblazers of Ukrainian Emigration to Canada: Wasyl Eleniak and Ivan Pylypow* (Edmonton: Brightest Pebble, 1997). For an example of commemorating the first immigrants, see also Harry Piniuta, *Land of Pain, Land of Promise: First Person Accounts by Ukrainian Pioneers, 1891–1914* (Saskatoon: Western Producer Prairie Books, 1978).

13. A primary example is Orest Martynowych, *Ukrainians in Canada: The Formative Period, 1891–1924* (Edmonton: Canadian Institute of Ukrainian Studies Press, 1991).

14. In its effort to profile the challenges and successes of the first Ukrainian Canadians, the Mundare Museum has followed other Ukrainian Canadian organizations (the Ukrainian Museum of Canada in Saskatoon, its branch in Toronto, the Heritage Village in Edmonton, and others) by presenting the same story in permanent displays.

15. Aiming to engage the local community in the life of the museum, Dagmar Rais continued this practice through the years of her curatorial leadership of the museum.

16. Author's field notes, near Mundare, Alberta, March 2, 2001.

17. John Lehr, "Kinship and Society in the Ukrainian Pioneer Settlement of the Canadian West," *Canadian Geographer* 29, no. 3 (1985): 207–19.

18. While there are other highly accessible cultural sites, including memoirs, autobiographies, paintings, and local history books, that readily profile the politics as well as local understandings of family, family histories concern themselves directly with the notion of kin, family, and their continuity. This is why I chose to focus on them.

19. Myron Momryk, *Annotated Bibliography of Ukrainian Canadian History Publications* (Ottawa: n.p., n.d.).

20. It is possible that some families wrote their history earlier, but prior to the 1970s not many family histories seem to have been published.

21. Stephen Cornell, "That's the Story of Our Life," in *We Are a People: Narrative and Multiplicity in Constructing Ethnic Identity*, ed. Paul Spickard and W. J. Burroughs (Philadelphia: Temple University Press, 2000), 41–53.

22. William J. Carlyle, "Farm Population in the Canadian Parkland," *Geographical Review* 79, no. 1 (1989): 13–35.

23. Joanne S. Stiles, "Descended from Heroes: The Frontier Myth in Rural Alberta," *Alberta* 2, no. 2 (1990): 27.

24. Kate Tichon, interview by Natalia Khanenko-Friesen, Mundare, Alberta, March 1, 2001.

25. Marilyn Mandiuk, interview by Natalia Khanenko-Friesen, Mundare, Alberta, December 16, 2000.

26. Cornell, "That's the Story of Our Life," 41–53; Anthony Wallace, "Revitalization Movements," *American Anthropologist* 58, no. 2 (1956): 264–81; Giddens, *Modernity and Self-Identity*.

27. Nico H. Frijda, "Commemorating," in *Collective Memory of Political Events*, 108. Similar observations have been made in relation to autobiographical narratives within

the framework of anthropology (see, for example, Vieda Skultans, *The Testimony of Lives: Narrative and Memory in Post-Soviet Latvia* [London: Routledge, 1998], 25–26), in psychology (see, for example, Bruner, *Acts of Meaning*, 11), and ethnic studies (see, for example, Cornell, "That's the Story of Our Life," 44–45).

28. Stiles, "Descended from Heroes."

29. Dagmar Rais, personal communication with the author, June 11, 2000.

30. The following families were selected: Chmelyk, Eleniak, Halas, Koziak, Vitiuk, and Weleshchuk (1891–1991), Romaniuk (1892–1992), Wojtas (1897–1997), Dobush, Gulevych, Koroliuk, and Uwyn (1898–1998), and Kolodychuk and Moszczanski (1899–1999).

31. Vladimir Propp, *Morphology of the Folktale*, 2nd rev. ed. (Austin: University of Texas Press, 1968), 23.

32. Steven P. Eleniak, ed. and comp., *Eleniak Family Tree* (Altona, Manitoba: Eleniak Heritage Society, 1991).

33. *Z rodu v rid* [From Generation to Generation] (1991), 153.

34. Steven Eleniak, personal communication with author, July 20, 2014. Note that the figures in this image are all male.

35. "Moszczanski Family Reunion Dinner Program," 1997.

36. Genealogy is commonly seen as one of the most popular leisure pursuits worldwide and is allegedly the second most common use of the internet, after pornography, according to Peter Warren ("Can't See the Net for the Trees—Genealogy Second Only to Sex," *Scotland on Sunday*, November 28, 1999, cited in Paul Basu, *Highland Homecomings: Genealogy and Heritage Tourism in the Scottish Diaspora* [Oxford: Routledge, 2007], 2).

37. Popular genealogy as social practice has been discussed by historians, geographers, and anthropologists since the 1970s, reflecting the new boom in genealogical research itself that occurred in this same decade. See, for example, Robert M. Taylor Jr. and Ralph J. Crandall, "Historians and Genealogists: An Emerging Community of Interest," in *Generations of Change: Genealogical Perspectives in Social History*, ed. Robert M. Taylor Jr. and Ralph J. Crandall (Macon, GA: Mercer University Press, 1986), 17–21.

38. Dallen J. Timothy and Jeanne Kay Guelke, "Introduction" to *Geography and Genealogy: Locating Personal Pasts*, ed. Timothy J. Dallen and Jeanne Kay Guelke (Aldershot, UK: Ashgate, 2008), 1.

39. Alex Haley, *Roots: The Saga of American Family* (New York: Doubleday, 1976).

40. Walter Rusel, interview by Natalia Khanenko-Friesen, Saskatoon, Saskatchewan, October 26, 2010; Radomir Bilash, interview by Natalia Khanenko-Friesen, Edmonton, Alberta, November 6, 2010; John-Paul Himka and Frances Swyripa, *Sources for Researching Ukrainian Family History* (Edmonton: Canadian Institute of Ukrainian Studies Press, 1984); Myron Momryk, *A Guide to Sources for the Study of Ukrainian Canadians* (Ottawa: Public Archives of Canada, 1984); John Pihach, "Introduction to Ukrainian Genealogical Research," *Saskatchewan Genealogical Society Bulletin* 15, no. 2 (1984): 74–76; *Researching Ukrainian Family History*, Research Report No. 6 (Edmonton: Canadian Institute of Ukrainian Studies, 1984); Frances Swyripa, *Oral Sources for Researching Ukrainian Canadians:*

A Survey of Interview, Lectures, and Programmes Recorded to December 1980 (Edmonton: Canadian Institute of Ukrainian Studies Press, 1985); Kathlyn Szalasznyj, *How to Research Your Ukrainian Ancestry in Saskatchewan* (Saskatoon: Ukrainian Canadian Committee, 1986); Muryl Andrejciw Geary, *Finding Your Ukrainian Ancestors* (Toronto: Heritage Production, 1998, 2000); Brian J. Lenius, *Genealogical Gazetteer of Galicia*, 3rd ed. (Anola, Manitoba: B. J. Lenius, 1999; available at www.lenius.ca/Gazetteer/Gazetteer.htm); John Pihach, *Ukrainian Genealogy: A Beginner's Guide* (Edmonton: Canadian Institute of Ukrainian Studies Press, 2007).

41. The release of Haley's novel was followed by its hugely popular television adaptation, *Roots* (1977), resulting in a cultural sensation in the United States. See Wikipedia, "Roots: The Saga of an American Family," http://en.wikipedia.org/wiki/Roots:_ The_Saga_of_an_American_Family.

42. "Directory of Resources," Library and Archives Canada, www.collectionscanada .gc.ca/databases/avitus/001069-110.01-e.php.

43. For example, the Alberta Provincial Council of the Ukrainian Canadian Congress is supporting the Alberta-Ukraine Genealogical Project and the Ukrainian Family History Portal.

44. Genealogy of Halychyna and Eastern Galicia, www.halgal.com, and Community and Family Histories of Ukrainians in Canada, http://communities.ukrainian genealogygroup-pei.org, are hosted by various online communities, the latter by the well-known web portal www.infoukes.com.

45. Himka and Swyripa, *Sources for Researching Ukrainian Family History*; Momryk, "Sources for the Study of Ukrainian Family History at Public Archives of Canada"; Momryk, *A Guide to Sources for the Study of Ukrainian Canadians*; Pihach, "Introduction to Ukrainian Genealogical Research"; *Researching Ukrainian Family History*; Swyripa, *Oral Sources for Researching Ukrainian Canadians*; Szalasznyj, *How to Research Your Ukrainian Ancestry in Saskatchewan*; Geary, *Finding Your Ukrainian Ancestors*. This list, for example, excludes the self-published *Genealogical Gazetteer of Galicia*, a compilation of maps and other resources covering the pre–First World War Austrian crownland of Galicia.

46. Equally there has been no critical exploration of Ukrainian genealogical research in other geographic contexts, either in the diaspora or in the homeland, though even in Ukraine genealogical research has surged in the last ten years.

47. John W. Adams and Alice Bee Kasakoff, "Anthropology, Genealogy and History: A Research Log," in *Generations and Change*, 53–78; David Lowenthal, *Possessed by the Past: The Heritage Crusade and the Spoils of History* (New York: Free Press, 1996); Eviatar Zerubavel, *Ancestors and Relatives: Genealogy, Identity, and Community* (New York: Oxford University Press, 2012); Timothy and Guelke, *Geography and Genealogy*; Basu, *Highland Homecomings*; Catherine Nash, *Of Irish Descent: Origin Stories, Genealogy, and the Politics of Belonging* (Syracuse, NY: Syracuse University Press, 2008).

48. Samuel M. Otterstrom, "Genealogy as Religious Ritual: The Doctrine and Practice of Family History in the Church of Jesus Christ of Latter-day-Saints," in *Geography and Genealogy*, 137.

49. Spencer W. Kimball, "The Angels May Quote from It," *New Era*, October 1975, cited in Otterstrom, "Genealogy as Religious Ritual," 147; Gawain Wells and Gayle J. Wells, "Hidden Benefits of Keeping a History," *Ensign* 26, no. 7 (1986): 47, cited in Otterstrom, "Genealogy as Religious Ritual," 147.

50. Walter Rusel, interview by Natalia Khanenko-Friesen, Saskatoon, Saskatchewan, October 26, 2010.

51. Alberta-Ukraine Genealogical Project, "Alberta-Ukraine Genealogy Project Launched," August 13, 2006, Ukrainian Genealogical and Historical Society, http://ukrainiangenealogist.tripod.com/alberta-ukraine.htm.

52. Radomir Bilash, interview by Natalia Khanenko-Friesen, Edmonton, Alberta, November 6, 2010. Bilash spoke to this matter in his presentation on the Alberta-Ukraine Genealogical Project at the Annual Meeting of the Canadian Association of Slavists, Victoria, June 1, 2013.

53. Ukrainian Heritage Village is an open air museum near Edmonton devoted to the preservation and conservation of the Ukrainian vernacular material and other cultural artifacts from the turn of the twentieth century.

54. See Alberta-Ukraine Genealogical Project, *A Fieldworker's Guide to Documenting Church Properties in Rural Communities in Alberta* (Edmonton: Alberta-Ukraine Genealogical Project, n.d.).

55. From the Alberta-Ukraine Genealogical Project flyer distributed at the Ukrainian Canadian Congress meeting in Edmonton, October 2010.

56. Most recently, the program was revised to recognize those early settlers who had no descendants and was expanded to include settlers of other ethnic backgrounds. See Alberta-Ukraine Genealogical Project, *Project Report, 2012–2013, Phase II* (Edmonton: Alberta-Ukraine Genealogical Project., n.d.), 13.

57. Catherine Nash "'They're family!,'" 181.

58. See also Lenius, *Genealogical Gazetteer of Galicia*.

Chapter 6. Homecoming

1. William Safran, "Diasporas in Modern Societies: Myths of Homeland and Return," *Diaspora* 1, no. 1 (1991): 83–99; Martin Baumann, "Diaspora: Genealogies of Semantics and Transcultural Comparison," *Numen* 47, no. 3 (2000): 313–37; Anders Stefansson, "Homecomings to the Future: From Diasporic Mythographies to Social Projects of Return," in *Homecomings: Unsettling Paths of Return*, ed. Fran Markowitz and Andres Stefansson (Lanham, MD: Lexington Books, 2004), 2–20.

2. David Harvey, *The Condition of Postmodernity: An Enquiry into the Origins of Cultural Change* (Oxford, UK: Blackwell, 1989); Arjun Appadurai, *Modernity at Large: Cultural Dimensions of Globalization* (Minneapolis: University of Minnesota Press, 1996); James Clifford, *Routes: Travel and Translation in the Late Twentieth Century* (Cambridge, MA: Harvard University Press, 1997); Anthony Giddens, *Modernity and Self-Identity: Self and Society in the Late Modern Age* (Stanford, CA: Stanford University Press, 1991); Kenneth

Gergen, *The Saturated Self: Dilemmas of Identity in Contemporary Life* (New York: Basic Books, 1991); Charles Taylor, *Sources of the Self: The Making of the Modern Identity* (Cambridge: Cambridge University Press, 1989); Dan McAdams, "The Case for Unity in the (Post) Modern Self: A Modest Proposal," in *Self and Identity: Fundamental Issues*, ed. Richard D. Ashmore and Lee Jussim (New York: Oxford University Press, 1997), 46–78.

3. Giddens, *Modernity and Self-Identity*, 75; Jerome Bruner, *Acts of Meaning* (Cambridge, MA: Harvard University Press, 1990), 115–16; McAdams, "The Case for Unity in the (Post)Modern Self," 48; Safran, "Diasporas in Modern Societies," 83–99.

4. Paul Basu, *Highland Homecomings: Genealogy and Heritage Tourism in the Scottish Diaspora* (Oxford, UK: Routledge, 2007), 162.

5. In this context, homecomings of other ethnic groups that have their homelands in the former USSR have also been subject to political control and limitations. See Great N. Slobin, "The 'Homecoming' of the First Wave Diaspora and Its Cultural Legacy," *Slavic Review* 60, no. 3 (2001): 513–29, and Tsypylma Darieva, "Rethinking Homecoming: Diasporic Cosmopolitanism in post-Soviet Armenia," *Ethnic and Racial Studies* 34, no. 3 (2011): 490–508.

6. Paul Basu is perhaps the leading commentator on homecoming. See also Chih-ming Wang, "Politics of Return: Homecoming Stories of the Vietnamese Diaspora," *East Asia Cultures Critique* 21, no. 1 (2013): 161–87; Katharina Schramm, "Coming Home to the Motherland: Pilgrimage Tourism in Ghana," in *Reframing Pilgrimage*, ed. John Eade and Simon Coleman (London: Routledge, 2004), 133–49; and Jung Ran Forte, "'Ways of Remembering': Transatlantic Connections and African Diaspora's Homecoming in the Republic of Benin," *Social Dynamics: A Journal of African studies* 33, no. 2 (2007): 123–43. Catherine Nash explores the homecoming experiences of the Irish; see her "Genealogical Identities," *Environment and Planning D: Society and Space* 20, no. 1 (2002): 27–52. On homecomings to the UK, see Anne-Marie Kramer, "Kinship, Affinity and Connectedness: Exploring the Role of Genealogy in Personal Lives," *Sociology* 45, no. 3 (2011): 379–95.

7. For comparative purposes, approximately 30 percent of Poles who arrived in the United States at the end of the nineteenth century and through the early twentieth century returned to Poland. See Wikipedia, "History of the Poles in the United States," http://en.wikipedia.org/wiki/History_of_the_Poles_in_the_United_States.

8. Andrij Makuch, personal correspondence with author, September 12–14, 2002.

9. The project was coordinated by myself and Dr. Teresa Zolner, department of psychology, St. Thomas More College, University of Saskatchewan.

10. Lara Verny, interview by Anastasia Tataryn, Saskatoon, July 7, 2002, tape 2002-01-30, audio file PCUH-UCP-UZBb, Oral History of Sociocultural Change on the Prairies: The Ukrainian Canadian Experience, Shannon Library, St. Thomas More College, University of Saskatchewan. Lara Verny is a pseudonym.

11. It was Hayden White's work that first shaped my understanding of narrativization; see his "The Value of Narrativity in the Representation of Reality," *Critical Inquiry* 7, no. 1 (1980): 5–27.

12. I discuss the extreme case of folkloric narrativization of the earliest narratives of departure (and arrival) in my essay on the Pylypiw and Eleniak families' stories of departure, "From Family Lore to a People's History: The Role of Oral Culture in Ukrainian Claims to the Canadian Prairies," in *Orality and Literacy: Reflections across Disciplines*, ed. Keith Carlson, Kristina Fagan, and Natalia Khanenko-Friesen (Toronto: University of Toronto Press, 2011), 177–96.

13. Natalka Husar's work is documented in such exhibition catalogues as the *Aptechka* [First Aid Kit] (Kyiv: Rodovid, 2009) and others. See Janice Kulyk Keefer's book *Green Library* (New York: Harper Perennial, 1996), and John Paskievich's documentary *My Mother's Village*, DVD (Montreal: National Film Board of Canada National Film Board, 2001).

14. Author's field notes, Rozhniv, Ukraine, May 22, 1996.

15. Author's field notes, Rozhniv, Ukraine, May 25, 1996.

16. Anne Dobry is a pseudonym.

17. George is Anne's husband and Rodney is their son.

18. [. . .] indicates omitted text and . . . indicates pauses in conversation.

19. Molodiia is a village in Western Ukraine.

20. Anne was referring to Hankivtsi, for we were looking at pictures of the village as we were talking.

21. Anne Dobry, interview by Natalia Khanenko-Friesen, Mundare, Alberta, June 5, 2001.

22. Mircea Eliade, *The Sacred and the Profane: The Nature of Religion*, trans. Willard Trask (London: Harcourt Brace Jovanovich, 1959); Victor Turner, *The Ritual Process: Structure and Anti-Structure* (New York: Aldine De Gruyter, 1969); Maurice Bloch, *From Blessing to Violence: History and Ideology in the Circumcision Ritual of the Merina of Madagascar* (Cambridge: Cambridge University Press, 1986).

23. For more on the idea of parallel kin, see chapter 2.

24. Mary Ellen P., personal communication with the author, 2000.

25. Vera A., interview by Natalia Khanenko-Friesen, Catskill Mountains, New York, July 2000.

26. Anne Dobry, interview by Natalia Khanenko-Friesen, Mundare, Alberta, June 5, 2001.

27. Ibid.

28. See, for example, Petro Krawchuk, *Bez Nedomovok: Spohady* [Without Abbreviations: The Memoir] (Kyiv: Literaturna Ukraïna, 1995), 271–73.

29. Wasyl Pylypiw was the son of the first immigrant to Canada, Ivan Pylypiw; Wasyl visited Nebyliw in 1966.

30. A driver drove the two of them; Olha did not drive Wasyl.

31. Petro Krawchuk, a procommunist Ukrainian Canadian leader, organized the 1991 homecoming tour to the village.

32. Olha Velychko, interview by Natalia Khanenko-Friesen, Nebyliw, Ukraine, June 28, 2002. Olha Velychko is a pseudonym.

33. See Krawchuk, *Bez Nedomovok*, 270–73. Our interview was conducted in Ukrainian. The translation is mine.

34. "Heritage Tour III to Ukraine: Highlight of Centennial Summer," *Ukrainian Culture*, September 1991, 14–15.

35. Krawchuk, *Bez Nedomovok*, 270–73.

36. Ibid.

Chapter 7. Into the Twenty-First Century

1. Extract from a poem by Tamara Lavruk Moroshan, *Ia pryïshla v tseĭ svit liubyty: Poeziï* [I Came to This World to Love: Poems] (Cascais, Portugal: n.p., 2008), 5–6. Moroshan, a teacher and journalist originally from the village of Mykhal'cha, Chernivtsi Oblast, Ukraine, now lives and works in Cascais, Portugal.

2. BAM, or Baĭkalo-Amurskaia magistral', is a Soviet railroad in Siberia, and at the time of its construction (1974–84) was known as the project of a century.

3. Olena Huzar, personal communication with author, July 17, 2013.

4. Natalia Khanenko-Friesen (Shostak), "'Value Village' in My Village: Western Ukrainians and Overseas Kin," *Anthropology of Eastern Europe Review* 17, no. 2 (1999): 53–8.

5. "Hey, guys, do not sit still, start the *kanada* dance / 'Heĭ Hop Kanada' // no old women please // we want only young ones // and keep playing music."

6. Vasyl' Mel'nykovych, "Kolomyĭka Emihrantam," a song from the album *Hutsul Hooligan* (Ivano-Frankivsk Recording Studio "Six Seconds," 2004).

7. Anthropologists debated at length and in depth on the meanings of the notion of postsocialist transition. See, for example, Michael Burawoy, and Katherine Verdery, "Introduction," in *Uncertain Transition: Ethnographies of Change in the Postsocialist World*, ed. Michael Burawoy and Katherine Verdery (Lanham, MD: Rowman and Littlefield, 1999), 1–18; Katherine Verdery, *What Was Socialism and What Comes Next?* (Princeton, NJ: Princeton University Press, 1996); Catherine Wanner, *Burden of Dreams: History and Identity in Post-Soviet Ukraine* (University Park: Penn State University Press, 1998).

8. "FMS Chief: Number of Labor Migrants from Ukraine to Russia Amounted to over 1.3 m in 2012," *Kyiv Post*, June 25, 2013, www.kyivpost.com/content/ukraine/fms-chief-number-of-labor-migrants-from-ukraine-to-russia-amounted-to-over-13-m-in-2012-326155.html; Marta Jaroszewicz, "Poland More Attractive for Ukrainian Economic Immigrants," *Osrodek Studiow Schodnich*, www.osw.waw.pl/en/publikacje/analyses/2013-06-12/poland-more-attractive-ukrainian-economic-immigrants; Migration Policy Centre, "Migration Facts Ukraine," www.migrationpolicycentre.eu/docs/fact_sheets/Factsheet%20Ukraine.pdf; Pavlo Sadoka, interview by Natalia Khanenko-Friesen, Lisbon, Portugal, November 12 and 19, 2012; Natalia Khanenko-Friesen, "Is There a Hyphen in 'Ukrainian-Portuguese'?," *New Pathway*, January 31 and February 6, 2013; Embassy of Ukraine in the Republic of Turkey, "Ukrainians in Turkey," http://turkey.mfa.gov.ua/en/ukraine-tr/ukrainians-in-tr; Olena Malynovska, *International Migration in*

Contemporary Ukraine: Trends and Policy (Geneva: Global Commission on International Migration, 2004), 14.

9. The early debates on labor emigration were summarized at "Economic Migration from Ukraine: The Reasons and Outcomes," a round table organized by the Institute for the Study of Diaspora in Kyiv in April 2003. See Instytut Doslidzhen' Diaspory, *Ekonomichna Emihratsiia z Ukraïny: Prychyny i Naslidky* [Economic Migration from Ukraine: Reasons and Outcomes] (Kyiv: Geoprint, 2003). Also, see Mykola Shul'ha, "Mihratsiia z Ukraïny" [Migration from Ukraine] *Ukraïns'kyi Rehional'nyi Visnyk* 21 (2001): 10–11.

10. Irina Pribytkova, "Trudovye migranty v sotsial'noi iierarkhii ukrainskogo obshchestva (nachalo)" [Labor Migrants in the Social Hierarchy of Ukrainian Society (Part 1)], *Sotsiolohiia: Teoriia, Metody, Marketing* 4 (2002): 156–67; Irina Pribytkova, "Trudovye migranty v sotsial'noi iierarkhii ukrainskogo obshchestva (okonchanie)" [Labor Migrants in the Social Hierarchy of Ukrainian Society (Part 2)], *Sotsiolohiia: Teoriia, Metody, Marketing* 1 (2003): 109–24; Myroslava Keryk, "Labour Migrant: Our Savior or Betrayer? Ukrainian Discussions Concerning Labour Migration," http://migrationonline.cz/en/labour-migrant-our-savior-or-betrayer-ukrainian-discussions-concerning-labour-migration; Ivan Hnybidenko, "Problemy Trudovoï Mihratsiï v Ukraïni ta ïkh Vyrishennia" [The Problem of Labour Migration in Ukraine and Its Solution], *Ekonomika Ukraïny* 4 (2001): 19–22; Instytut Doslidzhen' Diaspory, *Ekonomichna emihratsiia z Ukraïny*; "Teenagers without Parental Care Due to the Parents Work Abroad: Who Are They?," Ternopil Nongovernmental Youth Organization Share Warmth webpage, http://ternopil.iatp.org.ua/teplo/research.htm.

11. Natalia Khanenko-Friesen, "Robinson Crusoes, Prostitutes, Heroes? Constructing The Ukrainian Labour Emigrant in Ukraine," in *Hyphenated Histories: Articulations of Central European Bildung and Slavic Studies in the Contemporary Academy*, ed. Andrew Gow (Leiden: Brill, 2007), 103–20.

12. Khanenko-Friesen, "Robinson Crusoes, Prostitutes, Heroes?"; Natalia Khanenko-Friesen, "Searching for Cinderellas, in Naples and Beyond: Popular Culture Responses to Labour Migration from Ukraine," *Spaces of Identity: Tradition, Cultural Boundaries and Identity Formation in Central Europe* 6, no. 2 (2006): 18; Natalia Khanenko-Friesen (Shostak), "On Diasporic Tourism, Homecoming and Making the Other: Canada-Ukraine Trajectories," in *Ports of Call: Cultural Transfer between North America and Central Europe*, ed. Susan Ingram and Markus Reisenleitner (Frankfurt am Main: Peter Lang, 2003), 121–54.

13. Natalia Khanenko-Friesen, "Trudova Mihratsiia ta Literaturna Tvorchist': Na Porozi Transnatsional'noho v Ukraïns'komu Kul'turnomu Prostori" [Labor Migration and Creative Writing: Carving Transnational Spaces in the Field of Ukrainian Culture], in *Skhid-Zakhid* [East-West], vols. 16–17 of *Neo-antykolonializm vs Neo-imperializm: Relavantnist' Postkolonial'noho Dyskursu na Postradians'komu Prostori* [Neoanticolonialism vs. Neoimperialism: The Relevance of Postcolonial Discourse in the Post-Soviet Space], ed. Gelinada Grinchenko and Tetiana Dzyadevych (Kharkiv: Kharkiv National University, 2013), 488–519.

14. I was assisted in this search by many of my colleagues and informants in Ukraine, Italy, and Portugal. Many publications are not known outside of the regions where they were published and, as a rule, until recently, information about them was not easily available in the public domain of the internet.

15. The word *zarobitchanstvo* encompasses an array of meanings, and roughly compares to the English phrase "the phenomenon of labor migration." The word's root is *zarobitky*, which can refer both to earnings and the experience of earning. At the root of *zarobitky* is the verb *robyty*, "to work / to do / to labor." Traditionally, the word *zarobitky* connoted going elsewhere, outside of one's community and taking up unskilled labor.

16. This bibliography was completed in the summer of 2012, along with an analysis written in Ukrainian; see Khanenko-Friesen, "Trudova Mihratsiia ta Literaturna Tvorchist'," 488–519.

17. Eight publications in the bibliography are listed without a year of publication and are not included in this figure.

18. George Markus and Michael M. J. Fischer, *Anthropology as Cultural Critique* (Chicago: University of Chicago Press, 1999).

19. Author's field notes, Lisbon, Portugal, December 2012.

20. Yar Slavutych, "Ukrainian Writing," *Canadian Encyclopedia*, www.thecanadian encyclopedia.com/articles/ukrainian-writing. See also C. H. Andrusyshen and Watson Kirkconnell, eds. and trans., *The Ukrainian Poets, 1189–1962* (Toronto: University of Toronto Press, 1963); Jars Balan, ed., *Identifications: Ethnicity and the Writer in Canada* (Edmonton: Canadian Institute of Ukrainian Studies Press, 1982); Mykyta Mandryka, *History of Ukrainian Literature in Canada* (Winnipeg: Ukrainian Free Academy of Sciences, 1968); and Yar Slavutych, comp., *An Annotated Bibliography of Ukrainian Literature in Canada, 1908–1986* (Edmonton: Slavuta, 1987).

21. Rostyslav Kramar, "Do Pytannia Fol'kl'oryzmu ta Fol'kloryzatsiï Trudovykh Emihrantiv" [On Folklorism and the Folklororization of Labor Emigrants], *Narodna Tvorchist' ta Etnohrafiia* 3–4 (2007): 60–65; Olena Hinda, "Poetychni Novotvory Ukraïns'kykh Mihrantiv v Italiï iak Predmet Fol'klorystychnoho Doslidzhennia," *Mifolohiia i Folklor* 2–3, no. 3 (2009): 27–36.

22. Going for *zarobitky* to Russia and on short trading trips in the near abroad preceded the migration to Western Europe.

23. I discuss the results of this review in "Robinson Crusoes, Prostitutes, Heroes?"

24. Vasyl' Potochniak (chief editor of *Do Svitla*), interview by Natalia Khanenko-Friesen, Rome, Italy, December 14, 2007.

25. Iryna Kalynets', *Dity Emihrantiv pro Sebe: Spovidi, Dumky, Sudzhennia . . . Bil'* [Children of Emigrants on Themselves: Confessions, Thoughts, Verdicts . . . Pain] (Lviv: Artos, 2008, 2009). A number of popular Ukrainian writers have turned to the theme of labor migration in their works without having personal experience of labor migration. Iren Rozdobud'ko's *Rankovyi Prybyral'nyk* [Morning Cleaner] (Lviv: Literaturna Ahentsiia Priamida, 2004) and *Ia Znaiu Shcho Ty Znaiesh Shcho Ia Znaiu* [I Know That You Know That I Know] (Kyiv: Nora-Druk, 2011) are two examples.

26. Two other researchers who briefly reflect on migrant poetry are Ukrainian folklorists, both of whom emphasize the folkloric nature of this creativity and seek to locate these poetic texts within the existing framework of other well-known verbal folklore; see Rostyslav Kramar, "Do Pytannia Fol'kl'oryzmu," and Olena Hinda, "Poetychni Novotvory."

27. A few male poets have taken up contemporary political issues in their poetry. Ukrainian poet Anatoly Panchenko, who is well known in Portugal and beyond, is illustrative here.

28. In Portugal, over the course of two research trips in December 2011 and December 2012, I met with and interviewed eleven poets whose lives in Portugal seemed to be fully enmeshed in the poetic word. Ten of my respondents were women.

29. See, for example, Alexandra Hrycak, "Women as Migrants on the Margins of the European Union," in *Mapping Difference: The Many Faces of Women in Contemporary Ukraine*, ed. Marian Rubchak (New York: Berghahn Books, 2011), 47–64.

30. Pani Viktoria is a pseudonym.

31. Author's field notes, Rome, November 3, 2011.

32. Julie Cruikshank, *The Social Life of Stories: Narrative and Knowledge in the Yukon Territory* (Lincoln: University of Nebraska Press, 1998).

33. Having emerged at the intersection of many cultural planes, poetry writing among Ukrainians abroad seems to stand out from the cultural means that other ethnic groups have drawn on to sustain themselves in their new homelands. The mass scale of migrant poetry writing appears to be a uniquely Ukrainian phenomenon when compared to how other ethnic groups and communities advance themselves in their new homelands of southern Europe. Marianna Soronevych, the editor of the *Ukraïns'ka Hazeta* in Rome, Italy, shared with me her observation that among all sixteen ethnic groups that are being served by the news production company that publishes *Ukraïns'ka Hazeta*, only Ukrainians have been engaged so actively in the production of literary texts, both poetry and prose. Other editors in her office expressed their surprise at the number of poetic and literary submissions *Ukraïns'ka Hazeta* receives on a regular basis (Marianna Soronevych, interview by Natalia Khanenko-Friesen, Rome, Italy, November 3, 2011).

34. I have discussed this matter at in "Robinson Crusoes, the Prostitutes, the Heroes?"

35. Bohdan Lepkyĭ and Levko Lepkyĭ, "Chuiesh, Brate Miĭ" [Listen, My Brother], in *Zoloti Kliuchi* [The Golden Keys], vol. 2, ed. Dymtro Revuts'kyi (Kyiv: n.p., 1927), 12, http://proridne.com/pisni/ЧУЄШ,БРАТЕМІЙ.html.

36. As observed by the anonymous commentator, Lepky's song was promptly embraced by the people, and some of its words were changed (and now remain as part of the song). The poem also acquired a new name: "The Storks" (Kuntseve General Education School website, http://kuncevo.ucoz.ru/index/ukrajinska_mova_10_19_ch_2/0-).

37. Heorhiĭ Petruk-Popyk, "Zhuravli Bohdana Lepkoho" [Bohdan Lepkyi's Cranes], in *Dumaiu Vholos* (Kyiv: Radianskyĭ Pys'mennyk, 1990).

38. Nadia Baranovs'ka, interview by Natalia Khanenko-Friesen, Lisbon, Portugal, November 12, 2011.

Epilogue

1. Arjun Appadurai, "Global Ethnoscapes: Notes and Queries for a Transnational Anthropology," in *Recapturing Anthropology: Working in the Present*, ed. Richard G. Fox (Santa Fe, NM: School of American Research Press, 1991), 191–216.

Index

64; syntagmatic relations in, 225–26n31; vernacular, 139, 199

longing for homeland: as archetypical feature of human life, 230n7; corporate nature of, 155; imagined versus real relations with the old country and, 97; versus longing for kinfolk, 76–77; in migrant poetry, 207–8; parallel longing for Ukrainian others and, 218; perseverance of, 97; private versus public, 86, 88; Soviet impenetrability and, 155; Ukrainian Canadian identity and, 97; in-between zone and, 214, 218

Lowenthal, David, 7

Lubkemann, Stephen C., 221n5

Luzhany, Ukraine, 25–29, 48, 69

Lviv, Ukraine, 186

Lysyk family, 91–92

Madagascar, Merina ritual in, 84

Mahleiros, George, 207–8

Maidanyk, Yakiv, 106–7, *107*

Makuch, Andrij, 158

Mandz'o, Genka, 227n14

Marchuk, Volodymyr, 108

Markus, George, 194

Martynowych, Orest, 80–81, 241n13

Medwidsky, Bohdan, 33, 34–35, 226n39

Mel'nokovych, Vasyl', 189, 190

memoirs and family histories, *126*; academic attention to, 135; accessibility of to researchers, 135, 241n18; anniversary and centennial celebrations and, 144, 146; in archives, 237n25; Basilian Fathers Museum and, 138–39, 242n30; Canadian focus of, 32; contents of, 140–42; distance between Canada and Ukraine and, 99; ethnic reflectivity and, 99, 235n1; family trees in, 142, *143*; firsts in, 234n50; versus genealogy, 145–46; individuals excluded from family trees and, 144; longing for homeland and, 155; metastory of the beginning and, 31–32; multiple purposes of, 144; natural flow of family lore and, 97; numbers of by decade, *136*; old versus new country in, 96–97; post–World War II changes and, 136–37; at Prairie Centre

for the Study of Ukrainian Heritage, 235n1; produced by Ukrainian Canadians, 19–20; spatial metaphors in, 94–95; structure of, 139–40, 141–42; Ukraine as depicted in, 140–42; value of to researchers, 241n18

Memories of Mundare (local history book), 18, 91–92, 93–97

Merina ritual (Madagascar), 84

Métis status, 6, 144

Molochansk, Ukraine, 4–5

Molodiia, Ukraine, 168, 246n19

Momryk, Myron, 135–36, 147–48

Mormons. *See* Church of Jesus Christ of Latter-day Saints

Moroshak family, 169

Moroshan, Tamara Lavruk, 190, 205, 247n1

Moszczanski family, 142, 242n30

Mott, William, 14–15

Mundare, Alberta: author's choice of for ethnography, 86–87; Basilian Fathers Museum in, 90, 102, 130–31, 133; beauty of physical setting and, 96; choir in, 233n39; churches and monastic communities in, 89, 233n36; community and family narratives of, 90–92; as earliest Ukrainian Canadian settlement, 133; fiftieth anniversary of Ukrainian immigration held in, 89; generations of Ukrainians in Canada and, 131; geographical location of, 93–94, 232–33n35; history of, 88–92, 136; landscape of, 95; lifeworld of, 89–90, 93, 95, 97; local history book produced by, 18, 91–92, 93–97; mural in church in, 87, *88*, 232n34; notion of generations in, 132; place names and, 94, 234n54; predecessors of residents of, 93–94; Ukrainian commemorative events and, 233n41; Ukrainian Greek Catholic parish in, 87, *88*, 89, 130; Ukrainianness in, 129–30

Mundare murals, 87, *88*, 232n34

Museum of Folklife and Architecture (Kyiv), 229n42

Nash, Catherine, 152

National Archives of Canada, 135–36

Soviet Union (*continued*)
    territory added to, 79, 80, 232n32; visits to
    villages prohibited under, 103–4, 162
Spain, labor migrants to, 190
Stafford, Charles, 32–33, 52–53, 71, 157
Stets', Stepan, 59, 67
Stetskos family, 140
storytelling, 29–30, 164
Struk, Bohdan, 186, 189, 213
Swyripa, Frances, 80, 147–48
Sych, Oleksandr, 108
Szalasznyj, Kathlyn, 147–48

Tatarchuk, Hanna, 176, 177
technology: audio letters and, 25–26; changes
    in diasporic imagination and, 77, 79; fusion
    ethnography and, 25; in rural versus urban
    communities, 227–28n16; shortened dis-
    tance between diaspora and homeland
    and, 182, 207; social media and, 210; TV
    news from Ukraine and, 77; video record-
    ings and, 213–15, *215*
Terletsky family, 169
Ternopil, Ukraine, 103, 162–63, 186–87, 197–
    98, 247n2
Ternopil National Pedagogical University, 103
Ternopilska Hazeta (newspaper), 198
Thomas, William I., 109
Tichon, Kate, 134
Tovarystvo Obiednanykh Ukraïntsiv Kanady
    (TOUK), 177–79
Trach, Nadia, 65–66, 102
Tsarist Russia, 6, 50, 82–83
Turkey, labor migrants to, 190
Turner, Terence, 34
Turner, Victor: on antistructure of myth and
    ritual, 171; on liminality, 42, 226n38; on
    ritual and separation, 34, 71, 157

Ukraine: author's roots in, 3; celebration of
    independence and reunification of, 81,
    83, 84, 86; communication technology
    in, 227–28n16; departure and separation
    in oral lore and songs of, 32; diasporic
    dimension of Ukrainian culture and, 187,
    216, 217; genealogical research and, 150,
    152; historical German settlements in, 4;

incorporation of into Soviet Union, 79,
    80, 232n32; independence of from Soviet
    Union, 178, 179, 180; *khustka* from parcels
    as currency in, 235n9; labor migration
    and, 22, 191, 207; as land of ancestors, not
    living family, 172; landscape of, 4; maps
    of, 93–94, 152; versus old country, 87; or-
    ganized tourism to, 20–21; post-Soviet
    economy of, 189–90; post-Soviet emigra-
    tion from, 189–90; primacy of song and,
    190; primacy of the collective and, 14;
    prohibition on travel to ancestral villages
    in, 162–63; Russian language in, 161;
    Soviet collectivization of agricultural
    communities in, 116, 118; Soviet impene-
    trability and, 155; study abroad in, 186;
    surveillance of correspondence with rela-
    tives abroad in, 103–4; times of mass
    emigration from, 223n6; traditional
    needlework in, 214; in Ukrainian Canadian
    family histories, 140–42; in Ukrainian
    Canadian politics, 79–80; Ukrainian
    Canadian public ceremonies and, 82–84;
    Ukrainian Canadians' reclamation of an-
    cestry in, 152; wedding ceremonies in, 42;
    white stork metaphor and, 45–47, 208–9
Ukraine Society, 178
Ukrainian Americans xii, 80, 173
Ukrainian Canadians: Canadianness of, 24;
    centennial of settlement and, 138–39; days
    of commemoration among, 81–84, 86;
    demographics of immigrants and, 79–80,
    231n13; diversity among, 230–31n10; fam-
    ily histories produced by, 19–20; first im-
    migrants and, 133, 224n16, 241n12; focus
    of stories of, 31–32, 224n16; genealogical
    continuity for, 129; generations of, 130;
    homecoming as rite of passage for, 157;
    homecoming in lifeworlds of, 170; home-
    land in politics of, 79–86; identity projects
    of, 77; individuals excluded from family
    trees and, 144; liminality of, 43; meanings
    of Ukrainian homeland for, 230–31n10;
    motif of departure for identity of, 32;
    organized tourism to Ukraine and, 20–21;
    origin narrative of, 43; origins of diasporic
    practices of, 12–13; popular genealogy

FOLKLORE STUDIES
IN A MULTICULTURAL
WORLD

The Last Laugh: Folk Humor, Celebrity Culture, and Mass-Mediated Disasters in the Digital Age
(University of Wisconsin Press)
Trevor J. Blank

A Vulgar Art: A New Approach to Stand-Up Comedy
(University Press of Mississippi)
Ian Brodie

The Painted Screens of Baltimore: An Urban Folk Art Revealed
(University Press of Mississippi)
Elaine Eff

Improvised Adolescence: Somali Bantu Teenage Refugees in America
(University of Wisconsin Press)
Sandra Grady

Squeeze This! A Cultural History of the Accordion in America
(University of Illinois Press)
Marion Jacobson

Ukrainian Otherlands: Diaspora, Homeland, and Folk Imagination in the Twentieth Century
(University of Wisconsin Press)
Natalia Khanenko-Friesen

The Jumbies' Playing Ground:
Old World Influences on Afro-Creole Masquerades in the Eastern Caribbean
(University Press of Mississippi)
Robert Wyndham Nicholls